THE BOY
FROM TIGER
BAY

THE BOY FROM TIGER BAY

CERI JACKSON

Little
a

Published by Little A, Seattle

www.apub.com

Amazon, the Amazon logo, and Little A are trademarks of Amazon.com, Inc., or its affiliates.

EU Product Safety contact:
Amazon Publishing, Amazon Media EU S.à r.l.
38, avenue John F. Kennedy, L-1855 Luxembourg
amazonpublishing-gpsr@amazon.com

ISBN-13: 9781662510489
eISBN: 9781662510496

Cover design by Emma Ewbank
Cover image: © travelib prime / Alamy Stock Photo

Printed in the United States of America

To those who refuse to turn a blind eye

'Murder, though it have no tongue, will speak.'

Hamlet, William Shakespeare

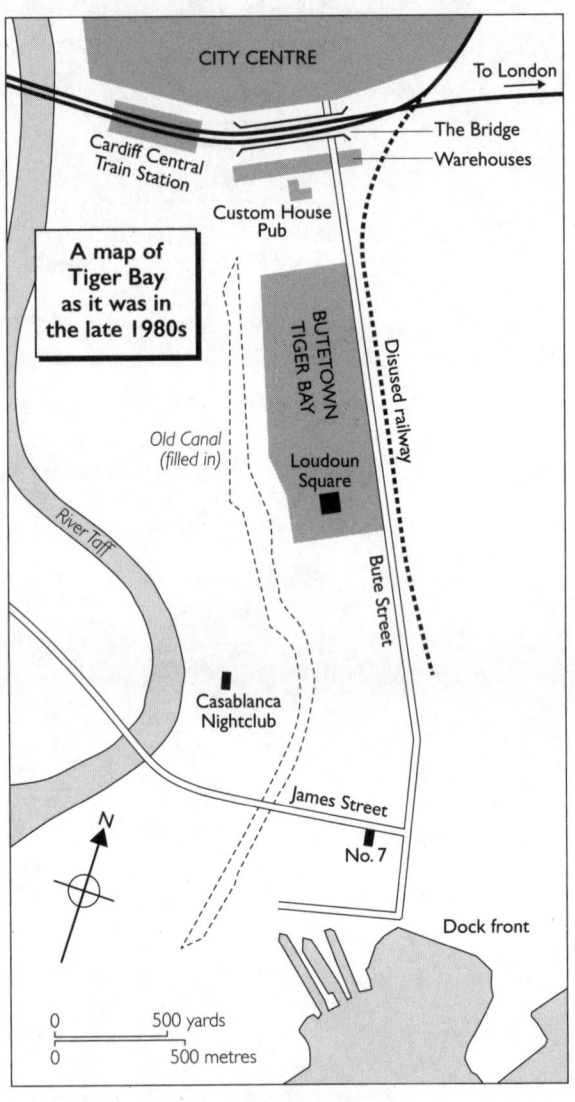

CITY CENTRE

To London

The Bridge

Warehouses

Cardiff Central
Train Station

Custom House
Pub

A map of
Tiger Bay
as it was in
the late 1980s

BUTETOWN
TIGER BAY

Old Canal
(filled in)

Loudoun
Square

River Taff

Disused railway

Bute Street

Casablanca
Nightclub

James Street

No. 7

N

Dock front

| 0 | 500 yards |
| 0 | 500 metres |

WHY TELL MY STORY?

For me, the prospect of this book was, initially, a daunting one. To grant a writer carte blanche to delve into your innermost thoughts, to prod at the fears that keep you awake at night, and to lay bare the good, the bad and the ugly, has not always been comfortable. But that discomfort pales by comparison to the fictional stories and gossip that have been heaped on to my name over the decades. My aim has always been to set out the truth of what happened to me and my co-accused, to silence those who still think us guilty and to recognise the loved ones who suffered alongside us. For me, this is for my mother, Maria, and brother, Stephen, both now gone but whose support I remember every day with love and deep gratitude.

—John Actie

Preface

It was in the autumn of 2017 when the story of the so-called Cardiff Five first drifted on to my to-do list. In the February of the following year, it would be thirty years since the death of Lynette White and the first stirrings of a murder hunt that would beset the criminal justice system like no other.

By that stage, the case had only just reached its legal climax, the flurry of reports in its wake deemed to be the final utterances of a scandal that had absorbed its rightful share of TV documentaries and column inches over the decades.

As the landmark anniversary loomed, a difficult question hung in the air: what was there left to say?

And so, the editor of BBC Wales's investigations unit, where I worked as a journalist, commissioned me to write a long-read for the news website, a canter through the story's head-spinning twists and turns in a few thousand words.

As I embarked on my research, I knew little about the case beyond the cursory.

The name Lynette White had been hardwired into my mind ever since the day when, aged nineteen, and only a few months younger than her, I had seen the headlines about her murder emblazoned on the news-stands of the *South Wales Echo* street-sellers.

When the 'breakthrough' in the case finally came, I recognised the names of a couple of the five men charged. Cardiff is a small city, and was much more so in the 1980s. Growing up there, it was not so much a case of six degrees of separation, more like two or three.

Everyone knew John Actie's name. You would be in a nightclub and a friend might nudge you, furtively gesturing in his direction. His towering stature aside, John Actie's presence seemed to emit a charge like that of an incoming storm. His reputation for fighting was notorious; he was not a man to be crossed.

Every town or city has that one family whose surname is widely recognised and more feared than any other. The city then was a warren of large, extended families interconnecting its various districts and suburbs. But none held quite the same sway as the Acties, of whom John was the most prominent scion.

While I did not know Tony Paris, I knew of his cousin, a popular figure who worked on the doors of one or two nightclubs at the glitzier end of a vibrant and diverse social scene. In the 1980s, Cardiff had a flavour distinct from its modern rebranding. Down-at-heel and lacking identity maybe, but its DNA was riven with a swagger redolent of its bygone glory days as an eminent and infamous seaport.

Indeed, the remains of the city's dockland, viewed by many who grew up outside it as a crime-riven ghetto, plays a prominent role in what happened in this story and why.

Not long after the arrests, I left my home to begin journalism training. Nothing ever happens in Cardiff was my firm belief as I headed for London, where, in my young and mistaken mind, everything happens.

Over the years, I read the latest reports as they flitted in and out of the news. The case's fits and starts, the drip-feed of instalments, many years passing between them, had served to diminish the full force of its astonishing entirety.

As I waded into the BBC's news archive to begin my research, I was quickly swept away by a riptide of intrigue, one that would soon carry me out into the depths of fixation.

Before returning home to Cardiff after some years away, I worked as a feature writer on a national newspaper, delving into the human fallout, the nuances and complexity of stories that lay beyond the headlines. It was that aspect of journalism that interested me, and on meeting the surviving members of the Cardiff Five, I stumbled upon far more than I had ever bargained for.

I met Tony Paris first at his small flat on the outskirts of the city centre, where he had agreed to give me an interview, the first of many as it turned out. As was his wont, he had painted on a smile and presented a jokey and sanguine demeanour.

It was only over time as trust was built that his mask would slip to reveal the full horror of an experience that had not only ruined his life but also cruelly burdened him with an inconsolable pain that should never have been his to bear.

John Actie, I had been told, distrusted journalists, so I was apprehensive about how my intrusion in his life would be received. Surprisingly, it was welcomed, and I soon realised that while he had clearly mellowed with age, his fearsome reputation was little more than a caricature of a complex and multi-faceted character who, his phosphorescent anger notwithstanding, was considerate, smart and polite.

No one, he said, has ever given us a chance to tell our story. And he was right. No one ever had.

When I later met Stephen Miller, whose life, it was clear, had become stuck in an interminable loop of all that had happened in the aftermath of the murder of Lynette, his girlfriend, he was mourning the death of his mother. He said he had given up hope that anyone cared. His late mother, he was convinced, had a hand in sending me his way.

Telling the story through the voices of the men, my long-read quickly expanded to ten thousand words. It seemed a lot but barely scratched the surface. I had to do more.

I was an avid listener of deep-dive podcasts at the time and a colleague suggested it would be an ideal platform for such an epic story. I pushed for a small budget and set out on a wing and a prayer. Aside from a brief stint as a radio reporter many years before, I had zero credentials in this particular storytelling specialism.

Spare time became a thing of the past as evenings and weekends were spent recording upwards of one hundred hours of interviews with the men, their families and friends, along with a host of legal experts.

Much to everyone's surprise, most of all my own, the thirteen-episode podcast series – *Shreds: Murder in the Dock* – was a success and paved the way for a three-part BBC TV documentary, which I co-produced.

But even after all that, I still felt dissatisfied, the thought that too much had been left unsaid nagging in my mind. The devil of this story is in its detail, the depth of which is not easily conveyed within the constraints of broadcasting.

In preparation for writing this book, my house became overtaken by thirty-five boxes of case files stacked in towers amid a sea of yellowing paper, reports, transcripts and police statements, every one of which I had read with the same relish as I would a best-selling page-turner. It has been an exercise in restraint filtering their detail in telling this story.

I have chosen not to write it in a reportage style but instead afford it the type of storytelling perhaps more suited to a stranger-than-fiction tale. But what is strictly journalistic is the sourcing of facts within it. Not a single detail has been presumed or gilded.

4

Lynette striking matches, for instance, as you will read about, was taken from two police statements from men who had used her services as a sex worker in the weeks before her murder.

Whether it be the phase of the moon and the weather on a given day, or the behaviours, thoughts, gestures, emotions or words spoken, every inclusion is corroborated by research, the accounts of the surviving men, the families of those who have since died, lawyers, psychologists, police detectives and news archives, as well as the case files.

Sadly, Tony Paris died in September 2022, leaving only John Actie in Cardiff, and I have written chiefly from John's perspective with his full sanction and support.

As for Lynette White, hers is not my story to tell – that belongs to her family, who have suffered horrendously. Out of respect for the Whites, I have striven to be mindful of that at every turn and have written about Lynette separately at the end of this book.

It is also important to stress that the telling of this story is in no way aimed at gratuitously knocking South Wales Police. Within its telling is an example of some of the finest detective work ever conducted by the force. Every person that has contributed is unequivocal in their respect and support of good policing. A dangerous and thankless job so vital to the health of our society, it is a role imbued with immense trust and power and, as such, accountability is its cornerstone.

More broadly, this is not a story about a murder investigation, but about the dark side of human nature, of blind judgement and prejudice and the radiation of its toxic fallout. It also lifts the lid on events in the 1980s and their impact on our lives today, far beyond the nostalgia of fashion and music.

Importantly, it also reveals a version of Wales and its capital, a heterogeneous and multicultural city, too often eclipsed by homespun and reductive stereotypes.

But above all it is the story of five men – John Actie, Tony Paris, Ronnie Actie, Stephen Miller and Yusef Abdullahi – snatched from their lives and families to be thrown into a nightmare from which they were never allowed to escape, one that is widely recognised as the UK's greatest miscarriage of justice. To afford them some long-overdue respect, I have deliberately referred to them by their first names throughout.

My shock at how this shameful series of events unfolded in my home city, a place I believed while growing up to be safe and just, was profound.

If stories are a means of helping us to better understand our world, then this has led me to the certainty that terrible injustices, which we often console ourselves only ever happen elsewhere, are often the reality of someone much closer to home.

Drawing attention to a wrong as old as human cognition itself, Roman emperor and Stoic philosopher Marcus Aurelius wrote: 'You can commit injustice by doing nothing.'

My hope is that this book will contribute in some way to the resonance of his words by bringing awareness, the undoubted first step towards any form of change.

Prologue

Butetown is a small, square-mile district enclosed on all four sides like the confines of a jail cell. It is a territory set apart from the rest of Cardiff, the capital of Wales, a compact city with a soul-stirring history.

At the top, Butetown's entry point and unofficial border is a metal bridge carrying the Great Western Railway's main Cardiff-to-London line. Beyond it, the city streets bustle as the outside world goes about its business turning a blind eye.

Underneath the bridge, two lanes of traffic, the black railings of raised walkways either side, emerge on to Bute Street, the district's main drag, which runs straight as an arrow from top to bottom.

By day, the top of Bute Street is a jumble of warehouses and spit-and-sawdust pubs. By night, though, well, that is a different matter.

To the east is another railway, elevated atop a high stone wall, like a prison yard's, dirty and slippery with damp. Its obsolete tracks are buckled and clogged with reedy grass.

On the west side, an old canal has been drained and filled. Only the crumbling remnants of lock gates and bridges remain, protruding on to a colourless strip of wasteland.

In its centre, a concrete jungle is rundown and cracking at the seams. Its high-rises, maisonettes and houses are sliced into blocks by a warren of graffitied side roads and alleyways strewn with litter from unemptied communal bins.

Then, at the bottom, running perpendicular to Bute Street, is the other main artery, James Street. And behind that, the sea, once home to a tumultuous dockland, now as still as the dead who had dreamed it into life.

Crying gulls float on the wind above the dock's harbour, gouged, as if by a giant claw, from the convolutions of the south-east Wales coastline, providing a funnel for the Severn Estuary's deadly quicksilver tides. An undulant slick of mudflats one moment, a swirling brown cauldron buffeting the high sea walls the next.

The dockland is a ghost town. What old buildings remain, the recognition of their historical importance having spared them from the wrecking balls, are desolate, boarded up and choked with vines.

Hard to imagine now, but for a spectacular moment in history this strange, anomalous corner of South Wales set the world on fire.

This was the legendary Tiger Bay.

The busiest coal port in the world, its reputation was unrivalled, its stories of wonder and iniquity carried by the wind across the Seven Seas.

Like the Klondike during the gold rush some decades later, it sprang into life in the mid-1800s, when an insignificant village close to an area once described as a 'direful swamp . . . of little value' morphed into a city at the centre of the world.

Twenty or so miles north, the coal, iron and steel from the South Wales Valleys had ignited Britain's Industrial Revolution. Torrents of 'black gold', prized anthracite and steam coal, thundered down the railway tracks to the docks to fill the holds of a myriad ships bound for far-off shores.

The docks quickly expanded to nearly seven miles of quayage, so crowded it was said a monkey could swing from rigging one end to the other.

It was, wrote Tiger Bay historian Neil Sinclair, like a Saudi Arabia of coal. It was no exaggeration. The docks reportedly made the man who bankrolled them, aristocrat and industrialist John Crichton-Stuart, the second Marquess of Bute, the richest man in the world.

At the hub of its teeming financial quarter, second only in importance to London's Square Mile, the thronging trading hall of the palatial Coal Exchange set the price of coal worldwide, turning fortunes on a dime and witnessing the signing of the first ever million-pound cheque.

Bute's architects had built grand stuccoed townhouses around elegant garden squares to rival any of London's, homes for its sea captains and merchants. Further up was a model village of terraces for its workers, tucked away from the high commerce and splendour of the dockland's banking halls and shipping headquarters – a stately waterfront procession of Georgian, Victorian and Edwardian-style magnificence befitting the world's coal metropolis.

A cosmopolitan marketplace burgeoned, enveloping the shops of Bute Street and James Street, their fronts festooned with all the finery and exotica under the sun, with intoxicating aromas billowing from a profusion of international restaurants, delicatessens and cafes.

As darkness fell amid the unceasing cacophony of whistles and foghorns, police patrolled in the safety of twos, the roar of barroom brawls, banter of 'street girls' and the strains of calypso, blues and jazz from backstreet speakeasies reverberating into the night air.

As to how the area came by the name Tiger Bay, well, there are differing theories. One, more respectable, claims Portuguese sailors described its notoriously difficult tides as akin to sailing through a bay of tigers.

Another, perhaps more persuasive, holds that the murder and mayhem, gambling, opium dens and innumerable brothels earned it prominent use of a once generic term long used by sailors for raucous ports everywhere.

But the Bay had something more distinctive that set it apart from the sailor towns of the rest of the UK's thriving docklands at the time.

With its high demand for labour and its designation as the UK's discharging port, it teemed with seamen from ports across the British Empire, many of whom settled, sending word to their compatriots of the area's racial tolerance and hospitality.

There was no place quite like it on earth, Neil Sinclair remembered of his childhood – a league of nations, an Aladdin's cave, a flavour of a kasbah with, at one time, fifty-seven different nationalities living in mutual respect and celebration of one another's customs. That was the true Tiger Bay, a community apart from the chaos of the dock front.

Walking through its streets, a journalist at the time reported, was like 'taking a trip around the world'.

A crucible of diversity, argued to be the UK's oldest black district, Tiger Bay had flourished into a cheek-by-jowl rainbow nation.

Gradually, as the wealthy departed the Bay for more verdant suburbs expanding around the growing city of Cardiff, its workers and boarding houses spread into the salubrious buildings left behind.

A short walk from the docks, nestled amid the workers' terraces, was Loudoun Square, a beautiful garden fringed by fine townhouses, the heart of Tiger Bay. Old men would sit on its walls reading racing tips as children played on swings under the tall, shading domes of sycamore trees.

Their mothers, predominantly white women, were local or had been drawn to the area to work in service. For the ignominy of marrying men of colour, they were commonly disowned by their families of origin. The stigma seemed to bond the outcast community more strongly, giving rise to a distinctive culture of its own – communal, unrepressed and egalitarian, derided for being at odds with the accepted British way of life.

The rest of the city was unapologetic in its loathing of Tiger Bay. Newspapers were full of scaremongering and racist headlines, condemning its miscegenation, a perceived hyper-sexuality of black men and the aberration of their 'half-caste' children.

In 1919 boiling resentment erupted in some of the UK's bloodiest race riots. With the area scapegoated for post-war hardships, a baying mob of outsiders spilled from under the bridge to ransack its streets. After that, the men of Tiger Bay, as established as any other inhabitants of the city, and on whose backs vast riches had been made, were stripped of their jobs and ordered to register as aliens. The Bay became a fortress.

By 1932, in the depth of the Depression, coal prices plummeted. The boom had been glorious but now came the bust as oil claimed the fortunes of coal.

As the years of crippling unemployment and neglect rolled by, the district, still strong and proclaiming itself the happiest and most cohesive in the city, fell into dilapidation, with health workers reporting TB as rife among children.

What happened next Neil Sinclair described as 'one of the most torrid pages of meanness and spitefulness to be found in the annals of Welsh history'.

The city fathers wanted Tiger Bay eradicated. They declared it a slum and, rather than modernise it, ordered that the entire area be razed. In 1960, the piledrivers tore up the garden in Loudoun Square to build high-rise flats, into which a portion of the community were decanted, the rest dispersed to newly built council estates on the outer fringes of the city.

And so, the 'shame' of Tiger Bay was resigned to the past; in time, the rest of the city would never have heard of it, many dismissing it as folklore. Even though the name Tiger Bay proudly and doggedly stuck among its own, the area was only recognised officially as Butetown, and more widely referred to as 'the docks'.

'Under the bridge' was a term used to describe entry into what children grew up believing to be an edgy and dangerous area. Deep-seated discrimination meant 90 per cent of Tiger Bay's young people were denied jobs, left with nowhere to go, nothing to do, no money to spend and nothing to lose. The knocking-down of Tiger Bay had been a disaster, the local authority conceded. One slum had been cleared only to create another.

In the early 1980s race riots against oppressive policing erupted across the UK in socially deprived, mainly black areas. No trouble here, Cardiff claimed, patting itself on the back as a paragon of historical race relations.

But that was not true.

In the summer of 1981, there was a flashpoint. A police raid on a blues party in the Bay resulted in a kickback by a group of young men, who built barricades around Loudoun Square and hurled petrol bombs at a battalion of police cars lining Bute Street.

The threat of a full-blown riot was only eased by the intervention of community elders, who brokered a meeting between police chiefs and the youths, who complained of heavy-handed treatment and unfair stop-and-search practices around the bridge. No arrests were made and a news blackout on the unrest was ordered.

But for one of the men involved, nineteen-year-old John Actie, the grandson of a fondly remembered and respected seaman originally from St Lucia, it was a Pyrrhic victory.

A few weeks later, as he walked through the centre of town, he was arrested for allegedly damaging a nightclub door. 'You were throwing bottles at me down the docks a few weeks ago, Actie,' an officer told him.

From there he said he was taken to a police station, dragged to the cells, beaten up and charged with assault. The case went to court. Both sides gave their accounts. All charges against John Actie were thrown out.

All was not well between the dock's boys and the police.

The old narrative persisted; this was very much a tale of two cities.

The dock's boys were not welcomed in clubs in town, but outsiders seeking a taste of the ghetto life would regularly file under the bridge to one place in particular, the legendary Casablanca. A former chapel turned reggae club, the 'Casa' was as renowned for live music as for its free-flowing supply of cannabis.

But that was not Butetown's only pull for outsiders. Sex was for sale.

As the sun dropped and darkness pervaded, the top of Bute Street near the bridge stirred into life as the city's red-light district, the kind where women loiter on pavements outside pubs smoking cigarettes, their faces lit by the predacious headlamp beams of cars driving slowly by. Men from all over the city, and way beyond it, would regularly drive under the bridge.

It seemed that providing what happened in Butetown stayed in Butetown, the authorities did not seem too bothered.

But things were about to change.

In 1987, Cardiff, a city in the throes of a post-industrial rebrand, unveiled the jewel in the crown of its vision for the future:

to transform its desolate seaport into a brand new 'Cardiff Bay'. The city wanted its docks back.

With millions of government money set aside, many millions more were sought from private investors and a slick sales pitch went into overdrive.

Then something happened that no amount of PR wizardry could gloss over.

What unfolded as a result is, as with everything else to do with the story of the Bay, hard to believe at times.

How it all began, though, the events of that fateful day in February 1988 – that was, sadly, all too common.

Chapter One

Lynette White struck a match and paused for the flare to settle, her hand and face, the sapphire blue of her eyes and the bleached highlights of her brown hair lit with its flickering gleam as she walked the few steps to the narrow, walled staircase.

It had been a cold and wet Saturday night and, despite a break in the downpour, water from the rain-soaked streets continued to stream into storm drains as the clock ticked into Sunday 14 February, Valentine's Day.

Out on the harbour, a waning crescent moon cut between breaks in the cloud, casting glints of silver light on the black flux of the incoming tide, presenting a scene as romantic as any to mark the occasion.

But affairs of the heart had been a sore point for Lynette White of late, perhaps making the events of that fateful night even more tragic, if that was at all possible.

That weekend, she had planned to go to London with her boyfriend of two years, Stephen Miller. The couple had talked about leaving Cardiff to move to his home in Brixton. His mother had agreed they could stay with her while they found their feet and he was keen to introduce Lynette to her.

But for reasons that are not entirely clear and can only be speculated on, over the past five days Lynette had cut all contact with Stephen, and with everyone else she was close to, for that matter.

It was likely sometime after midnight, possibly around 1 a.m., that she had turned along James Street, a long stretch of old shops, many boarded up, their carved-stone façades shabby with grime, mixed with new-build flats and a smattering of pubs and takeaways.

Number seven, an upmarket stationery shop to the great and good of the docks fifty years before, had receded into a gaunt, unprepossessing townhouse of three metal-windowed flats stacked one on top of the other above a betting shop.

Lynette stopped outside and reached for her key from the pocket of her long brown leather jacket. The jacket belonged to Stephen, and she had taken to wearing it, the way women like to do; his scent and the coat's expansive, heavy drape around her small frame made her feel safe.

The lightbulb in the cramped, pitch-dark communal hallway of the flats had blown and, forever losing her plastic cigarette lighter, she had resorted of late to using matches to light her way.

A couple of steps up the staircase, she extinguished the dwindling flame, stopping to hurriedly strike another, and then a third before she reached the first-floor landing. From there she could make out the silhouette of the door to Flat One which she pushed open with her shoulder.

The electricity supply inside had been disconnected not long after Christmas but the front room, empty except for a low, bare mattress and a few cardboard boxes, was lit sufficiently by the yellow haze of the streetlamp directly outside one of its windows.

It was her usual practice to light a candle and partially draw the curtains. Maybe she had a bad feeling, a foreboding from deep within urging her to get out of there as quickly as possible. Not that she had ever lingered in the flat; she hated the place. It was cold and dirty, its walls mottled with damp. Whatever the reason, Lynette did not waste time with the bother of a candle that night.

◆ ◆ ◆

Sylvia Leyshon lived in a ground-floor flat in Louisa Place, a two-storey block of buff-brick flats on the edge of a small estate, where only a small walkway of no more than twenty-five yards separated her window from the side of 7 James Street.

As Sylvia was suffering from ill health, her niece, Peggy, had come to stay for the weekend in order to assist her, and the two women had stayed up until 1.30 a.m. watching the late film.

Despite the cold, Sylvia's windows were open as she disliked the effects of central heating. She was born and bred in the area, so had no qualms about security and had become used to filtering out the noise from the street outside.

Sporadic squalls of passers-by broke the whisk of traffic on James Street and the muffled, vibrating thud of bass speakers drifting on the wind from the Casablanca nightclub nearby.

It must have about been twenty minutes later, as the two prepared for bed, that Sylvia stopped in her tracks on hearing a woman scream. So loud, she did not have to strain to hear the screams stopping and starting about three times, the silence in between punctured by frantic calls for help. She could not be sure exactly how long they had lasted but it was a good while, five minutes, she later told police, after which time they stopped.

The women were so disturbed that Peggy took her Alsatian dog outside into the garden to check if she could see anything.

A mist had begun drifting inland from the sea, carrying with it the lament of the Flat Holm foghorn as a group of couples passed by at the end of a night out. Peggy remembered the unsteady scrape of one of the women's stiletto heels on the pavement. She scanned the area close by but could see nothing untoward. And so, the women retired to bed, putting the screams down to a drunken domestic; after all, they reasoned, it was normal to hear all manner of shrieking and shouting on the weekends after the bars and clubs emptied.

As she spoke with police later that week, Sylvia Leyshon said that she had known Lynette White because she had been friendly with her daughter for a time. She had no idea she was connected with the James Street flats next door and said that the last time she had seen her was about a fortnight before, when she had called out to her through the window to ask if she would get some cigarettes. Lynette duly returned from the shop and, as Sylvia handed her money, she seemed her normal happy self.

But Sylvia Leyshon and her niece were not alone in hearing the screams. A short distance away, another woman described being awoken around the same time. 'It was a frightening, piercing scream,' she said, 'which, to me didn't seem to be someone fooling around.'

Unnerved, the woman had got out of bed to look out of her window towards a nearby pub on the dock front but it was in darkness.

Most of the pubs in the area were long closed by then. The only club still going strong at that hour was the Casablanca, where promoters were holding a Valentine's evening. Lover's rock reggae singer Sandra Cross from Brixton, supported by Birmingham's Stereo Classic sound system, had drawn a sizeable crowd including two coach parties from out of town.

Popular with students and locals and all sorts in between, a diverse crowd was drawn to the Casablanca's distinctive blue-and-white-painted brick exterior. It stood in the old financial quarter of Mount Stuart Square, next to the Coal Exchange, now virtually derelict except for its historic trading hall, where rock concerts were held.

The Casablanca had originally been Bethel Baptist Chapel, built in the mid-1800s, its ornate Italianate style reflecting its high status at the time. After falling out of use as a church in 1955, the building had taken on new life as a cabaret and strip bar before being bought by a Bajan entrepreneur who had settled in Cardiff.

Its fame quickly grew far beyond the city limits as a legendary live music venue, with some obligatory Tiger Bay notoriety thrown in for good measure.

Despite its reputation, trouble or the threat of it was no more prevalent in the Casablanca than any other club in the city, with the important caveat that if it was trouble you were looking for, then make no mistake you would find more than you could handle in Tiger Bay.

But on Valentine's Day 1988, the extent of any trouble had been the singer being booed off stage when her PA system broke and a woman the worse for wear being helped off the floor by bouncers.

After stopping for a nightcap, the staff had, as usual on a busy weekend, locked its doors at around 3.30 a.m. and filtered through a nearby gully to walk the few minutes to their homes around Loudoun Square.

It was just before 9 p.m. later on Valentine's Day, as the weekend shift at Butetown Police Station, due to clock off soon, were preparing their handover, when a member of the public, a young woman, walked through the entrance and up to the front desk.

Her name was Leanne Vilday, a slim nineteen-year-old with long brown hair scraped back off her face and tied in a pony tail.

It was concerning a friend of hers, she explained, Lynette White. She had not seen her for days. Every night without fail, Leanne would bump into Lynette at the Custom House, but no one had seen hide nor hair of her. The Custom House was a landmark pub close to the bridge, a nexus of the city's sex trade, one every police officer in the area was familiar with.

Leanne Vilday told how she had lent her friend the keys to a flat she had recently rented at 7 James Street. She had just come from there; on finding the door locked, she had looked through the letterbox and there were a couple of things that did not seem right – doors shut that were usually tied open. She just had a feeling something was wrong.

Ordinarily the officers would have logged her report and passed it on to the night shift, but the more experienced of the two, a sergeant who had policed the docks for nigh on twenty years, intuited something from the woman's agitated, shaking demeanour. It unnerved him. The flat was barely four hundred metres down the road. The sergeant instructed his constable to fetch the patrol car from the back car park.

At 7 James Street the officers led the way upstairs by torchlight, with Leanne Vilday following behind. The handle of the door to Flat One was loose, and with a sharp kick, the door sprang open. Inside, they traced their torch beams over a small hallway, the floor scattered with rubbish, and scanned the three internal doors, all of which were firmly closed.

The nearest opened into a kitchen leading through to a bathroom at the far end. Along the entire rim of the bath, a row of spent matchsticks and cigarette butts stood on their ends, had been oddly arranged in an alternating pattern.

Doubling back to the hall, the police opened a second door. The room contained just two mattresses propped against the wall.

Approaching a third door, the officers gestured to one another as the cone of light picked up smudges of blood on the paintwork. Inside, lying between the mattress and the streetlight window was the body of a woman. There was no mistaking it: she was dead.

As the sergeant radioed for back-up, describing the grim discovery, Leanne Vilday, who had been ordered to wait outside the flat, cried out and began sobbing loudly.

Within a short time, the area around 7 James Street was alive with the flashing blue lamps of patrol cars as officers, uniformed and plain clothes, rifled through the gardens of nearby flats, lifted drain covers and emptied street bins.

Locals walked by, craning their necks, and traffic backed up as drivers slowed down, distracted by the commotion, a blur of red brake lights shrouded by a miasma of white smoke rising from tailpipe fumes and hitting the cold night air.

The duty detective inspector, Richard Powell, had not long arrived from Cardiff Central Station where he was based, a couple of miles away in the city centre. He had secured the scene, where efforts were being made to restore power to Flat One, and was busy taking preliminary statements from the tenants of the two flats above.

The phone had rung late on Sunday night at Home Office pathologist Professor Bernard Knight's home. Sudden deaths did not observe office hours and in his decades of experience, collecting his kit and leaving his house in the northern suburbs of the city at a moment's notice whatever the time of day or night, had become second nature.

He had conducted upwards of twenty-five thousand autopsies in his career, many thousands of them examining the ravaged lungs of coal miners to evaluate pneumoconiosis. There had, of course, been countless murder cases on his books, and this, he had thought to himself, was another sad story of a lady of the night who had succumbed to their version of 'industrial disease'.

He had dealt with a number of such cases around the docks over the years. One of the most prominent was that of thirty-one-year-old Nora Wilfred, regarded by neighbours in the Newport area, twelve miles east of Cardiff, as a devoted wife and mother-of-four. But for two or three months prior, her husband had been dropping her off close to the Custom House pub two or three nights a week, doing so for the final time on a rainy night in December 1972.

The following day, Nora Wilfred's body was found dumped on wasteland, 'curled up as if she was praying', police reported. Judging by her injuries, she had put up a fierce struggle before succumbing to multiple stab wounds.

On the day of her murder, Cardiff had been besieged by thousands of sports fans for prominent rugby and football fixtures, as well as droves of Christmas shoppers. Despite substantial rewards for information and an exhaustive police investigation, the case of Nora Wilfred remained unsolved, one of only two unsettled murders in the city over the preceding twenty-five years.

The murders of sex workers are notoriously difficult to solve, the aftermath of an explosion of rage during a fleeting meeting between strangers with no traceable connection. Its victims are often isolated and vulnerable, and the men that use them are unwilling to come forward for fear the exposure of their shadowy avocation will damage their reputations and family lives. In the case of Nora Wilfred, that is precisely where police had laid the blame: on a 'wall of silence' from the vice community.

Fingers would inevitably and unfairly point to Tiger Bay. The majority of the women and clients came to the area from outside, but that was a fact easily overlooked.

Back at James Street, after waiting for what seemed like an eternity in the bitter cold and wind for scenes-of-crime officers to finish up, Professor Bernard Knight finally climbed the stairs to the flat at around 3 a.m. The crime scene was illuminated by tall lamps powered by a generator, its carpet protected by a walkway of thin metal sheets.

There was blood everywhere.

Lynette White lay on her back in the left-hand corner of the room underneath the window, her head turned towards one side, partly exposing a severe wound to her throat.

Her right arm stretched outwards, as if reaching for the foot of the nearby bed, her left bent upwards at the elbow, her bloodstained open palm almost touching her injured face.

Kneeling down, Professor Knight noted that the body was fully clothed, dressed in a leather coat, grey stone-washed jeans, white ankle socks, a black T-shirt worn under a grey sweatshirt, its large motif no longer discernible due to heavy bloodstaining and lacerations.

Her right shoe, a flat, black, lace-up pump, lay close to her head, a few inches from a black wristwatch, its strap broken.

Professor Knight helped remove the coat needed for fingerprint analysis, noting that only Lynette's left arm was through the sleeve. The right sleeve and the rest of the coat had wrapped and tightened like rope around her chest, likely the result of a struggle before her body was rolled or dragged.

Lynette White's body had been moved in extremis, of that there was no doubt. The pattern of blood spatter clearly showed an initial injury to her neck had been inflicted a few metres away. Professor Knight could also see the rips and tears on all areas of her clothing had become displaced from the knife wounds underneath.

Inevitably, one of the first things the police would want from him was the likely time of death. Theories on estimating that accounted for the most common research projects in forensic medicine. He had authored the only book in the English language on the subject at the time. Running to three hundred-odd pages, it concluded, more or less, that you cannot reliably do it.

The nonsensical statements of pathologists in TV police dramas – 'he must have died at twenty past two last Tuesday' – would drive him up the wall. If you get the right day, you are doing pretty well. There are just too many variables.

Signs of rigor mortis were of little use. The only hope of getting anywhere near a time of death, Professor Knight would tell his students, is body temperature. When somebody dies the body's temperature starts falling, but at different rates depending on a number of factors – the size of the person, whether they are fat or thin, the temperature in the room when they breathed their last breath. If the central heating goes off or on or someone opens a window, the whole picture is shot to pieces.

Working stringently within parameters of inaccuracy, the best his expertise could deduce was that Lynette White had been killed somewhere in the region of twenty-four hours before.

Arrangements were made to transport the body to his mortuary a few miles away at Cardiff Royal Infirmary's Institute of Pathology, where he would perform the autopsy without delay.

Before he began, Lynette's remains were identified by her next of kin. South Wales's most senior investigator, Detective Chief Superintendent John Williams, escorted her distraught father, forty-one-year-old Terry White, into the mortuary. He had been awoken at his home in the Rumney area of the city at 4 a.m. by police knocking on the door.

As the start of his examination, Professor Knight switched on the handheld tape machine he used to record fragmentary notes. 'The body is that of a normally built girl of about the stated age, height 5ft 4 ins,' he said. 'She has shoulder-length brown hair with areas of bleaching . . .'

He then began the process of placing small white adhesive labels next to each decipherable wound.

'These are numbered for identification, though as many of the wounds are overlapping, description is difficult,' he continued.

Professor Knight enumerated fifty major and distinguishable wounds to Lynette's body, the majority of which had been inflicted to her chest and most of which appeared, due to lack of bleeding, to have been made perimortem, at or near the time of death. But it was a conservative estimate, and he readily accepted that the total number of injures, allowing for overlapping and defensive wounds to her hands, could easily be as many as seventy.

He wrote up his report immediately after. The cause of death: cut throat and multiple stab wounds.

◆ ◆ ◆

By the time Detective Chief Superintendent John Williams arrived back at Cardiff Central Police Station from the mortuary, the city's TV, radio and newspaper reporters had been primed for a press conference that morning.

It left little time to prepare but he was unfazed. The 'golden hour' countdown had begun. The success of any criminal investigation hinged on progress made in the time immediately following the crime. With so many unanswered questions, an inquiry of this nature was contingent on a hard-hitting public appeal for information, one that was spread as widely as possible.

His deputy, Detective Superintendent Ken Davies, convened an early briefing of East Division's Serious Crime Squad. Two incident rooms were now in operation in the city centre and the docks. Over fifty officers had been assigned to three teams: house-to-house inquiries, victim's background and connections, and persons to be traced, interviewed and eliminated.

Lynette White's boyfriend had already been picked up and was at the docks police station. He was fully cooperative and not thought to be a suspect.

Meanwhile, calls were put in to the South Wales Criminal Intelligence Bureau for a steer on possible prime suspects, the port authority for shipping lines in and out of the docks, and neighbouring forces for any parallels with recent murders of young females on their patch.

Detective Inspector Richard Powell, the duty officer who had first arrived in James Street, provided an update of statements taken by other occupants of the flats, the long and short of which was that they had heard absolutely nothing untoward on the night of the murder.

As for Leanne Vilday, a friend of the victim, they were suspicious that she knew more than she was prepared to say. She had rented the flat at 7 James Street but was saving to buy furniture and, in the meantime, she and her baby son were lodging with another woman across the road.

Nothing at that stage was clear. From what Professor Knight had concluded, Lynette White may well have lain dead for longer than a day. But there was one early clue.

The wristwatch recovered from the floor near Lynette White's body, a present from her boyfriend, looked like it had been torn from her wrist during the attack, its clock hands having stopped between 1.45 and 1.50 a.m.

It had been sent for examination and, when opened up by a horologist, the quartz crystal inside suddenly vibrated, springing the mechanism back into action, the tick-tick of the second hand audible once more. The simplest explanation, in his opinion, was that shock had caused it to stop.

As signs go, it was fairly convincing.

Chapter Two

John Actie swung open the front gate of his home on Bute Street and stepped into a cold and hazy Monday morning, when he crossed paths with a neighbour, who broke the news that would fast become the talk of the city.

A creature of habit, at the same time every weekday around 8 a.m., John would finish his tea and head out to the shops for the morning newspaper. The convention may well have jarred with his reputation but, nonetheless, the fact remained that John Actie, just like his father, Charlie, before him, was unstinting when it came to keeping abreast of current affairs.

'Did you hear about the murder?' his neighbour asked him.

'Murder?' John replied. 'What murder?'

'Lynette White.'

'Who's Lynette White?'

John turned the name over and over, scrolling through his mind. Lynette White . . . Lynette White . . . The name meant nothing. Found above the bookie's on James Street, John. Crawling with police. A young girl apparently. Terrible. Just terrible.

The blaze of squad cars John had seen the night before now made perfect sense. He had been walking the few minutes from his home to the Casablanca when he had bumped into a friend. Rumours had begun to circulate about something happening at the betting shop, possibly a robbery, and the two men diverted their route to walk past the scene and check out what was going on. At no stage had anyone even suggested anything about a murder.

John backtracked into the house and up the stairs to the bedroom where his partner was sleeping. Born and bred in Tiger Bay, Taryn was young, mid-twenties; maybe the name Lynette White would ring a bell with her. But she too drew a blank.

There were a few Whites in the area but then it was a common enough name. They would know more soon enough. Nothing gossip-worthy stood a chance in hell of staying under wraps in Tiger Bay for long.

Besides, there were more pressing matters at hand. Taryn, two days over her due date, prayed for the early grip of labour to take hold; the sooner the baby arrived, the sooner she could begin to feel her old self again. In the meantime, she resolved to sleep a little longer, letting her first-born, just four and not long started school, sleep late. Thank God it was half term.

Beyond the bridge, the early sun started to rise and drew away the cloud, rousing the city. A stir of commuters had built to stop-start jams along the high streets. Metal shopfront grilles clattered open, a ripple of office strip lights blinked into action across town and the hissing hot water spouts of fogged-up cafes screeched into metal tea pots, heralding the start of a new week.

On the northern reaches of the city's bustle, Cardiff Central Police Station, a brutalist concrete-and-glass fortress serving as the headquarters of South Wales Police's Eastern Division, was a hub-bub of activity. Major Crime Squad briefings were in full flow as press officers beetled around the in-house social club, setting out chairs and dragging a table between the bar and an upright piano to serve as a press conference bench.

At 9 a.m. sharp, Detective Chief Superintendent John Williams took to his stage. If he was feeling the effects of a sleepless night, it did not show. Pristine in a blazer and freshly pressed shirt and tie, his eyes, small and flinty, flitted around the assembled battery of reporters and TV crews.

An avid cross-country runner and rugby coach, Williams's physique belied his fifty-one years, but his face, brooding and hawkish, but not unpleasantly so, ringed with a dark, receding horseshoe hairline, gave the game away.

Experienced and unruffled in the media spotlight, he spoke slowly, rhythmically, pausing dramatically mid-sentence, as if his enunciated words, dressed in the full regalia of his archetypal Welsh accent, were keeping time to a single, ominous, martial drum beat.

On the streets of Tiger Bay, Williams may as well have hailed from a different country. The distinct Cardiff patois, a fusion of the tongues of its immigrant forebears, from Ireland to Timbuktu, was faster, more tense and flat, lacking the sing-song of its hinterlands. To the people of the Bay, Williams was a 'Taff', an out-of-towner, bland and parochial, a dyed-in-the-wool Welshmen who belonged to a different tribe, one, history had made it painfully clear, the likes of them had no place in.

Nearly thirty-five years had passed since he had joined the force as a sixteen-year-old cadet from Neath – a market town forty miles west surrounded by heavy industry and, back then, a cultural galaxy away from Cardiff. Williams, whose intensity at times verged on seething, perhaps justifiably, had climbed the ranks, navigating the mounting debris of man's inhumanity to man with every rung.

A devoted family man, he would retire very soon to spend more time with his wife and await a brood of grandchildren to dote on. The murder of Lynette White would be the swansong of an exemplary career. It was, the thought undoubtedly having crossed his mind, one hell of a case to bow out on.

Lynette White was twenty years of age, he began, and had been living in a shared house with her boyfriend in Grangetown, an area contiguous with the docks. Williams skirted around questions about

Lynette's occupation for some unknown reason. He had replied euphemistically that 'she is a Cardiff girl, a popular girl who is fairly well known in the docks'. But the media had already cottoned on and soon so would everyone else. Lynette White had been a sex worker.

'I can tell you,' he added, 'that she has been brutally murdered in what was almost certainly a vicious, frenzied, sadistic attack . . . death has been caused with a sharp instrument, a knife or a piece of metal, with which her upper body has been repeatedly and savagely attacked.'

What the police were urgently appealing for information about was Lynette White's whereabouts in the days leading up to her death. The last positive sighting of her had been on Tuesday, 9 February.

'She had not been seen at her Dorset Street home since this time neither do we have any sightings of her in the dockland area,' Williams continued. 'It's imperative to our inquiry at this time that we find her movements between then and yesterday which was, of course, St Valentine's Day . . . and we will endeavour today through your good offices to try to get people to ring in to see if we can re-trace her movements and that is the inquiry as it stands at the moment.'

The murder hunt had got off to a vigorous start. Three miles away, on James Street, industrial vacuum machines had been towed in to pump the sumps of roadside storm drains in the plausible belief the killer had discarded the knife through the grates as he left the scene.

Police photographers' cameras whirred as shots were taken of every possible angle of the immediate area outside. Groups of officers wearing protective gloves paced hurriedly, clutching brown evidence bags, while a helmeted constable brandishing a clipboard stood guard at the front door of Number Seven, logging the to-and-fro of crime scene investigators in white paper suits.

At the foreshore, sub-aqua divers had mobilised to scour acres of mudflats. Close by, a sweep of beat officers, thankful at least for the dry weather, bear-crawled shoulder to shoulder, combing the estuary bank, a senior officer wearing a trilby hat barking instructions from the sea wall as they turned every stone in their path or at least as many as they could before the tide rushed back in.

Locals surveyed the scene with a mixture of confusion and fascination, pointing out directions to police unfamiliar with the area. Knocking on doors, braces of uniformed and plain clothes officers alike processed basic questionnaires. House-to-house calls were a standard initial strategy of any major crime investigation. A sight or sound that might be brushed aside by a civilian as banal and incidental could provide vital leads to a time-sensitive inquiry.

Meanwhile, just the other side of the bridge at Thomson House, home to the city's newspapers, the first edition of that evening's *South Wales Echo* rolled off the presses and on to the newsstands by early lunchtime.

'Cardiff woman, 20, murdered in frenzied attack', screamed the front-page. Underneath it, a black-and-white head image of a strikingly pretty girl, her brown, shoulder-length, typically 80s hair, worn big and permed with a shaggy fringe hugging her kohl-smoked eyes.

On seeing it, John, never one to shy away from drama, had gasped loudly. 'Oh my God,' he said, 'it's Pineapple's girlfriend!'

Pineapple, otherwise known as Stephen Miller, was a nickname that aptly described his dreadlocks, piled on top of his head and tied in a band so they splayed like the leaves of a pineapple.

John knew him, but not well, as Stephen had not lived in the area for long, maybe two years. He might bump into him in the Casablanca and pass the time of day. A few times he had seen him driving around with his girlfriend, who he would nod acknowledgement to, maybe, if he saw her walking along Bute Street, but he had never conversed with her. There would have been nothing to say.

While there were a number of clubs and pubs in Tiger Bay – the Paradise, the Dowlais, the Packet, the Paddle Steamer, the Bosun, the list goes on – there were two that loosely defined distinct factions in the area: the Casablanca and the North Star. John would frequent the former, and Lynette the latter.

A single-storey former seaman's mission near the dock front, the North Star, dirty white with a soulless black door, was as windowless as it was unprepossessing. The uninitiated might have mistaken it for a lock-up, the sort found in railway arches. The initiated, however, would call it what it was: a roughhouse dive.

Serving only cans of lager from the local cash and carry so no glasses were required, the club would open around 9 p.m., the night's appointed DJ setting up in his booth, complete with flashing lights, an hour or so later. The proprietor, a tiny, grey-haired woman by the name of Eileen, in her late sixties, would arrive by taxi around midnight to preside, along with her doormen, until 3 a.m. or maybe 4 a.m., depending on how busy it was.

A drinking hole for the few overseas sailors who still docked in Cardiff, as well as gay men and lesbians who were on the fringes of society at the time, the North Star also offered a refuge for the working girls, somewhere to kick back in the relative safety of its tatty bench seats to recall the night's dramas and then drink to forget them.

At the end of every working night, Lynette would arrive by taxi to meet Stephen. As she waited for him, she would flirt with the old-timers, clutching a can of Breaker and a packet of Embassy Regal, and spill on to the postage-stamp dancefloor.

But the North Star was not for John Actie. Not that he had a problem with the sex workers – that was all part of the rhythm of life in the docks as far as he was concerned. It did not make them bad people, it was just that side of street life held little interest for him.

The extent of his connection with the North Star was the infrequent occasions in the past that he had deigned to darken its door in order to hustle or scam, selling 'weed' to sailors, a fiver or a tenner in exchange for a fold of paper sprinkled with nothing more than dried thyme, which he bought in bulk bags from the delicatessen in one of the arcades up town. He would be in and out as quickly as possible.

Stephen Miller, though, tended to straddle the two worlds, socialising with the few friends he had made in the Casablanca and retiring to the North Star to meet Lynette at around 1 a.m. every morning. It was where the two had met during a visit to Cardiff to see his older brother Anthony, who had moved to the city from Brixton in south London, and set up home with a local girl.

It was in fact his younger brother, Mark, who had first introduced them. During frequent visits to South Wales, Mark had begun seeing Lynette, but their relationship had dwindled after a few months and he had since moved back to London. Stephen and Lynette hit it off immediately and during the fortnight he stayed in Cardiff, they grew close.

Keeping in touch on the phone after he left, within a few months Lynette called with the news that she had found him a place to stay and so he moved to Cardiff to see if they could make a go of things. Although a former girlfriend had borne Stephen's son, it had only been a fleeting liaison. Lynette was his first serious relationship.

For him, Butetown was a different world compared to south London, the only other place he had ever known in his twenty-two years. Its village atmosphere, where everyone seemed to know everyone else, was a novel experience for him and he enjoyed its lively nightlife and the warm welcome it gave to strangers, regardless of the colour of their skin.

It was a far cry from the ever-widening racial fault lines of Brixton, which he had witnessed erupting into race riots in recent years. And, of course, he liked to think that hailing from London afforded him a certain status, one under which his true nature – shy, more than a bit nervous and socially ill at ease – could hide.

Stephen had been in the North Star on Valentine's Day looking for Lynette. He remembered it being between eleven and midnight when there was a knock on the club door and two detectives walked in and asked for him.

He was seen crying as he was escorted outside after being asked to come with them to the station, where he was shown into an office containing a table and chairs, and told to wait.

After staring at the four walls for an hour, his mind racing, the door was opened by an impeccably dressed officer. He introduced himself as Detective Inspector Richard Powell and proceeded to take down some rudimentary details. It was only later in the conversation that he told Stephen he had some bad news: they had found Lynette's body in 7 James Street.

The words 'Lynette' and 'body' seemed to swirl and collide in Stephen's head, and he struggled and failed to make sense of the news. He later recalled feeling like a part of him was not there. Then after a while, almost as if on auto-pilot, he jabbered pell-mell about London, something about his home, how he and Lynette were due to travel there that weekend.

Powell left the room, and after remaining stock still for another few minutes, Stephen turned to the window overlooking the streetlamps on James Street, broke down and began sobbing.

During subsequent questioning, Powell made no bones about it, reminding him frequently that his girlfriend had been mutilated, cut up, her body left in a terrible state. Stephen gasped back tears, wiping his eyes and face, thanking a uniformed officer who had brought him a cup of tea.

Did he know 7 James Street? He knew James Street but not Number Seven. It was a flat above the bookmaker's, he was told. Yes, he knew where the bookie's was but he had never been inside and he was at a loss as to why Lynette would be there. As far as he knew, she would take any clients to a friend's flat elsewhere in the city.

Wanting to do anything and everything he could to help, Stephen willingly stripped off his clothes, each item placed in a sealed bag for testing, and held out his arm when the doctor arrived to take a sample of his blood.

Stephen remained in the room dressed in his socks and a boiler suit. In the early hours of Monday morning, after what seemed like an eternity of questions, he asked if he could go home to feed Lynette's dog. He would try to get some rest and come back the next day.

No, he was told, they would like him to stay as there were more questions. Officers said he could use a mattress in the station's cell if he wanted to get some sleep. Stephen declined, opting instead to try to sleep resting his head on his folded arms. Even though he had not been arrested and was not thought to be a suspect, when he wanted to use the toilet he was escorted there and back by an officer, who would then leave, locking the door behind him.

In line with what everyone associated with Lynette, her friends and acquaintances, had told police, the last time he had seen Lynette was the Tuesday before. She had a bath, and the two of them had watched television and played the card game Hearts.

As usual, they had left home, a room in a shared terraced house, and Stephen had given Lynette a lift in his blue Ford Cortina, dropping her near the Custom House early evening and arranging to meet later as usual in the North Star.

The couple, Stephen explained, had argued on the previous Sunday night after Lynette had accused him of being with another woman. He had shouted at her and she had left the North Star, staying elsewhere that night, he presumed at one of her aunties' houses. But by the Monday, she had come home and they had patched things up, had some dinner and watched a film.

They argued from time to time, like everyone, he said, but Lynette had seemed happy as they parted. He had waited for her in the North Star on Tuesday night but she never showed up.

Every day that week he had searched for her, dropping in and out of the North Star, seeking out her friends and quizzing them, each swearing blind they had not seen her. In each shop, bar and club he went into, he would ask everyone, 'Have you seen Lynette?'

At the Casablanca, somewhere Lynette did not frequent, only on occasion asking at the door for Stephen, he had asked so often that it had become something of a joke, the likes of John Actie and others in there rolling their eyes and ribbing him that she had left him for another man.

Paul Coombes, the couple's landlord, who also lived in the Dorset Street house, had asked around, calling at the Custom House and a few pubs nearby, but he too drew a blank. After he and Stephen had phoned around hospitals, they agreed to give it a few more days before reporting her missing.

The only explanation Stephen could come up with for her sudden disappearance was that Lynette had been scared about having to give evidence at a court case. Two cases in fact. One involved a fight between two sex workers at the North Star. She had been due to give evidence at the trial on 12 February but had not showed up and a witness summons had been issued by the judge. A second trial involved two men accused of prostituting a fifteen-year-old girl. But detectives had made inquiries into both cases, and while they were keeping an open mind, they doubted there was any connection.

Maybe it had all got on top of her, Stephen had said. Lynette was also being chased over the non-payment of fines for soliciting. It was usual practice that the girls would appear in court on a rotation basis; vice squad officers gave them a particular date to turn up and they would plead guilty and receive a fine. A blind eye might have been turned to the flagrant prostitution around the Custom House but the police had to be seen to at least go through the motions of trying to curb it.

Stephen admitted that Lynette would give him money but vehemently disagreed with the officers' accusations that he was her pimp. According to his logic, Lynette had been working on the street long before they had met.

A pimp, in his book, was someone who forced a woman to work the streets. On the contrary, he had been jealous of her being with other men and had tried many times to persuade her to stop, telling her she could do better. A couple of times she had relented, taking up jobs leafleting or doing bar work but the pay was miserly and each time she would relapse, appeasing her boyfriend by saying it was 'easy money' and that it would not be forever.

Before long, they settled into a routine of Lynette giving him money, often also meeting him halfway through the night so he could buy weed and sate a burgeoning cocaine habit. But, he argued, she did so of her own free will and he was categorically not a pimp.

While being held at the station he had sobbed uncontrollably when asked if he had killed her. Giving a full account of his whereabouts on the weekend she died, he said he had watched sport on TV before driving to a friend's house and on to the pub before heading to the Casablanca after 11 p.m. He had played pool and flitted between there and the North Star, still looking for Lynette.

After two days in the police station, Stephen was not coping. Upset and confused, the officers finally agreed he could go home. Still dressed in a boiler suit and socks, he was driven in a patrol car to Dorset Street.

He went upstairs to their bedroom to find it had been wrecked, the wardrobes emptied of his and Lynette's clothes. Drawers had been pulled out and their contents tipped on to the bed and floor. As he started to clear up, he switched on the portable TV on the chest of drawers next to a small bear holding a red love heart, last year's Valentine's gift to Lynette.

The news was on. John Williams was appealing for the city's prostitutes to come forward and assist the murder hunt. There was no escape.

Everyone in the docks and the rest of the city was talking about the murder. For John Actie, though, the fervour of speculation had been eclipsed by the arrival of a healthy baby girl, Remi, two days after Lynette White had died.

After a troubled youth, everything had come good, Remi's arrival turning the page on a brand-new chapter in his life. He had found a woman he loved, become a stepfather to her young daughter and now had a baby of his own. And if there was one thing John loved more than his beloved dogs, it was children.

Behind his colossal stature and a reputation for fighting of such mythical proportions that opponents, including the likes of Cardiff's senior Welsh heavyweight champion-turned-professional boxer Rudi Pika, would seek him out and challenge him, there was another side to John. Those that knew him well would be more likely to highlight his wide, full-face smile than his brute force.

John Actie was someone you definitely did not want to be on the wrong side of, but he would not gun for you to be his enemy. If you upset him, though, make no mistake, you would know about it. John was upfront and in your face. Mess with his family or a friend and chances are you would, quite literally, not know what hit you.

John's size became apparent from a very early age. Things had started out well for him as a boy. Standing head and shoulders above his schoolfriends, John's prowess on the rugby field, a combination of lightning speed and deadly heft, marked him out for success.

For his sports-obsessed father, Charlie Actie, John was a prodigy. He watched proudly in the stands of a twelve-thousand-strong crowd at Cardiff Arms Park as John swept St Cadoc's Roman Catholic School under-11s rugby side to victory and lift the coveted Del Harries Memorial Cup. Sitting at his father's legs as the family watched excerpts of the match on television the following day, part of coverage of an international game that same weekend, John recalled his father's pride at the commentary. The memory remained the highlight of his life.

'*Two minutes from the end, as a result of a penalty kick taken on the 25-yard line, a try was scored by John Actie and converted. The score at the end of the match was 10–4.*'

While a strict disciplinarian at home, making John and his older brother, Stephen, dig the garden for the slightest indiscretion, Charlie Actie, a hulk of a man with hands as large as shovels, would lavish time on his second son, travelling all over the city and the furthest stretches of the Valleys to see him play for Cardiff Youth.

Known to grab any spectator who dared utter a racist slur at his son during play and lift him by the collar into mid-air, Charlie Actie abhorred discrimination of any kind.

If there was one thing he had instilled in his young son above any other, it was to never back down in the face of fear. As one of the very few black families on a predominantly white council estate, his son needed to learn to stand up for himself. If John came home distressed about being picked on by the older boys, he would be ordered back outside to confront them. 'You never back down from a fight, son. Never!'

Charlie Actie was one of eleven children who had grown up in Tiger Bay's heyday, the son of Sarah Jane, of Welsh and Bajan descent, and Robinson John Actie, who had docked from St Lucia in 1916, all 6 feet 8 inches of him. John Senior, known as the 'gentle giant', had been a thinking man, active within the civil rights movement following the race riots of 1919.

A prolific letter writer, his correspondence with influential African-American scholar and activist St Clair Drake, whom he met during Drake's studies in Tiger Bay, are still held in the New York Public Library.

Robinson John Actie also campaigned with the League of Coloured Peoples to end the colour bar, which not only racially discriminated when it came to jobs and housing but also in restaurants and hotels, many of which refused to serve black people.

Living in Tiger Bay at that time were more foreign and ethnic-minority seamen than the combined total of all Britain's provincial ports; aside from London, it had the largest number of residents from overseas in the UK.

It was a world Charlie Actie had grown up in, and he had been on the receiving end of racial discrimination more times than he cared to remember.

At his wedding to Maria Quinn, an eighteen-year-old former swimming champion, ten years his junior, the feelings of his in-laws were made painfully clear. They stayed away. Countless times, a young Maria had been warned by her parents, 'Stay away from that bridge. We don't want some big black man stealing you away.'

The Quinns were a family whose lineage was as much a part of the history of the city as coal. Originally from the Newtown area, otherwise known as 'Little Ireland', their antecedents were among the swathes of Irish who had sailed to Cardiff to escape the ravages of the potato famine. They were given homes by the Marquess of Bute in return for building his burgeoning dock. While the Quinns treated their grandchildren as their own, Charlie Actie, on account of his colour, was persona non grata.

After many years at sea, Charlie gained steady employment as a steel erector, working on the early phases of the Severn Bridge's construction at the time of John's arrival into the world in early October 1961.

By then, the demolition of Tiger Bay was in full flow, and not long after, Charlie and Maria took up the offer of relocation to the council estate of Llanrumney on the eastern reaches of the city, settling into family life in Parracombe Crescent, a fan of spacious semis with garages and generous gardens, built around a central green.

As a member of one of the very few black families living on the estate, even as a child John had always felt like a fish out of water, feeling a much stronger connection with his birthplace. On weekends and school holidays, he would stay with his grandmother in Tiger Bay, his grandfather having died some years before, waking up to the comforting mews of circling gulls.

But not long after the arrival of their seventh child – Charlie and Maria had three sons and four daughters, including twin girls – Charlie Actie became unwell and was later diagnosed with lung cancer.

Following surgery, he was given the all-clear, much to the relief of his celebrating family, only for the disease to return to his throat. By the age of twelve, John had unknowingly visited his father in Holme Towers hospice in Penarth, on the other side of the bay, for the last time. Forty-three-year-old Charlie Actie had reprimanded his son for playing up his mother, a final memory, the regret of which John would forever struggle with. Maybe he had done so subconsciously, but it seemed John had directed his life in such a way that he had been told off ever since.

He had been at the home of his best friend David Bishop, who would go on to don the red jersey and play rugby for Wales, when a relative telephoned and asked that John come home immediately. Unaware of the reason, John raced round the block on his red Raleigh Chopper, bursting through the door to be confronted by the entire Actie clan assembled in the front room. He immediately clocked the photograph of his parents' wedding day was missing from the mantelpiece. His crying mother was nursing it in the back room. It was one of his uncles who took him to one side to tell him his father had died.

Screaming and in tears, John ran outside and careered up the drive chased by relatives. Losing his footing in his blind panic, he tripped, crashing into a wall and, as his younger sister Donna recalled, was knocked unconscious. When he came round a short time later, life as he knew it was irrevocably changed.

At the vigil for Charlie Actie in the family's front room during the Christmas week of 1973, John struggled to reconcile the contrast of his Dada, once so strong and seemingly invincible, the protective force who would tuck him behind his imposing frame to shield him from the wind and rain as they walked home from rugby training, now laid waste in a white shroud, his once handsome, dark-skinned face ashen and famished. The agonising image burned deep into his young mind.

On the January day of his father's funeral, John had been dressed in a new suit as the cortege set off on the fifteen or so-minute drive to Tiger Bay's St Mary the Virgin, on Bute Street, the church and its surrounding streets lined with mourners.

During the burial at the city's Cathays Cemetery, John's uncles tried to console him as he howled, watching his stricken younger sister being restrained as she screamed and fought to lie down on top of the lowering coffin. Everything was finished. Nothing, John thought to himself, could ever be as bad as that day.

His father had been his touchstone, and the trauma of his loss seemed to have imbued John's chemistry with such a fury at the injustice of his early death and its resulting sense of futility that he seemed to become a living, breathing testament to the scientific principle of like attracting like.

As Maria was forced to take on cleaning work to meet mortgage payments while raising seven children, John imploded. Refusing to play rugby now his father was not around to watch, he would idle away hours climbing on to the garden shed roof with his air rifle, taking potshots at the backsides of schoolchildren cutting through a nearby lane from the bus stop.

Regularly truanting from school, on the occasions he did make it through the gates of St Illtyd's Catholic High, at the time run by monks, he would be disruptive, stealing sweets and dinner money from other pupils and swearing at teachers when chastised. Eventually, John was excluded after he punched a teacher who was dragging him by his hair to the headmaster's office for another caning.

Made a ward of court, much to Maria's horror, John was dispatched to a series of approved schools. Desperately homesick, he would regularly run away, making his way across fields of open countryside in the howling rain to the nearest train station and somehow back home.

As the rest of the family were eating tea, he would suddenly appear at the kitchen window. 'Mum! Mum! John has escaped again,' his siblings would shout. Maria would be tearing her hair out, part of her wanting to hide him away but the better part of her knowing she had to call the authorities.

From there it was on to a detention centre, where on arrival John was beaten up at the reception for not calling the warden 'sir'. He soon became inured to racial abuse and violence. Being forced to move around in bunny hops for long periods, punished if he faltered and used his arms to steady himself, was part of normal life but one that bred within John a hatred of authority and its systems.

The boys were made to scrub flows with house bricks and forced to play a game called 'murder ball'. Separated by ethnic groups, white and black, staff would watch from the gymnasium sidelines as the lads punched and kicked for possession of the ball, some requiring hospital treatment as a result.

John graduated to borstal, where he was racially abused and beaten on a daily basis for fighting with other boys, spending the majority of his time in solitary confinement. Having witnessed the lifeless bodies of other boys who had hung themselves with belts from dormitory doors, he knew his experience, however traumatising, paled by comparison. Many of them, John knew, had been victims of sexual abuse meted out by some of those in charge.

By the time John had finished his 'schooling', the die was cast. Then, like a coming of age or graduation, at sixteen came his first term of detention, three years for robbery.

But there was more to come.

In February 1984, trains from the Valleys and across Wales spilled a sea of red jerseys from every rugby-mad town and village on to the streets of Cardiff city centre. The national stadium resonated with the sonorous capacity crowd battle-cry rendition of the national anthem, 'Hen Wlad Fy Nhadau' ('Land of My Fathers') before Wales v. France kicked off on a bright, fine afternoon.

Just before half-time, three teenagers from Port Talbot, an industrial town thirty-six miles west of Cardiff, left the stadium having grown tired of the crush in the stands. They wandered under the bridge, a fabled portal for visiting rugby fans on international days, to get a pint. Disappointed to see the pub was closed, they sat on the kerb waiting for it to open. As they did so, two 'coloured men' walked by asking if they wanted to buy ganja. They declined but then grinned at one another before calling the men back.

'Come with us,' said the taller of the men, bearded with long dreadlocks. 'We've got Leb, black, Morocco, bush, grass, you can have a quart for £14.'

Tearing off a strip of a rugby programme, the tall man emptied an amount of what looked like grass and wrapped it up, also handing over a small block of a darker substance before he yelled at everyone to run. As they did, three plain-clothes officers jumped out of a parked unmarked white car.

Lab tests showed the 'grass' to be a 'green herbal material', likely thyme, but the solid substance was confirmed as cannabis resin, enough for a single joint. The tall man with dreadlocks had been identified as John Actie and he was asked to come in for questioning.

He did so but was belligerent, demanding his solicitor be called. When told to calm down, John brandished the back of his hand, waving it menacingly in the face of one of the officers. Through gritted teeth, he hissed, 'Do you want this?' before clenching his fist and jabbing it towards the officer's face, sending him reeling backwards in fear of a blow.

On being charged, John had grinned: 'When no one's around, I'm going to have you. You may think you have me on this rubbish but I'm going to have you.' It is no exaggeration to say that the police were terrified of John Actie.

Sentenced to a year in jail, his first term in an adult prison, this was only the start of a pitched battle between John Actie and the police.

◆　◆　◆

At 9 p.m. on Thursday, 17 March 1988, the streets of Tiger Bay had emptied as everybody, John and his partner Taryn included, sat glued to their television sets.

With its instantly recognisable theme tune, an urgent blend of chopper-blades, drums and droning synthesisers, *Crimewatch UK*, a monthly live broadcast on BBC One, regularly attracted audiences of thirteen million. Well known for its dramatised reconstructions of unsolved crimes, senior detectives would also feature to appeal to viewers to phone in with information.

Among the police officers that month were John Williams and his team from South Wales Police. Securing a slot on such a high-profile show early in the inquiry was something of a coup.

The reconstruction opened with a panoramic shot of the Bay, the host describing Lynette White as a practical girl who had turned to prostitution to make a living after a troubled childhood. Seven nights a week, the viewers were told, she would be seen working the area, often taking clients to the flat in James Street before meeting friends at a nearby club in the early hours of the morning.

The scene cut to the North Star, where a regular, a taxi driver called Jack Ellis, talked fondly of Lynette White. In his police statements, though, he said he had seen a marked change in her during the final weeks of her life. She had lost her spark. No longer her chatty and bubbly self, Ellis remarked that she had become 'sloppy', dressing in the same clothes, jeans and jacket.

The film showed how confirmed sightings of Lynette White had been around 11.30 p.m. on Saturday 13th, when two acquaintances had briefly chatted to her as she stood outside the Club Mont Merence, known as Monty's, a no-frills disco in the city centre.

She was still circulating in the area around the home where she and Stephen lived, as earlier that day, as she did every Saturday morning, she had called in at the local pharmacy to buy her usual: condoms and deodorant.

The reference to her troubled childhood pointed to Lynette White's parents, who never married, having split up when she was a baby, her mother, Peggy, returning to her native Essex with Lynette's sister, who was a year older. Terry White's large birth family, originally from the docks, his sister, also called Lynette, and his mother in particular provided what little stability Lynette had with her father moving around for work and in and out of prison over the years for short stretches.

When Lynette White was four, Terry White remarried and in time they moved away from the docks to the Rumney area of Cardiff. His daughter, he said, got on well with her stepmother, Carol, who later had two children, a girl and a boy. Around the time Lynette White started comprehensive school, she had been devastated by the death of her paternal grandmother, a woman who had been the one constant in her young life.

Remembered as a chatty and pleasant pupil, her school life was unremarkable until she began truanting, which caused rows with her father. Soon after she left home at sixteen, Terry White found out she had become involved with sex work and the two became estranged.

He was devastated by her death, putting up a £1,000 reward for any information about her killer. And on *Crimewatch* that night, the odds of finding the killer looked good, as an early and compelling lead was revealed.

During the round of house-to-house calls, a teenage girl living close to the murder scene told police she had seen a strange man as she walked her dog past the James Street flat on the afternoon of Valentine's Day, a few hours before Lynette's body was discovered.

Leaning against the wall next to the front door, the man's arms were crossed around his chest, and she could see his right hand was bleeding. As she passed by, he was shaking, mumbling incoherently and crying. As she continued on her walk, she encountered the man a second time, a couple of feet away, sitting near an old capstan close to the water, his injured hand now hidden in his pocket.

This man must be a prime suspect, the show's host asked John Williams. Indeed, he is, Williams replied.

A forensic artist's impression was shown of the wanted man, who Williams described as white and distinctive, slightly built and fairly young, with a chubby face, pointy chin, long sideburns and a shadow of stubble. A long fringe was swept across one side of his forehead, and his collar-length hair was greasy and black.

South Wales Police had taken an encouraging eighty or so calls as a result of the TV reconstruction. A proportion of them reported seeing the same man. A description given by an off-duty police officer, out for a Sunday drive with his wife, matched the young girl's description, adding that he looked 'Asian or part-Asian, light skin'. A group of nuns had seen him sitting on steps rocking back and forth, as had a young mother pushing a pram, who said the hairs on the back of her neck stood up on making eye contact with him.

A barmaid of a pub frequented by sex workers said the photofit resembled a man who frequently came in and stood at the back of the room staring at the women. He appeared to be a loner, and an odd character, she said, who wore thin-rimmed glasses.

The landlady of one of the dock's oldest pubs, the Packet Hotel, had also called police to say she had seen a man who looked identical to the sketch, noting the long, swept fringe, foraging around on wasteland nearby a week after the murder.

He had cycled up to a patch of land and spent three minutes searching through bushes and rubble as if looking for something, furtively glancing around him from left to right to check if anyone could see him.

Her report must have been of some interest to detectives at the time as it pointed to a fact they not revealed to the public. On the exact same strip of land, Lynette White's keys and green frog fob had been found in the days following the murder.

Despite repeated calls to the city's taxi drivers to 'rack their brains', only one had come forward with anything of note. He said Lynette White had flagged him down at the city centre ice rink at 10 p.m. that night and he had dropped her at the James Street flat. The man with her, he noticed, had been gripping a rolled-up bag, like a tool kit, but unlike the photofit he had a moustache and full, scraggy beard.

As the calls continued to flood in to the incident room in the early stages of the investigation, John Actie, like everyone else around the Bay and further afield, had never thought the photofit of the prime suspect was anyone other than a client of Lynette White's; one of countless men who had slipped under the bridge that fateful night in search of a salve unavailable to them beyond the dangerously vulnerable and undiscerning.

Chapter Three

As the investigation ambled on over the next few months, the clos-est to any firm developments was an appeal by police for men in the area to participate in a forensic sweep in order to eliminate them. A number had responded, among them John Actie, who had volunteered a blood and hair sample.

But for an investigation that had stormed out of the traps, by the end of the summer the initial burst of bravado appeared to have waned. The media smelt a rat.

By early September, journalists had little to publish beyond headlines such as 'We will catch you, killer warned by police'. John Williams had been giving regular interviews to keep the inquiry in the public's mind, to apply pressure to the conscience of anyone withholding vital information. But the steady stream of rhetoric was beginning to push into the realms of bluster.

The telltale signs of stress, certainly of irritation, seemed to be showing in Williams's previously implacable demeanour. Every inquiry has its ups and downs, he had said crossly, when asked about an apparent lack of progress. Rest assured there is a 'ground-swell of feeling', with everyone on the inquiry, from himself down to civilian staff, convinced that this man would be caught.

But no murder weapon had been found, no motive established, journalists pressed, and why had they not found the bloodstained man seen outside the flat? Williams sidestepped the question with assurances that confidence levels were as high as they had been in February, his vehemence only further fuelling scepticism.

Confidence may well have remained at February levels, the press kicked back, but any tangible progress in the case remained at February levels too.

While there had been fourteen different sightings of Lynette White around the city in the week before her death, police still did not even know where Lynette White had been in the five days leading up to her death. She clearly had some sort of base as, according to people who had seen her, she had been dressed in a variety of different clothes, leading to the suspicion that she may have been shielded by a secret boyfriend.

Williams pointed to one of the most difficult tasks he faced, that of breaking down the 'wall of silence' among the vice community. He once again urged sex workers, whom he insisted could well hold the key to the inquiry, to cooperate with his officers. Former clients were assured of confidentiality and warned it was in their interests to come forward rather than wait to be tracked down. Williams said he had no desire to 'upset matrimonial homes'.

'[The vice community] is a tight-knit community not prone to helping the police,' he said. 'Someone among them knows the score and the reasons behind why this happened.'

As part of the investigation, vehicles spotted with suspicious frequency in the vicinity of the Custom House were being noted or pulled over. One of the drivers had turned out to be a vicar; another protested his innocence by claiming his car's top speed was ten miles an hour.

In April one driver had come forward to explain he was a medium and had only visited the pub because he had been 'directed by my spiritual guides to go there'.

Psychics have proven in some cases to be eerily on the mark, but the fact that three months into the murder hunt the driver was subsequently escorted to the murder scene twice, claiming to have 'vibrational contact' with the victim, maybe illustrates the lack of any firm direction in the investigation. What information the medium relayed to detectives has never come to light.

Then in early September, in response to Williams's headline warning, a man called up the city's newspaper office claiming to be the murderer, an anonymous caller, a feature of many murder investigations. The caller sounded young, softly spoken with a local accent, and maybe a bit drunk. The murder weapon, he said, could be found at a house in Meteor Street, in an area close to the city centre.

Detectives identified a young man living on the street, raided his flat but found nothing.

A few days later, the caller phoned again. 'I'm too clever for you,' he said. 'I won't get caught . . . I shall treasure that knife. I am not ashamed to tell you that I killed her, she deserved it. If the police are that good at solving murders, they would have caught me by now. The trail has gone cold and they will never find me now.'

On BBC Wales's evening news programme, Williams reacted peevishly when asked to deny suggestions that police were dragging their feet. The police had 'a tremendous amount' and 'masses of information' from the public, he countered, but they only had limited resources and they were still in the process of evaluating it all.

Behind the cameras, John Williams was even more rattled. The inquiry was stalling and, as head of CID, it was down to him to provide it with a much-needed shot in the arm.

That eventually came in the form of a newly promoted detective inspector who had taken over the reins of the murder hunt by the autumn of 1988. Graham Mouncher had made a name for himself as a tenacious, uncompromising and experienced investigator who, crucially, got cases over the line.

Hopes that his arrival would galvanise the team had been realised, as within weeks things were moving apace.

Immediately after the murder, the South Wales Criminal Intelligence Bureau had identified a list of twelve possible suspects that fitted the bill, a list that detectives had systematically whittled down to two or three. Mouncher took that a step further and homed in on one in particular.

The individual, who hailed from Pontypridd, a mining town just twelve miles north of Cardiff, fitted exactly with a criminal profile, an investigative strategy then in its infancy in the UK, which police had commissioned pioneers at the University of Surrey to come up with.

The profile had drawn from characteristics typical of killers at the time. A curious phenomenon identified that a huge proportion of murderers were in fact between the ages of twenty and twenty-four. Murder results from relationships with others, from individuals who do not get on with others and struggle to express anger or frustration.

By extrapolating and analysing research, the psychologists strongly suggested the suspect likely had difficult forming relationships, worked in a low-skilled job and had a problem with drink or drugs. The probability that he was familiar with the Butetown area and had used prostitutes before was high.

Further, they postulated that the victim represented something that angered the killer, the manic nature of his attack, a sudden, explosive outburst, pointing to the possibility of an argument over payment that had got out of control. This man was likely, the report concluded, to confess if asked directly.

Mouncher had scoped out his suspect, a former client of Lynette White's with a criminal record for sexual violence who would become known as 'Mr X', and following a preliminary and voluntary interview, he had become even more convinced he was their man. A blood sample had been taken and while he waited the week or so for results to come back, Mouncher continued with a surveillance operation, tracking his every move.

But in early November, the laboratory had phoned with some bad news: a DNA profile, an emerging technology at the time, showed the suspect's blood did not match spatter found on wallpaper at the crime scene. It was a hammer blow. Ten months on, in November of that year, South Wales Police were back at square one, no nearer to solving the biggest, most widely publicised crime for decades.

Pressure was building on all fronts. Aside from the media, an entirely different, arguably more powerful force was, implicitly if not explicitly, bearing down on the investigation: a political one.

Throughout the 1980s, the UK government, complying with the free-market ideology of its then prime minister, Margaret Thatcher, had set up the Urban Development Programme to regenerate deprived and rundown inner cities. Using money from the government, the taxpayer, to kick-start the venture, it would then attract buy-in from private investors, who could cover the upfront costs, for which they would reap dividends in the long term.

A transformed London docklands, previously in a state of severe decline, now boasted million-pound riverside properties, sought after by the 1980s social phenomenon of 'yuppies'.

Yuppies, which stood for young, upwardly mobile professionals, was an emerging demographic synonymous with greed and conspicuous consumption – young, champagne-swilling high-earners, who typically worked in the City's stock markets. By the late 1980s, a backlash had grown against them, as working people were driven from their homes, no longer able to afford to stay in a newly gentrified area.

In April 1987, the Welsh Office, headed by a member of Thatcher's cabinet, wanted in on the action and unveiled sweeping plans to revive Cardiff's fortunes, the cornerstone of which was none other than Tiger Bay.

The Cardiff Bay Development Corporation set up camp in Mount Stuart Square, close to the Casablanca nightclub, with a clear mission statement: 'To put Cardiff on the international map as a superlative maritime city which will stand comparison with any such city in the world, thereby enhancing the image and economic well-being of Cardiff and Wales as a whole.'

The corporation assured the people of Tiger Bay that fears of being segregated further were unfounded – far from it, its members said, they would not only benefit with new jobs but improved amenities as well.

Inspired by the success of Baltimore with a comparable history, Cardiff's desolate seaport was to be transformed into a brand-new, shiny Cardiff Bay. But with its success contingent on attracting upwards of £2 billion in private investment, the brutal and unsolved murder of a young woman jarred with the glossy sales pitch.

The clock was ticking.

◆ ◆ ◆

At 6.30 a.m. on Friday, 9 December 1988, it was still dark. Looking at the sky, you would have been forgiven for thinking it was a moon-less night over Tiger Bay. It shone from behind the cover of cloud, which spun a web of drizzle around the crisp early morning air.

John Actie, dressed only in boxer shorts, leaned out of the upstairs bedroom window of his home, 145 Bute Street, the end of a small clutch of two-up two-down new builds not far from Loudoun Square. He was shouting at five overcoated figures standing outside his front door. Inspector Tommy Page had braced himself before knocking.

'What do you want?' John bellowed. 'Get away from my door!'

Inspector Page was known to everyone in Tiger Bay. In over-all control of the docks' police station, he had been charged with maintaining community relations and would often be found in and out of the pubs and clubs, bantering with locals over a pint while keeping his ear to the ground and cultivating sources, informers or 'snouts' as they were known.

Page looked up at John and in a nervous, placatory tone asked if he would come downstairs, as he needed to have a word.

The murder squad detectives had sent Tommy Page to collect John that December morning, thinking his familiarity would be less incendiary. But John made no effort to conceal his dislike of Page.

He was just one of a number of the docks' officers that he had clashed with over the years.

Inspired by his father's example, no doubt, John had taken his advice about never standing down from a fight to extremes, regularly stepping in to defend teenagers he saw being picked on by officers, getting embroiled in other people's fights. He had continually butted heads with the police, notching up a dangerous number of victory marks against them.

No matter how many times he was warned by one of his uncles – 'Don't push it, John, they'll come for you' – John would brush it off. How could they come for him if he had done nothing wrong? Besides, now aged twenty-seven and at a pivotal point in his life, a time when, as a young father, he had finally found some equilibrium, his need to excessively battle had mellowed.

John slammed the bedroom window shut and ran downstairs to speak with Page.

The officer explained that the superintendent had requested he be brought down to the station. What for? John asked. It was to do with Lynette White, came the reply.

John felt as if a bomb had exploded in his stomach; heat coursed through his chest and his heart hammered so loudly he could hear it. Then his entire body went cold, all strength draining from his legs, which he feared might buckle.

A couple of days before, on the Wednesday, everyone had been talking about a handful of guys police had pulled in for questioning, his cousin Ronnie Actie among them. No one had taken it seriously. John had met a girlfriend of one of them at the shops the day after. She was crying and he had comforted her, telling her not to worry. You know what the police are like, he had said, they are just fishing around and her boyfriend would be home soon.

Now they had come for him and a sickening sense of foreboding overwhelmed him.

John made it clear he was going nowhere. Page reasoned with him. If he did not come, they would send back-up and he did not want to have to do that with John's partner and children in the house. John told him to go and wait in his car.

Throwing on some clothes, he bent down to kiss Taryn. 'What do they want?' she asked.

'Haven't got a clue. Something to do with the Lynette White murder. Let me get down there and I'll be back in an hour.'

Eight officers in three cars were waiting around the corner of the house. John climbed into the back seat of a yellow Morris Marina, next to Page.

At Butetown Police Station, Page went through a basic questionnaire to get details of his whereabouts on the night of the murder.

Like everyone in the area, John had fully complied with door-to-door inquiries in the days following the murder. He had invited the constable into his home. So soon after the event, he clearly recalled to him that he had been working at the Casablanca, where he had remained until walking home at around 3.30 a.m.

But ten months on, his recall of that night was not so clear and John Actie made an initial, albeit innocent, mistake. He gave Page an account of his whereabouts the weekend before, explaining that he had been due to see a particular sound system from Birmingham at the Casablanca but had fallen asleep watching TV at home.

Left alone in the room, John looked out on to James Street, where the early morning traffic was starting to build. He noted a flat roof under the windows and a dialogue ran inside his head.

They're fitting me up. No, they wouldn't do that, not for murder. Would they? Go on, John, just go. Open the window, jump on to the porch roof and bam! You're gone. No, no, you can't do that. It'll be all over the news: 'Do not approach his man, he's a murderer.' Hang on a minute. You'll be OK . . .

The door flew open, crashing into a filing cabinet nearby. Eight officers, including the chief, John Williams, walked in.

'John Arthur Actie,' Detective Inspector Richard Powell announced, holding a Perspex ruler in one hand and slapping it repeatedly on the palm of his other, 'I am arresting you on suspicion of the murder of Lynette White.'

John turned to Powell and looked him in the eye. He swore loudly. 'You're fitting me up,' he said.

◆ ◆ ◆

Tony Paris had not been asleep for long when he was awoken at 11.30 a.m. by loud banging on his front door and the shouts of police to open up.

He had been out the night before and had returned in the early hours to his flat, midway up Nelson House, one of two fourteen-storey high-rises in the middle of Loudoun Square.

Still half-drunk, it took a few seconds for his fogged mind to clear and determine that he was not dreaming. He sighed, a mixture of irritation and amusement, thinking it was one of the boys messing around.

Naked, save for his glasses, he swung open the door and without a moment to focus, he reeled backwards against the wall as four men barged their way inside, telling him he was under arrest on suspicion of murder.

Tony's mind spooled through countless possibilities of what the bloody hell they were on about. In a split second he replayed the previous night's events in his mind. He had been to the Dowlais, a club not far from the Casablanca, with a friend. Everyone had been cool. Sure, he had got 'blocked up', drunk, but had returned home in the early hours without incident.

'Murder? What murder? Who's dead?' he said.

'Lynette White.'

Tony's incredulity quickly turned to anger. 'Let's get down to the station and sort this out,' he said.

Escorted from the building in handcuffs, Tony looked around in bewilderment. The entire building, outside the lifts, the concourse and the square itself, was guarded by police.

Knots of bystanders gawped as he was driven away in a police car, a mid-morning development guaranteed to send the Tiger Bay grapevine into meltdown.

Like John, Tony was led into a small room to answer questions about his whereabouts on the night of 13/14 February. Working at the Casablanca, collecting glasses, he said, as he had told the police doing house-to-house inquiries. He had got there at about 9 or 10 p.m. and stayed until it closed.

The police said they did not believe him. He knew more about the murder, an officer said, pushing photographs of Lynette White's body in the mortuary towards him.

It was widely held that thirty-one-year-old Tony, barely 5 feet 2 inches tall, with milk-bottle-thick glasses and tipping the scales at not much over eight stone wringing wet, had once fainted at the sight of his own blood. Apocryphal though it undoubtedly was, the fact remained that Tony Paris's level of squeamishness was renowned.

Tony pushed the photographs away in disgust and as he did so the officer, one he did not know, bellowed at him that the girl was dead and they had come to believe that he knew something about it.

Look, Tony said, I do not get involved with trouble, all the police round here know what I am like. Go and get one of them and they will tell you. An officer Tony had known for years, one who he used to have a joke around with, walked into the room and Tony pleaded with him to vouch for him. 'Think of yourself now, Tone,' the officer replied. 'Think of yourself.' And with that, he turned around and left.

It was at that point Tony's hopes of being in and out in ten minutes, having cleared up an unfortunate misunderstanding, faded fast.

By Tiger Bay standards, the Paris family were relative newcomers. Tony's parents, Arthur and Isabelle, known as Jean, had arrived in Cardiff from the island of St Kitts and Nevis, shortly before his birth in August 1957.

The second eldest of eight siblings, Tony was a sweet, football-mad kid, plagued with poor eyesight and asthma. The extent of any rebellious behaviour while at school was sneaking a swig of communion wine as an altar boy at St Mary's.

'If you can't love yourself, Tony,' his father, Arthur, a former dock worker, would tell him, 'how can anyone else love you?' And Tony learned to love Tony. To his mind, he gave off a good vibe with his long leather coat, two-tone suits, and dreadlocks, which he had had cut off a few years before.

Others might feel insecure about being so tiny but not Tony. You see, he would say, his stature, or lack of it, had imbued him with the power to instantly detect the charge of impending trouble and the foresight to move the hell away from it. Tony Paris was a glass-half-full guy, an optimist in all aspects of life, including the potency of his charm when it came to chasing women.

Regularly working in the Casablanca for his friend, who was the manager, Tony had no grand ambitions or dreams. He had left school at fourteen, having fallen behind due to his poor eyesight and had been accepted on to an apprenticeship at a nearby engineering works. But after a couple of years, he grew bored and drifted into a more freelance line of work.

Tony had married for the second time in 1987, and to support his wife and two young sons, one from each marriage, Tony would shoplift.

He would regularly do his rounds of the docks, calling in people's houses with goods to sell or to pick up wish lists from which he would steal to order from shops in town. Women would describe the dress they wanted, what floor it was on and what size, and off he would go wearing a specially tailored donkey jacket, lined from left to right with a gigantic pocket into which he would smuggle his swag.

On one occasion, he had been followed outside by a store detective. He had held his hands up and pleaded guilty, and had never lived down the headline in a local paper – 'Rasta caught shoplifting'. Tony paid the fine and that, apart from a driving offence, was the long and short of any criminal record.

He had known Lynette White, not well but she had seemed a nice enough girl and they had chatted on occasion. Through the pub pool league he played in, he had got to know her late uncle, a popular figure locally, as well as her father.

A party boy with a loving family and a tight group of friends from multiracial backgrounds, Tony Paris was delighted with life. Cardiff was the best city in the world and Tiger Bay the jewel in its crown. Tony was a 'Bay Boy' and for that reason alone, he felt among the luckiest men alive.

By the time of Tony Paris's arrest, Yusef Abdullahi, known as 'Dullah', had been in custody for nearly two days.

He had been in the top-floor flat he rented in a six-storey block on Bute Street, not far from the junction with James Street, when at 3 p.m. on Wednesday, 7 December, the door burst open and he was wrestled to the ground.

'Don't move! Stay down on the floor!' an officer shouted, jamming a knee into his back. Plain-clothes and uniformed officers ransacked the flat, pulling out drawers, emptying cupboards, searching pillowcases and mattresses, ripping back carpets and lifting ceiling panels into the roof. From the corner of his eye, he could see objects being put in brown envelopes. He did not have a clue what they were looking for.

Midway through the search, Dullah's sister, Yasmin, who lived in the flat, arrived home and was ushered into her room and ordered to stay there. Anytime Dullah so much as jerked his head to see what was happening, he would feel a knee in his ribs.

After a while, he was dragged down the flights of stairs and wrestled into one of a line of four or five police cars parked outside.

Dullah had only ever stayed in that flat off and on. His more permanent home was in Louisa Place, a housing estate of flats and terraced houses at the back of James Street, which until recently he had shared with his partner of five years, Jackie Harris, the mother of his two children.

Jackie had fled to a women's refuge with her three young children, the eldest from a previous relationship, to escape Dullah's violence a few months before. Returning to the house having got word of his arrest, she found the door taken off with a sledgehammer and a stream of police and forensic teams tearing up every inch inside and outside the property.

To say Dullah and Jackie's relationship was stormy was an understatement. An attractive couple – she, a petite, vivacious and unfailingly polite pale brunette and he, black-haired, olive-skinned and handsome – their propensity for drama was off the scale.

The previous year, in the midst of another argument, Dullah had broken a restraining order and taken his oldest child, Joseph, to spend some time with him for a few days. The next thing he saw was Jackie's tear-stained face on the evening TV news and the front page of the *South Wales Echo* under the headline, 'South Wales boy, 3, snatched from bed'. The couple had subsequently made up, but for how long exactly was anyone's guess.

Dullah's life had been troubled since childhood, when his parents, Cardiff-born Pauline and Somali-born former seaman Ameed, had moved from the docks to the newly built estate in the area of Ely in the west of the city.

One evening, after returning from his shift at the steelworks, his father complained of feeling unwell and had retired to bed, where he suffered a catastrophic heart attack. With no landline in the house and the nearby phone boxes vandalised, his mother frantically ran from neighbour to neighbour pleading for help, but she watched helplessly as people turned away or drew their curtains.

The local police station refused to call an ambulance, advising her to contact her out-of-hours GP. Eventually she ran to the home of one of the few white women in the area married to a black man. She had ushered her inside to use the phone but by the time the ambulance crew arrived, it was too late.

That, on top of racist graffiti daubed on their house and the refusal of any local nursery to enrol her youngest child, prompted Pauline Abdullahi, a pub cleaner, to return to Tiger Bay, much to the relief of her four children, Yusef the eldest of three brothers and a sister.

While Pauline worked four jobs to support her family, refusing to sign on the dole, Dullah and his brother Rashid would use time out of school to indulge their passion for animals. Rearing chickens and dogs and liberating a string of horses from a local travellers' site, deeming them ill-treated, the two would while away hours riding bareback, thundering across the wastelands of the docks.

After dropping out of school with ambitions beyond the confines of Tiger Bay, fuelled by a self-belief in his obvious talents with horses, at eighteen, Dullah, whose only conviction had been for a motoring offence, left Cardiff for Newmarket, home to one of the UK's most famous racecourses, to work as an apprentice jockey.

But it was a short-lived dream. During a weekend visit home, a year or so later, as he was walking along Bute Street, a fight broke out between a friend and his father returning from the pub. Jumping to his friend's defence, Dullah became embroiled, a knife was produced and the thirty-eight-year-old father suffered three stab wounds.

Serving eighteen months of a four-year sentence, given remission for good behaviour, Dullah picked up his life in the docks on his release.

The unemployment rate among the area's young men at the time ran at 90 per cent. Any attempt to get a job in town proved both hopeless and humiliating. On applications forms for dishwashing in hotel kitchens, youngsters would amend their surname and change their address and postcode to be in with a chance of an interview. But even if they got that far, the ill-disguised look of surprise on the interviewers' faces on seeing the colour of their skin was swiftly followed by rejection on the basis they were deemed 'overqualified'.

The exclusion had led to the emergence of a black-market economy in the docks, mainly weed and some cocaine. Unlike John Actie, Dullah was firmly in the Custom House and North Star faction of the docks. As resident DJ of the latter, he would supply the working girls with cannabis, speed and cocaine to those who could afford it.

But away from that, Dullah would help out at the Custom House, where his partner's stepfather was the landlord, and get whatever work was going: labouring, running market stalls, working nightclub doors.

The violence regularly meted out to his partner aside, many who knew Dullah might have suggested that his biggest crime was that of hubris. Enjoying the spotlight, he had a propensity to run his mouth, tell lies and spin all manner of tall stories.

He had had a previous brush with the Lynette White murder hunt in the June of 1988, thanks to Leanne Vilday, whom he knew from the North Star, and to whom he regularly sold drugs. They had recently fallen out. Dullah, perhaps fancifully, claimed tensions had built over his rejection of her advances on occasions, and that she owed him money for baby clothes, one of his many business hustles at the time.

The incident in question was a drunken outburst by Vilday in the Custom House pub. Drowning her sorrows from a break-up with a girlfriend, Vilday had taken speed, a drug she used every day, and had been, in her words, 'knocking back double gins', to the extent that she had become so disruptive she was ordered to leave the premises. On being escorted outside, she had shouted that Stephen and Dullah had murdered Lynette White. Later saying she could barely remember the incident, she explained that she had only shouted this because she was aggrieved that Stephen had gone back to London and escaped the constant pressure by the police which had become her everyday reality. As for mentioning Dullah, she said the only reason she could think of for doing so was because he had never liked Lynette.

Dullah was duly brought in for questioning by police and denied any involvement, explaining he was labouring on a ship in Barry Docks at the time. He agreed to a blood test and that, for six months at least, was an end to the matter.

Ronnie Actie, aged thirty at the time, had been walking to his sister's house at 1.15 p.m. on Wednesday, 7 December when a police car pulled up alongside. Two officers got out and arrested him, cautioning him that he was to be questioned about the murder of Lynette White.

'I've been arrested for some things,' Ronnie said, 'but this beats the can.'

Of all the men picked up that week, Ronnie was the one who spent the least amount of time around the docks. As the first-born grandchild of the Actie clan, his family connections with the area were strong, but he and his nine siblings had grown up on a council estate in the Gabalfa district, north of the city centre, where he had a close group of friends.

His sister, Michelle, had returned to live near Loudoun Square some years before, and Ronnie, close to her children, close to all his nieces and nephews for that matter, would stay there often.

Earlier that day, Michelle, who was heavily pregnant, was opening the door to her house when two plain-clothes police officers strode towards her. They asked where Ronnie was and she said she had no idea; she had been out all day. One of the officers pushed past her and asked her four-year-old son if he had seen his uncle Ronnie. The little boy pointed upstairs to the bedroom Ronnie used when he stayed. See, the officer said to Michelle, children never lie. They checked upstairs but Ronnie was not there.

Uncharacteristically for the toweringly tall Actie clan, Ronnie was shorter, 5 feet 7 inches, but even so, he was a man known for being more than capable of standing his ground. As a child in school, he had excelled in art, regularly coming home to present his mother with another picture, but his interest in football had soon taken over everything.

Having left the local Welsh-language school at the earliest possible chance, Ronnie collected his dole cheque every two weeks and as long as he had his music, sport and family around him, he was happy enough. He had started getting into trouble at the age of fifteen and by his late twenties had clocked up two stints in prison, one for assault and another for breaking into the local bingo hall.

Girlfriends had always been in steady supply but none had led to commitment. Over the Christmas period of 1987, he had been in the North Star when he met Leanne Vilday. Despite the fact that Vilday tended to have romantic relationships only with women, the two had begun seeing one another casually, hooking up on the weekends.

He had been as shocked as anyone when he saw the television reports about the murder of Lynette White, whom he had first met five years before; he would bump into her now and again and the two would catch up fleetingly.

When his parents received the devastating news of their son's arrest, the reaction of his father, also called Ronnie, a 6-feet-3-inch former nightclub doorman who had more recently cleared houses for a living, was emphatic: they have been set up, he said.

◆ ◆ ◆

By the time Ronnie was processed through custody, it had been twelve hours since two unmarked South Wales Police cars, flanked either side by four blue-lighted outriders, sped along the Westway out of London and on to the M4.

In the back seat of one of the cars, Stephen Miller, his hands cuffed behind his back and a detective either side of him, stared out of the window, shrugging in disbelief at the car travelling alongside where his brother, Anthony, was similarly shackled, also under arrest and bound for questioning in Cardiff.

It was the last place Stephen wanted to be. After two months of 'running around like a blue-arsed fly' for the police investigating Lynette's murder, and having secured a new home for Lynette's dog, he had made the decision to leave Tiger Bay, a place he had come to loathe, in April 1988. Feeling too anxious and depressed to travel alone, he phoned his younger brother, Mark, who agreed to meet him at Cardiff Central Bus Station and accompany him on the coach trip to London.

His contact details were left with Detective Inspector Powell, who had become exasperated by his incessant visits to the station, reporting back in minute detail, as promised, the most incidental pieces of information he had gleaned from the area, and his almost daily questions about updates in the inquiry. Powell was, quite frankly, relieved to see the back of him.

During the weeks following Lynette's murder, Stephen had given umpteen further statements, expanding on and confirming details of their relationship: the lock of his hair she had tied to the left belt loop of her jeans; the pawn shop receipt for her two rings found in the glove compartment of his car; the visit he paid to his girlfriend's close friend, Leanne Vilday, pleading for information on her whereabouts during her initial disappearance.

He described the small knife attached to a corkscrew that Lynette carried for self-protection on the streets, the extent of his coke habit, the watch he had bought her from a late-night garage, her daily routines, the face cream and deodorant she used, the brand of cigarettes she smoked, whether she used a lighter or matches. The details were exhaustive.

To say Stephen Miller was compliant was an understatement. But then he was running true to form. The fourth of Jamaican-born Madge and Clive Miller's children, Stephen had followed first-born Anthony, oldest sister Janet and another sister, Donna, born a year before him with spina bifida. Only ten months after his arrival, his parents' marriage was foundering, and Madge left the family home to live with her aunt, giving her husband custody of the siblings.

It was not until Stephen was seven that he returned to live with his mother. By then, he was shy and withdrawn, his mother noticed, but otherwise impeccably behaved, regularly attending school and bringing home favourable reports.

His civility endured throughout his years at secondary school, which he left at sixteen to join the government's Youth Training Scheme. By the following year, having failed to secure regular employment, Stephen signed on at the job centre in between sporadic bouts of labouring on building sites.

Growing up in Brixton, he was understandably wary of the police, going out of his way to keep out of theirs. On the evening of 28 September 1985, Stephen had been invited for tea at his friend's mother's house. As the teenagers later walked together along Stockwell Road, they were stopped by a roadblock. In the distance, billows of smoke rose into the air in front of a distant but discernible line of riot shields.

A traffic officer stopped the men, telling them they could not come any further as there was a disturbance further down the road.

'No problem, sir,' Stephen had replied. 'We don't want any problems.'

Glued to the TV news that night, Stephen learned about the flashpoint of the riot: the shooting of thirty-seven-year-old Dorothy 'Cherry' Groce in her home. Lying in bed at the time, she had been targeted by the Metropolitan Police in the mistaken belief she was hiding her son, Michael, who was wanted for a firearms offence.

The memory of rioting four years earlier in 1981, a kickback against the oppressive stop-and-search policy – the so-called Sus or 'suspected person' law – and outcry at the institutional racism faced by the black community, endured in Stephen's mind.

Witnessing trouble unfolding had been a daily occurrence for a young Stephen who, anxious by nature, had grown fearful of anyone in a uniform. His abiding image of the police was primarily of them masked, armed and caving someone's door in.

The one occasion Stephen had been in trouble was aged fifteen, when a local character known to be a bully had picked on him relentlessly. Ignoring his pleas to leave him alone, Stephen walked away but was followed and later held his hands up in court to a wounding offence, insisting it was in self-defence but respecting his twelve-month punishment in a youth detention centre.

He had never been in trouble since and in his final weeks spent in Cardiff, Stephen, then aged twenty-two, wanted to ensure that continued. He had stopped taking coke and, never a drinker, allowed himself the occasional spliff as he spent his time alone, walking Lynette's dog and helping to bring his girlfriend's killer to justice.

Haunted by memories, he had moved out of the room they had shared and into temporary accommodation, purposefully chosen for its proximity to Butetown Police Station. That way, he reasoned, he would quickly be on hand in the event of any breakthrough in the case.

Once he was back home at his mother's house, Madge would try to talk to him about the murder but each time she did, he would break down. Locking himself in his room, he had become a virtual recluse and eventually acted on his mother's advice and arranged to speak with the family GP.

Slowly over the next few months, Stephen began to venture outside and in September had begun a relationship with a girl, Debbie, whom he had met in a wine bar. She was with him in Camberwell, when, at midday on 7 December, he and his older brother were approached by two South Wales Police detectives.

'I am Detective Constable Seaford,' they were told, 'and this is Detective Constable Greenwood. We are from Cardiff. We have made further inquiries into the murder of Lynette White and we are arresting you for being involved in the murder. We will be taking you back to Cardiff for questioning.'

Those names would come to haunt Stephen Miller in ways he never thought possible.

After ten months, the Lynette White murder investigation announced its long-awaited breakthrough. A white man had been seeing crying and bleeding outside the murder scene. The men arrested were all black or of mixed-heritage and all were from Tiger Bay, with the exception of the Miller brothers.

He did not yet know it, but John Actie was about to embark on the fight of his life.

Chapter Four

In a windowless basement, the Victorian cell complex was dimly lit, its floor-to-ceiling subway tiles cracked and yellow with age. As John Actie was led past a long corridor of cells, he emerged into an annexe where there must have been thirty or forty officers lining the walls.

His head pounding, he felt as if he was in a trance, the enormity of what was happening yet to fully sink in. The other four men – Tony, Stephen, Ronnie and Dullah – were already there, lined up. John was thinking clearly enough to notice that he was the only one among them restrained, each of his wrists handcuffed to two of the burliest police officers he had ever seen.

For the past three days, the arrested men – Anthony Miller having been subsequently released after his alibi checked out – had been bounced around different police stations, a steady stream of interviews broken up by long stints in a cell and trips to the magistrates' court for extra time to hold them.

John's nine interviews had been comparatively short, totalling four hours or so, the largest chunk of which was arguing over where he was the night Lynette White was killed.

He had got confused with the weekend before, when he had planned to go to the Casablanca to see a visiting sound system but had fallen asleep on the sofa watching television and had not woken up until late.

The passage of time had faded his memory. Taryn had given birth two days after the murder and he went virtually every weekend to the Casablanca, where there were always different sound systems and singers on the bill. Valentine's weekend did not stick in his memory prominently; there was no reason why it should have.

Detectives insisted John had been at the Casablanca. Convinced he was being fitted up, he refused to trust a word they said.

To clear things up, he had pleaded with them to find the questionnaire he had filled in during house-to-house inquiries. If detectives had given him a copy, he would, of course, have been reminded that he had been working at the Casablanca that night, drafted in as extra security, as he often was on big nights, arriving sometimes after 11 p.m. and leaving at around 3 a.m.

But the detectives kept saying they could not find it, that it had been mislaid. John suggested checking with the manager of the Casablanca for the diary of events. They did not know where he lived, they claimed. Of course, they knew where he bloody lived, John told them. That is when he realised they wanted to keep him confused; it suited them to keep him on the back foot, make him look as if he was trying to hide something.

Nothing he had ever experienced came close to the terror he felt. A doctor had been called after he had to return to his cell complaining of a debilitating headache. He had been prescribed migraine medication, which had eased it but still the pain nagged away.

People had come forward, detectives told him. They had seen him entering the flat at 7 James Street the night Lynette White was murdered. They told him the names of two women and a man. John had never heard of them. Shown a photograph of one of the women, he said he had never laid eyes on her. They're lying, he said.

'The police have got something to do with those statements,' John said. 'Someone's had a word with them off the record, told them what to say then the police write it up and the women signed it. As far as I'm concerned, they're all made up.'

'Are you saying we put words into their mouth?' the detectives asked. 'Do you seriously believe police would go out and get people into the station and tell them what to say?' Yes, I do, John replied. Those people must be imagining things. A hell of a thing to 'imagine', he was told.

Besides, Stephen Miller had confirmed it was all true, the police told him. Plagued by nightmares of seeing Lynette's dying face, Stephen, they said, could keep it secret no longer and had confessed. John struggled so hard to breathe he thought he might hyperventilate.

'Well, if he's said that, I don't know what you've been doing to him,' he told the detectives. 'It's you writing that down and him signing it.'

Stephen Miller had been interviewed in the same way that he had been, police assured John; his solicitor has been with him all the time and nobody has forced him to say anything.

You are fitting me up, John insisted. 'You read about it all the time,' he said. 'The police fit this man up, that man up. It happens all over the place and then two years later they are found not guilty. That's exactly what you're trying to do to me. You think I'm "big John" who runs everything down the docks. Let's get him away and everything will be quiet. You just want me out the way.'

Tony Paris had been there too, the detectives said. Little Tony Paris? Shoplifter, Tony Paris? If this had not been so serious, John might have laughed. 'Oh, fucking hell,' he said, holding his head in his hands. 'Tony Paris? His own baby would beat him up.'

Dullah was seen at the flat as well. Oh God, now they were just being ridiculous, John said. He would go nowhere with Dullah, he did not even talk to him, did not like him and anyway, he was always in the North Star. What about Ronnie, his cousin? He got on well with him and would stop and have a chat if he saw him out, but he had his own group of friends, he never socialised with him. Stephen Miller? He knew him to say hello to, he was new in the area and kept himself to himself.

The detectives outlined to John what they understood to have happened that night. The men had been in the Casablanca and, all of a sudden, Stephen Miller, who has been looking for his girlfriend for five days, gets wind of where she is.

For some reason, as yet undetermined, all five of them go down to the James Street flat, where there was a bit of a tussle between Paris and Lynette. He gives her a slap. Pineapple says, 'Hang on, that's my girl!', he pushes Paris away and next thing, a knife comes out. He stabs Lynette and she screams. That alerts one of the women from across the road, who runs over and sees John at the top of the stairs acting as a look-out.

Impossible, John said, he had never set foot in 7 James Street. You put a description out about a white guy, crying, walking up James Street and now it has changed to five black guys? All of a sudden, these people come forward out of the blue?

They have been living in fear, the police told him. That is why this inquiry has gone on for so long.

John insisted he had never set foot in James Street. What about the blues he used to run, asked the police, that was near James Street? Angered, John told them he had not run a blues – a commercially organised all-night party featuring DJs and selling unlicensed drink – for over a year and they knew it. He had only run a blues from a flat he rented on Bute Street for a few months and one of the beat officers on duty would regularly call in for a patty and a can of Red Stripe.

Why would he be in James Street with guys he never hung around with, some of whom he did not like? He had his own group of friends. That was what they were trying to find out, the officers told him.

There was another person as well: a woman had seen him outside the flat as she had driven home that night, had to swerve to avoid them all. A woman driving her car now, is it? John struggled to believe what he was hearing.

We know you did not commit the murder, the police repeatedly told him. They just wanted him to tell them what he knew; maybe he left when the knife first appeared and he had nothing to do with it. They said he was holding out on them because of his reputation, not wanting to lose face.

But this reputation of his, they went on, was not all that it seemed. They had been talking to his partner and seen his kids, 'little smashers', and there was another side to big John Actie, they said, a doting father and family man. It was time for him to get his loyalties right.

John knew what they were trying to do: soft-soap him into taking their way out or be charged for a murder.

'There comes a point of no return and that point is fast approaching, John,' he was told. 'You're not giving yourself many avenues to go down.'

'What do you mean avenues?' John said. He had fully cooperated with the inquiry, even agreeing to give a sample of his blood when police appealed for men to take part in a screening. 'If I knew something I would tell you! What, do you want me to lie? Is that what you want me to do, lie to you and say I was there? I've told you the truth hundreds of times. I wasn't there.'

At the conclusion of the interview, John was asked if he wanted to add anything for the tape.

'Yes,' he said. 'I haven't done anything and the police are fitting me up.'

The officers started laughing.

'It is a serious matter,' John said furiously. 'This is not funny. You're sitting there laughing and smirking.'

To say they were fitting him up was an outrageous thing to say, the detectives told him. So outrageous, John, that it deserved a smile.

◆ ◆ ◆

The difference in tone of the interviews with John compared to Tony's and Dullah's was like night and day.

If anyone had raised their voice in John's interview, then it was not any of the interviewing detectives. While Tony's may have started out reasonably conciliatory, it was not long before it degenerated into a verbally hostile and aggressive interrogation.

Unlike John, Tony did know the two women who had given statements about the night of Lynette White's murder. Leanne Vilday, the friend who led the police to the flat to find the body, had a baby by one of Tony's brothers. At the time, the arrival had caused ill-feeling, given that his brother was in a relationship. But Tony would always stop on the street and acknowledge the boy, fuss around him and buy him sweets.

The second woman was twenty-three-year-old Angela Psaila, whose brother Tony had been at school with. He had seen her on infrequent occasions in the past when he had visited the North Star. Psaila rented a flat in a block on the opposite side of James Street, set off the road slightly, down an alleyway called Ship Lane. She, like Vilday, was a convicted prostitute, but of late she had been paid to look after Vilday's son when Leanne was out at night.

Tony had told detectives he had been working flat out all night in the Casablanca on the night of the murder. And what would he be doing with those other guys anyway? They knew one another but he had his close group of friends. He would not be in their company. He was not a troublesome sort, he insisted, he would always be the one trying to calm things down and if he could not do that, he would turn on his heel. He was known for it.

'Do you know what I'm thinking now after what you just said?' one of the officers said to him. 'I'm wondering if you were on the door of that club and that gang went across there and you went after them to keep the blinking peace. I've got a sneaky suspicion you went to tell them to stop being so bloody stupid, to use a bit of common sense.'

Maybe he had been drunk or on drugs and might not have remembered where he had been that night. Tony told them he did not take drugs, maybe smoked a bit of weed but that was all.

I don't know how many times I've got to tell you, Tony said on repeat, I was not there.

Two-thirds of the way through Tony's ten interviews, their opinion of him shifted dramatically, soon after they revealed what Stephen Miller had said: that Tony was the one who actually attacked Lynette White.

Behind this peace-loving 'goody two shoes' lurked a secret, split personality that snaps and changes at night, the officers had yelled at him. There were a lot of people in the area who would say he was a bit of a head banger.

'OK, good for them,' Tony had replied.

'You're a bit cool today,' the officer responded. 'You're a lot cooler than I thought you would have been. I think you're ready to fly off the handle, you're controlling yourself.'

'Controlling myself? I'm fucking shaking!'

Tony's lawyer remonstrated with the officers for shouting and poking a pen near Tony's face.

He might as well own up to it. He was at 7 James Street that night, the officers continued. Tony was a violent pimp with no conscience about Lynette White's injuries, her throat and wrists cut.

Those girls were just pieces of meat to the likes of him. 'Animals, that's all you are,' he was told. 'The lot of you!'

Dullah's interrogation did not get off to a good start as he hit back at harassment, having been questioned a few months before. 'You're all licking arse to clean up the Bay. It don't mean to say you got to come and pick up every darky you suspect,' he told lead detective Graham Mouncher.

It had been cleared by head of CID John Williams and the Crown Prosecution Service (CPS) to initially question the men without the presence of a lawyer. Dullah refused to answer questions without one, adding, 'Oh you're dying to nick someone for [the murder]. I mean you'd pin it on anyone right now.'

When his legal representative eventually arrived, he denied over six hundred times having any part in the murder. 'I was on the *Coral Sea*,' he had repeated robotically ad nauseum. The *Coral Sea* was the name of the boat he had been working on which had docked in Barry, ten miles west of Cardiff. He had left to go there on Friday, not returning until later on Monday.

Get ready, Dullah was told, as they were about to blow his alibi 'sky-high out of the water'. Ronnie Williams, his partner's brother-in-law, had told police he had seen him in the North Star on the Saturday night. That was a lie, Dullah said, he was on the *Coral Sea*, working.

You are a disgrace to the human race, he was told, a vicious, evil, wicked man. He was not on the *Coral Sea* that night, he had come back to Cardiff, met up with those people and went with them to slaughter Lynette White.

'While you've walked the streets everybody has been in danger, haven't they?' Mouncher shouted.

'You're telling me that, are you?' Dullah replied.

'Yes, I'm telling you that as you've already slaughtered one girl!'

The dynamic with Ronnie Actie was different again. He seemed to be the one leading the questioning, picking holes in the police theory and telling them they were getting over-excited whenever they got riled.

Police had questioned him about the ethnicity of various people around the docks and his own, saying they did not want to be personal but, they told Ronnie, he was light skinned but still did not look white; he was 'foreign looking'.

Ronnie went on to explain that he had been with friends that night and had called to the docks and gone to a few of the pubs, including the Casablanca, but the first he had heard of Lynette White's murder was on the TV news the Monday after.

'This was a terrible murder,' he said, 'and people are trying to involve me. Why? I've been pacing myself to try to answer that. The truth will come out in the end. There are reasons for it.'

'If someone was trying to fit you up,' detectives said, 'it's becoming a very large bloody gang that's doing it.'

There was more evidence coming in by the minute, he was told. In addition to the two women who had given statements, police said two men had come forward to corroborate their accounts. Their names were Mark Grommek, who lived in the flat above the murder scene, and another guy called Paul Atkins.

Grommek, it was explained to Ronnie, had recently started working as a DJ in the North Star. He knew of him, Ronnie told detectives. Vilday had introduced them briefly, but he had not remembered his name. As for Atkins, Ronnie had seen him once in Cardiff Prison, and recalled him as a 'strange little guy'.

These men, Ronnie was informed, had told detectives that five men had been knocking on the front door of 7 James Street and that Grommek went downstairs to let them in and had seen them head up the stairs to Flat One.

Did he say we had gloves on or masks? Ronnie asked. Because if we were supposed to have all gone in the flat, where are our fingerprints, forensic evidence? The police brushed that point off.

The witnesses had told how Ronnie's green Cortina had been parked outside the flat. The problem with that, Ronnie pointed out, was that he had not bought the Cortina until April, and in February was still driving a red Triumph, all of which could be verified. And why would he park outside James Street if he had gone there to commit a crime? There was a car park around the corner.

There was a lot of 'wheeling and dealing' going on down the docks, detectives said, something had backfired, maybe something to do with drugs. Ronnie did not take drugs, explaining he drank bottled beer but never enough to get drunk.

As for Leanne Vilday, she was a compulsive liar. He had voluntarily gone to Butetown Police Station shortly after the murder and spent four hours talking to police, telling them that he had met up with her in the North Star in the early hours of Valentine's Day, that she seemed agitated, not herself, and had been talking about how worried she was about Lynette because she had not seen her.

At one stage she said to him, for all they knew, Lynette White could have been murdered and he had told her not to be stupid. Ronnie had told police everything he knew. Why would he do all that if he was supposedly involved in the murder himself? It made no sense!

If Vilday had been too terrified of him, how come she had been crying on his shoulder for weeks after the murder? She had told him the officer who found Lynette White had been physically ill. You are telling me, he said, that these people witnessed this horrific murder and kept it to themselves for ten months? That was impossible!

He had stopped seeing Vilday months ago, but they remained friends and he held her baby only a few weeks ago when they had bumped into one another. Did that sound like a woman who was terrified? Similarly, why would Grommek recently start working as a DJ in the North Star if in fear of his life? None of this made sense!

He was being a complete and utter fool to himself, the police told him; he had to save his own neck. Everyone is looking out for themselves at this point. John Actie's alibi had been cracked, same as Dullah's. The five of them had gone to James Street like a lynch mob. They had looked after one another for ten months and now it was all collapsing around them as 'half the bloody docks' had seen them.

Ronnie maintained the same throughout his eleven interviews: he had never set foot in 7 James Street; he did not even know Vilday was renting it. He liked Lynette White, she was a friend of his, and if he had found out anything about her murder, he would have gone straight to the police.

At lunchtime on Sunday, 11 December 1988, the door of John Actie's cell opened. As he was handcuffed, he noticed a surge in activity around the police station with officers rushing around. *They are going to charge me, aren't they?* John asked his solicitor, who nodded solemnly.

As he was driven to the central courts from the outskirts of the city, he could not yet get his head round the enormity of what was happening, distracting himself with the talk inside the police van of one of Wales's most humiliating defeats at the hands of the Romanian rugby team in the National Stadium the day before.

Now lined up with the other men, the room in front packed with police, as if, John thought, they were spectators watching from the stands, Detective Inspector Powell, flanked by his boss, John Williams, read from a sheet of paper.

'John Arthur Actie you are charged that between 12th February 1988 and the 15th February 1988, together with Ronald Actie, Anthony Paris, Yusef Abdullahi and Stephen Miller, you did murder Lynette Deborah White, contrary to common law.'

In his official statement, Powell wrote that after he had cautioned him, John gave no reply.

That was simply not true. John had gone berserk.

It was not until he had heard the words spoken out loud that the shock hit. As John thrashed and roared like an animal floored by a hunter's bullet, the officers shackled either side fought to restrain him as he was pushed kicking and screaming into a cell.

Inside, it was stiflingly hot and, gasping for breath, he paced up and down repeating over and over, 'Me? A murderer?' His solicitor reported that John was not in a stable condition and that he was threatening to harm himself. After John pleaded to be allowed to speak with his cousin, Ronnie was eventually allowed in to console him.

The thought of his mother, Maria, and how she would react hurt John the most. Unbeknown to him, she had arrived at the courthouse with his sister, who had gone in trying to find out what was going on. John's solicitor had told her he was being charged but advised her to take Maria to Taryn's house and he would come down and speak to them shortly.

When they parked up on Bute Street, John's sister broke the news. Maria had run screaming and crying up the road, as John had when told his father had died. John had always said nothing could ever be as bad as that. This came excruciatingly close.

He was allowed to make one phone call, and as he spoke to Taryn a verbatim note was made of the conversation by an officer acting as jailer.

'When they charged me,' John said of the detectives lined up in the room, 'they were all smiling.'

The city centre had been virtually closed down. As the van turned out of the prison gates, John Actie discerned the whirr of helicopter blades over the siren wails of an army of police patrol cars.

Peering through the small, wire-mesh window of the sweat box, he could see streams of traffic backed up and crowds of pedestrians corralled behind pavement cordons. Police motorcyclists in high-vis jackets bellowed as they fervently waved the van through.

It is like we are the mafia, he thought to himself.

Bearing all the hallmarks of a show trial, as the courthouse came into view, police officers could be seen positioned sniper-like on the roof, oddly armed only with cameras to record the arrival of the expected crowd from Tiger Bay, for what reason other than spectacle was never made clear.

It was February 1989 and the start of a hearing called an old-style committal; then part of the legal process used to test witness evidence before committing serious cases to Crown Court, they have since been abolished in favour of a more streamlined roadmap to justice.

The five men had only just been released into normal prison life. In line with Home Office policy, they had been classified as A-category prisoners, their escape deemed to pose the highest threat to public and national security, and had initially been segregated for six weeks, escorted at all times by a prison guard.

The men, who had initially been paranoid and suspicious of one another, talking behind each other's backs, wondering if one of them knew more about the murder than they were prepared to admit, had been prescribed beta blockers and temazepam to contend with the stress. Finally released into the rest of the prison population, the tension had eased slightly but each remained convinced of the others' guilt. When any one of them left the room, the others would talk behind their backs, discussing the latest ream of evidence sent through from lawyers.

John's older brother, Stephen, had drawn up a visiting rota, assigning daily slots to ensure John felt supported throughout. Each day, a handful of people would be waiting in the visitors' room laden with bags of food, most of it given away or left uneaten and piled high in John's cell, his embattled nervous system unable to cope with appetite at the time.

Each time his mother, Maria, came in, she would cry non-stop and, unable to cope with seeing her distress, John asked his brother to ensure she stayed at home; he would telephone her every day.

Taryn too would cry when she brought in the baby. John would distract her by hatching a plan for him to get to see General, his rottweiler.

The jail stood just beyond the bridge at the top of Bute Street. At prearranged times, Taryn, terrified of General, who was without question a one-person dog, that person being John, would brace herself before clipping on the lead and walking him to Queen Street railway station. There she would buy a platform ticket and head for the tracks adjacent and with a good vantage point to the prison wing John was housed in.

On spotting her in the distance, he would wave a towel through the window bars and shout over. Ignoring the stares from people waiting for their train, Taryn would shout back, her breath frozen in clouds by the January cold. Tearfully, they would call back and forth, 'I love you', 'I love you too.'

By 9.45 a.m. on that February morning, the prison van turned down a ramp to the cells complex for the men to be processed for the start of the committal. As John entered, he caught sight of Detective Inspector Powell at the far end of the corridor. They locked eyes. Not for the first time, he thought he saw Powell smirk, the same expression he recognised from the times he had laughed at John during his interrogation.

Anger flashed inside John. Tearing away from the line of prisoners, he ran full pelt towards Powell. Even if had the chance to escape, Powell, backed up against a locked metal security gate, had nowhere to turn. Grabbing him by the throat, John pushed him against the wall and punched him.

As officers wrestled with John, other prisoners shouted at them to leave him alone, two unrelated to the case lashing out at other officers as frantic calls for help echoed through the cell block.

Detective Superintendent Ken Davies, second-in-command of the murder investigation, deemed the defendants an escape risk. As well as ordering they be handcuffed while in the dock, he called for back-up to be drafted in to secure the court.

A crowd had gathered in the foyer of the public gallery, unable to gain access, every seat, aisle space and standing room taken, some by plain-clothes officers planted to furtively write a register of names.

In the centre of the court, where the legal teams assembled, matters were no less febrile. As John's solicitor, Stuart Hutton, prepared for the proceedings, Detective Superintendent Ken Davies approached.

Motioning contemptuously to an envelope of crime scene photographs on his desk, he said, 'Take a good look at them because that is what your clients have done.' Hutton did not flinch. He had represented members of the docks' community in court innumerable times over the years, and had grown inured to the municipal sport of dehumanising the rough and ready of Tiger Bay.

Finally, just after 11 a.m., John, Ronnie, Tony and Dullah, their right hands cuffed to the left of a police officer, filed into the wide dock. Only after they were seated, John Actie in the centre, was Stephen Miller led up separately, heavily guarded for fear of reprisals over his confession.

Directly opposite, the magistrates emerged from their chambers and took their seats. Anyone underestimating the chairman, Kenneth Ernest Spurlock, a jolly-faced, white-haired gent with a quiet self-possession, would be making a foolish mistake.

A former Chindits special forces officer captured behind enemy lines in Burma in 1943, Lieutenant Spurlock endured internment at Maymyo concentration camp and the notorious Rangoon jail in Myanmar. There could be few people, certainly on the area's magistrate circuit rota, more capable of presiding over Court Number Five that day.

As the two female witnesses, Leanne Vilday and Angela Psaila, appeared to give their accounts, it was the first time John had laid eyes on either of them. As the women told of witnessing the murder of Lynette White at the hands of the five accused, the court descended into uproar. As more reinforcements were drafted in, before long the entire circumference of the court was lined by uniformed officers.

Arguments broke out as police ordered people to clear gangways and exits. When one officer grabbed hold of John's brother's arm, the gallery rose to their feet in protest, surging forward to his defence.

'The entire gallery erupted in a frenzy,' the notes of one officer read. 'There was considerable screaming and shouting and general disorder, police being threatened with violence and at one point I feared that a riot would take place. People in the gallery jumping from their seats, those outside in the foyer trying to get in.'

Then, the officer continued, a shout from the public gallery echoed through the court: 'If you think this is anything wait until you see us organised.'

It was prescient. Unbeknown to anyone in court, the statement, time would tell, was arguably the single biggest truth uttered during the course of the entire hearing.

At one stage, as the court awaited the return of Angela Psaila to continue giving her evidence, there were audible gasps as she could be heard screaming from outside, 'How many times do I have to tell you? I wasn't fucking there!'

Ms Psaila, it was explained, was feeling unwell and had requested to see a doctor. An adjournment of half an hour was agreed.

It was at that point, from outside the court, she was heard to be crying hysterically, her screams audible in the court that 'I wasn't fucking there.'

With that, the doors opened and Psaila was forcibly dragged into court by Detective Superintendent Ken Davies and jostled into the witness box, as other officers sat and stood close by, John noted, glaring at her.

The five defendants, back in the dock, handcuffed, looked at one another in disbelief.

When asked by a defence barrister what she had meant when she shouted, 'I wasn't there', Psaila grew irritated, saying she had been referring to the doctor's examination room; someone had asked her if she had been there for her consultation.

In total, the prosecution case presented three other witnesses – Leanne Vilday, Mark Grommek and Paul Atkins – each of their accounts taken apart during cross-examination. While the defendants held on to the hope of the prosecution being thrown out, it was not to be the case.

Meeting the criteria for a prima facie case, a date was set for a pre-trial review a couple of months later in May.

In the belief that publicity around the case in Cardiff would be detrimental to the men receiving a fair trial, the Honourable Mr Justice Pill announced that the trial, likely to stretch over several months, would be held in Swansea, a city less than fifty miles away, whose history of multiculturalism was at the time, putting it mildly, limited.

John turned to Ronnie and said, 'We've got big problems now. Big problems.'

Chapter Five

As chief prosecutor David Elfer QC rose to begin his opening address in the trial of the murder of Lynette White at Swansea's Guildhall in early October 1989, he did so with a chutzpah that belied the weakness of his case.

An experienced criminal barrister, Elfer would have known only too well that the arena of a courtroom, as drama-filled as any movie theatre, is a battleground not of evidence per se but of an art form as old as human cognition itself: storytelling.

'Butetown,' he said, 'is a nocturnal, upside-down world where people wear knives as part of their clothing, the way that *we* might a handkerchief.

'When *we* come home from work, *they* get up to go to clubs. And when *we* get up to go to work, *they* return home to sleep . . . It is a fearful place into which the arm of the police and criminal law does not reach very far.'

It was a description that caused outrage. There was no mistaking it: the community of Butetown was being tried alongside the five men in the dock.

He would later apologise for it, but Elfer was no fool. He had set out to conjure a theme in the minds of the jurors, one that triggered the atavistic fear of the 'other'. The divisive power of tribalism had long served to dehumanise Tiger Bay, and in the psychological warfare of a trial it was an expedient advance.

Lifting the veil on a twilight world of violence, prostitution and drugs, he described to the packed court the brutal murder of a young woman in a dark, dank and almost empty flat, stabbed so frenziedly her top resembled lace. The crime scene photographs passed to the jury as he told of her throat being cut virtually from ear to ear must have been images indelibly imprinted on their minds.

Cornered by a gang of five men, he continued, her jealous and possessive boyfriend among them, Lynette White had put up a fierce struggle before enduring a terrifying and lingering death. Agreeing upon a 'code of silence', her murderers, Elfer said, had hampered a long but determined police inquiry.

John Actie saw the jurors look over at him. They must be thinking he was an animal. He cringed at the thought. Slumped forward, covering his face with his hands, he willed the ground to open up and swallow him. Utterly powerless, there was nothing he could do but sit there and endure it.

Two women, Elfer continued, who lived in a flat across the road, had been startled by a piercing scream. Realising it had come from 7 James Street, a flat occasionally used by their friend Lynette White, they rushed over to help, only to witness her death throes.

'We have all had a go,' the women were allegedly told. 'Now you will have a go too.' With a blade held to their throat, Elfer said their hands were forcibly wrapped around a second knife and in scenes akin to a ritualistic killing, the women were ordered to further cut their friend's body. You are part of it now, the murderers warned them; breathe a word of this to the police and you and your children will be next.

'They were made to cut Lynette in order to buy their silence,' Elfer intoned.

'It worked for ten months and they did not say anything. But then shame began to surface about their part in it all.'

Lynette White and her boyfriend, Stephen Miller, Elfer alleged, had a stormy relationship. He was her pimp, and she, one of the hardest-working sex workers in the area, would be out on the street in all weathers, Christmas Day and New Year's Eve no exception.

Earning upwards of £100 a day, in the early hours of the morning she would meet with her partner in the North Star club on the dock front, where she would hand over cash for him to buy drugs.

In the five days leading up to her death, he said Lynette White had been out of contact, likely upset about a summons to give prosecution evidence in a court case about an incident between two women outside the North Star. She was reluctant to do so, fearing people would think she had informed to the police.

Also, a week before her death, the couple had fallen out, Elfer said, alleging that Stephen had been seen dragging his sobbing girlfriend from the warmth of a pub.

'Get out or I will kill you,' he had shouted, a woman later told police.

Stephen Miller looked heavenward, his eyes fixed on a large skylight window in the coffered ceiling. In a metaphor befitting a cinematic scene, heavy clouds drew in and fused into an eerie, dark-grey mantle.

First into the witness box for the prosecution, pathologist Professor Bernard Knight consulted his report written following an inspection of the murder scene and post-mortem examination.

He told how an absence of blood under the victim's body and the partly worn coat having become tightly wrapped around her torso indicated that the body had been dragged or rolled to its resting place a few feet from where the first major and fatal wound had been inflicted.

At the end of the bed, where a large area of carpet was soaked with blood, he pointed to an arc of arterial blood spray on the wall above it. It was likely that Lynette White's head was pulled back and her throat cut at least twice, although likely three times, the depth of the wounds indicating the considerable force used. Professor Knight postulated that she would either have been on the ground at the time or had buckled to it shortly after.

This was the first major wound, he said. The remaining fifty to sixty injuries, he went on, barring defensive wounds, had been inflicted after death or about the time of death, explaining that a lack or absence of bleeding from them showed a fall in blood pressure after the carotid artery in the neck had been severed. Slashes to her wrists, for instance, had not bled at all and had certainly been made after Lynette White had died.

The most marked of a number of defensive wounds, which included bruising on the knuckles, were to the right hand, but cuts also on the left were all consistent with attempting to ward off a knife attack.

When asked for his overall impression of the wounds, Professor Knight said the victim had been stabbed in every area of her body from her face to her groin; those to her chest and face were designed to mutilate and disfigure.

'The concentration on the breasts, the lower abdomen, the upper thigh and, I suppose, to some extent the facial area, is characteristic of a mutilating attack with sexual overtones, I would have thought,' he told the court.

Next, the forensic scientists revealed several key facts. An opened but unused condom had been found on the bed and tests had revealed that the victim had not partaken in sexual intercourse for up to six hours before the attack.

Small change had been found scattered on the mattress and on the floor; three £10 and two £5 notes had been recovered, ruling out robbery as a motive.

As for any forensic clues linking the killer or killers, the jury was told that the hems of Lynette White's jeans were smeared with unidentified male blood, the marks likely made by the span of a gripped hand used to move or pull the body.

The same blood had been found in blood spatter at various points around the room although none on the mattress. 'I excluded the defendants with absolute certainty,' the scientist told the court. Moreover, not a single shred of any forensic evidence linked any of the five men with the murder scene.

This included fingerprints, the flat having been swept with a 'fine tooth comb', which lifted 140 marks. Among them was a significant left palm print found on the chimney breast wall close to the blood-soaked carpet. It was twenty-seven inches above the ground, suggesting someone had crouched down and placed their hand on the wall to steady themselves. While there were blood markings around it, there were none within it, strongly indicating that it was linked to the attack.

Immediately after the arrest of the suspects, their entire wardrobes had been seized but again, no trace of the crime scene was found among them.

And so, Elfer turned to the evidence that the Crown insisted did connect to the five men.

Throughout her five days of testimony, Leanne Vilday spoke quietly, fixing her stare downwards at a single spot on the dark wooden panels of the witness box, rarely, if ever, lifting her gaze to the judge, counsel, jury, defendants or public gallery.

For ten months, Vilday had sworn blind to the police that she knew nothing about the murder until there came a point when, she told the court, she could hide the truth no longer.

At around 1.30 a.m. on St Valentine's Day 1988, she said, she was returning from discarding rubbish into a communal chute on the veranda of St Clair Court, a block of flats tucked away from the main road opposite 7 James Street, when she was startled by three loud screams.

At the time, she and her eleven-month-old baby boy were lodging with Angela Psaila, who, inside watching television at the time, also heard the screams. Vilday backtracked to a point on the balcony from where she could peer over to the main road. She noticed the communal front door of 7 James Street was open, an address occasionally used by her friend Lynette White.

Vilday, originally from Barry, a seaside town once home to a busy port, ten miles west of the docks, had drifted into sex work a year or two before, and while she had seen Lynette White around the streets during that time, in the past six months the two women had grown close.

In November, Vilday rented Flat One of 7 James Street but had not yet moved in, as she was saving to buy furniture. In the meantime, she offered Lynette White the use of it, somewhere to take clients, where she could charge more for sex indoors.

Fearing her friend was in trouble, Vilday told how she and Psaila ran across the road to the flat, noticing a green Ford Cortina parked outside. Running up the stairs, she said, the women passed John Actie, who, standing on the small landing outside Flat One, made no attempt to stop them entering the flat.

She spoke of the vivid memory of seeing Tony Paris sitting astride Lynette White, who was not moving and was evidently dead, as he stabbed at her chest. Watching him, she said, from various positions around the small room were Ronnie, Dullah and Stephen.

The next thing she knew, she claimed, a knife was held to her throat by John Actie, who then forced another into her hand and guided it towards Lynette White's body, dragging the blade across Lynette's wrist. When asked in what position Lynette White lay, Vilday said she was unsure if she was on her back or her front.

Angela Psaila, she said, had shouted at the men and had been punched in the mouth. She too, Vilday alleged, was forced to cut Lynette White's other wrist.

When it came to Psaila's version of events, there were some inconsistences.

There were two exit points to her flat across the road, a back and front. Leanne Vilday said they had run down the back exit on to a short alleyway that opened directly on to James Street, but Psaila insisted it was via the front, the choice of which seemed nonsensical given it required a much longer and more circuitous route to James Street.

When Psaila ran up the stairs, she recalled that John Actie had in fact tried to stop them but they had effortlessly batted him away. Psaila said that, far from already being dead, Lynette White was fighting with Tony Paris, not on the floor but on the bed.

In Psaila's account, Stephen had first stabbed Lynette White, who then got off the bed only to fall, pawing at the window as if to summon help. Then, each of the men took it in turns to wound her further. Psaila then claimed Vilday was ordered to cut Lynette White – not her wrist but her throat.

Then, according to Psaila, another man entered the scene: Mark Grommek, the tenant from the flat above. This, however, did not align with Grommek's drastically different account.

Grommek had got home around midnight, and shortly afterwards a friend of his, Paul Atkins, had called round. The two men were drinking tea and listening to records when the doorbell rang. Not expecting any more callers, Grommek ignored it. But it rang repeatedly for ten minutes, prompting him to walk into the front room, unoccupied due to damp, which faced on to the road.

There, he climbed on to the windowsill in order to get a view of the front door, around which stood four strange men. Fearful they might have been coming to assault him, as he had experienced some hostility as a gay man, he told how he, somewhat counterintuitively, wandered downstairs and opened the door.

'Is there anyone in Flat One?' asked one of the men, who wore a tracksuit and baseball cap and whom Grommek later came to know was Dullah. Grommek had replied that he did not think anyone was in the flat, before heading back up the stairs, glancing backward to see Dullah following behind.

Retreating to the safety of his flat and shaking like a leaf, he said he and Atkins heard a man with a West Indian accent shout, 'Give it to me! You've got what I want.' Then a different male voice said, 'Give the man what he wants, you fucking bitch or he will fuck you up real good!'

A woman could be heard protesting, Grommek told the jury, followed by some shuffling and then a high-pitched scream, which 'rung throughout the house'.

On hearing the men leaving, Atkins decided to investigate. As Atkins was downstairs, Grommek leant over the bannister to see Leanne Vilday outside Flat One, looking stressed. Atkins, he said, returned as 'white as a sheet' and was violently sick in the toilet, saying he had seen a girl's body and that there was blood everywhere.

The two men, Grommek said, discussed the night's events, deciding it best not to go to the police for fear of any fallback on them.

Meanwhile, the court heard, Vilday and Psaila, by this stage back safely in their flat across the road, never spoke a word to one another about what had just happened. Instead, Vilday played with her baby, had a bath, put some make-up on and went to the North Star at 3.20 a.m. As she fled the murder scene, her then boyfriend, Ronnie Actie, had allegedly told her to meet him there.

Ronnie, she said, had told her to 'just keep smiling and look happy', but while later driving to stay the night at his sister's house near Loudoun Square, he had hit her and told her to forget about it.

The defence had some questions.

Over her five days of evidence, Vilday was cross-examined alternately by each of the five barristers representing the defendants.

The court heard that during the murder investigation, she had made a total of twenty statements to the police. The first was taken only hours after the discovery of Lynette White's body, which she now claimed had been an elaborate charade. She explained she had not seen her friend for several days, but was not initially worried as Lynette had talked about going to London, which is where Vilday assumed she had gone.

This was an account she stuck to until 6 December 1988. It was then Vilday had told the truth, after police said they already knew what had happened – Psaila had told them.

Had officers threatened that if Vilday did not comply, she would be charged and her son would be taken away from her? No, she said, on the contrary, detectives had reassured her that they would protect her and her baby.

In her statement on 6 December, she had named four men: Stephen, Dullah, a black man with long dreadlocks whom she did not know, and another man called Martin Tucker, a regular at the North Star. Tony Paris and John Actie were never mentioned. Could she explain?

The mention of Martin Tucker, that was a lie, she said. It was the first name that had come into her head; she disliked the man and planted him falsely at the scene because she was too scared to mention John Actie at that stage.

But hang on a minute, John's defence protested, in September of 1988 Vilday had certainly been prepared to name him in return for a £10 informer's fee from a detective when she claimed, falsely as it turned out, that someone had overheard John say a local woman knew where Lynette White was staying in the days before the murder. Highly unlikely she would have done so had she been terrified because of his behaviour in the murder room.

Defence counsel also pointed out that Grommek and Atkins had also lied about seeing Tucker. Had she conferred with the other witnesses? No, she insisted she had never spoken a word to any of them about the murder. In which case, they said, it was one hell of a coincidence.

That was not the only glaring discrepancy. In her statement of 6 December, Vilday said Psaila had stayed in the flat and only she, Vilday, had run over to James Street, an account that aligned with a statement from Psaila made on the same day.

But then a week later, after both women were taken in for questioning again, this time in the early hours of the morning for a period of eleven hours, they changed their accounts to say that *both* of them had gone over to the flat. Vilday's explanation was that she lied previously so as not to involve Psaila.

Their updated statements, made just hours before the defendants were charged, now also included the presence of John and Tony, with Martin Tucker disappearing from her account. Coincidentally again, the defence said, Grommek and Atkins also dropped Tucker from their updated statements signed that same day.

Had police put pressure on her to name certain men? No, but she did admit that detectives had told her that Tucker's alibi had checked out, leaving her with no choice but to confess to John and

Tony being there. Was she sure there hadn't been any discussion with the other witnesses? Once again, no, she was sure.

On more than one occasion during cross-examination, Vilday broke down in tears, at one stage being referred for a hospital check-up. The jury was told that she was around four months pregnant but that doctors had deemed her medically fit to continue.

The defence asked her about the protective custody detectives had arranged for her for the duration of the trial. She said she was living in a house within the compound of South Wales Police headquarters in Bridgend, where senior officers visited regularly but never discussed the case. Her food and rent were paid for, as was childcare, and she was chaperoned to collect her unemployment benefit and during frequent nights out in Swansea.

Vilday agreed that on one occasion she had stayed out for two nights. Was that the occasion she got pregnant? Yes, she said. Was the father a police officer? No, she replied.

Back to the matter at hand, Vilday said she had not seen much blood at the murder scene as it was too dark. When asked to look at a crime scene photograph, she refused and broke down again. After a forty-five-minute adjournment, Judge McNeill consoled her and offered to stand behind her as she looked at the image.

'I suppose there were times when you were doing your business when you just had to grit your teeth and get on with it,' he told her. Yes, she said. 'Would you like to do the same now?' he said.

When asked about the clothes she wore on the night, Vilday said both women had thrown them away in the communal rubbish chute. She remembered Psaila had spoken to a neighbour shortly after doing so. No doubt, the defence asked, they must have been heavily bloodstained. Vilday struggled to recall, but said there was 'a little patch' on her skirt and a few drops on Psaila's blouse.

After being told to keep her voice up several times, it was put to Vilday that in normal life she was in fact much louder, someone who generally made herself conspicuous. Yes, she agreed, at times that was true.

The defence highlighted a case in point in the June of 1988. Vilday had yet again been interviewed by police, something she had become sick and tired of, after which she had gone to the Custom House pub. Having downed a number of double gins, she became disruptive and was ordered to leave. As she was escorted outside, she shouted that Stephen and Dullah had killed Lynette White.

When detectives got to hear about the outburst, she told them she had no clear memory of it and that she had been drowning her sorrows after a row with her then girlfriend. She told them her claim was untrue, but that she felt resentful that Stephen Miller was in London, and away from the pressure of the police inquiry. Dullah's name, she said, had come into her mind purely because police had asked her about him earlier that day.

'If you don't believe me,' Vilday had said, 'hypnotise me.' The police took her up on the suggestion.

A fifty-minute video recording of Vilday at the Wigan office of Dr Una Maguire, a specialist psychologist and police consultant, was played to the jury. The grainy footage showed her sitting, her head to one side as if half asleep, as she was questioned by the softly spoken Dr Maguire.

On the night Lynette White was killed, Vilday said she had been working and had gone for a takeaway pizza in the city centre before meeting Ronnie Actie in the North Star, also recalling how she had looked through the letterbox of the James Street flat before going to the police station, details that matched her original police statement.

At the conclusion of the session, Dr Maguire can be heard telling police that Vilday, who made no mention of the murder scenario, had told them all she knew, although the video that was played in court cut off before this point.

Why, if she was harbouring a guilty secret she was terrified to reveal, the defence asked, would she volunteer to be hypnotised?

Vilday said she had not expected them to go through with it and claimed she had resisted any attempts to induce her into a hypnotic state and had play-acted, deliberately adopting a deeper, slower breathing pattern, leaning her head at an unnatural angle and speaking in a drowsy voice.

References were made to different letters she had sent during the months of the murder hunt, but one written to an old school-friend on Boxing Day 1988, later passed to John's solicitor, was extraordinary. An excerpt of it read:

> *Dear Nicky,*
>
> *Well love, hope you're ok and fine. I'm living in Newport with my girlfriend and her friends.*
>
> *Nicola, three weeks ago the police arrested me for the murder. Well, Nic, I know you knows me and if I would have done something like that, I wouldn't be able to keep something like that to myself. Well, anyway, after being locked up for a couple of days the police said they had three witnesses to say that the five boys locked up now for it was there and they said I must either go on the police's side or on the boys' side. That meant I either say 'yeah, I was there and I saw the five boys' and get out of the police station that day and then be a main witness to this fucking murder case, or the other option I had was to say the same as I've said from the day I found the girl which is the truth Nicky . . . If I would have said what I've been saying for 10 months which, honest to God, is the truth I would have been in the dock with them for the murder. So, I've lied to the police just so I*

could have got out of the police station . . . I just
can't believe that the boys in prison are the right ones.

That was all lies, Vilday told the court. She had desperately wanted to talk to someone about her ordeal but did not want her friend to think badly of her by admitting to her she was in the flat.

Other friends described how she had changed from a cheerful, bubbly girl to one who drank and took drugs to excess following the murder; she would sit in the corner of a pub crying that the police were threatening to take her son away from her, said one, telling another she only agreed to say she was at the murder scene for the sake of her child. More lies, Vilday claimed.

Another letter written to a male friend in July that year described how a commemorative drink to mark Lynette White's birthday had been interrupted by 'loads of CID in the Custom House threatening to lock up the girls over Lynette'.

Well, there was a bit of harassment, she said, but no threats to lock them up as such, more that they would keep moving us off the street if we were not forthcoming.

If the jury had any hope that the testimony of Angela Psaila would be more straightforward, it would not take long for it to be dashed.

Psaila, then aged twenty-four, the daughter of a taxi driver who had grown up locally, did not take lightly to her account being questioned. Evidently feeling under pressure, she frequently lost her temper, swore and barracked counsel, cheeking the judge on occasion and repeatedly referring to the defendants as 'the five monkeys sitting in the dock'.

When asked, for instance, why she had suddenly swapped Stephen Miller's brother Anthony with John Actie in her statements, she said she had simply been confused and denied it had anything to do with detectives telling her they had confirmed Anthony Miller's alibi.

When further pressed on the matter, she rounded on the cross-examining barrister, shouting, 'I have just said Pineapple's brother was not there and John Actie was. What's the matter with the lot of you?'

The contradictions in her account were perhaps even more startling than Vilday's.

Lynette White, she insisted, had been stabbed by several of the men while struggling on the bed and had, at a later stage, pawed at the window, an account that flew in the face of forensic evidence; no blood had been found on the mattress nor fingerprints on the window pane.

According to her recollection, Lynette White, although severely wounded, was still alive when Vilday was forced to cut her throat. This not only contradicted Vilday's insistence that she was evidently dead but also Professor Knight's expert opinion that the neck injury had been the first and not last major injury inflicted.

But there was something telling about Psaila's revelations that made John Actie and his co-accused wonder for the umpteenth time how her evidence had been allowed to get this far.

Psaila told the court that when interviewed in November, police had put to her the name John Actie, one she was unfamiliar with. 'They kept on about him all the time,' she said. The police had divulged to her that someone had seen him. Well, by her logic, if she did not agree with that then she would be calling someone else a liar.

In the case of Dullah, she said the police again had been told he was pacing around outside the James Street flat. She was asked, you went along with that suggestion? It was not a suggestion, she argued, it was a fact.

'It is like I said, the police had been told that they were all pacing outside the flat,' she said. 'Everyone you've got in that witness box was supposed to be there.'

Detectives refuted claims they used pressure or impropriety at any stage during Psaila's questioning. She is wrong, they insisted, if she says names were put to her.

As to why she had changed her account from Vilday running over to the flat to both of them going there, Psaila said it was because police told her that her blood had been found there.

In the same updated statement, she had included being hit in the mouth by one of the men, she could not remember which one, and described how blood from a split lip had dripped in the flat. The science behind that explanation, though, was more complex.

In early December 1988, Psaila had been the victim of an attack on the street while soliciting. The police investigated, and as part of that, a sample of her blood had been sent to the government-run forensic laboratory, where scientists were also working on the Lynette White murder case. It was noted that Psaila's blood grouping was fairly rare and that it was the same grouping as the unidentified blood found on Lynette White's clothing and on wallpaper at the murder scene.

But the blood on Lynette White's jeans contained a Y chromosome, meaning it was male. The prosecution called a forensic scientist, who said there were two possibilities: it was either male blood or Psaila's blood had become mixed with male blood.

It was a theory rejected out of hand by the defence. The blood in question had soaked parts of Lynette White's jeans. Even though Psaila claimed she had tugged on them while trying to help Lynette White, it was preposterous, they held, to apply the mixture theory to such a large area. And besides, none of the male blood belonged to any of the defendants or the other witnesses, so whose was it?

In February 1988, Mark Grommek, a thirty-year-old unemployed chef originally from the town of Pontypridd, twelve miles north of Cardiff, had only been living in the second-floor flat at 7 James Street for two months.

At the time, he was on probation for shoplifting and had been in trouble since boyhood. After a stint in borstal for stealing a £5 jacket, in 1979 he had served three years in jail for the attempted armed robbery of a shop in London, during which he had brandished a toy pistol.

Grommek had settled in the docks, where he socialised peacefully with a small group of friends living close by, occasionally visiting one or two of the city's gay bars to meet other men, but he had struggled with his sexuality to the point of depression, for which his GP had prescribed him medication.

On arriving home late on Valentine's Day to find his home cordoned off by police, he had been taken to Butetown Police Station, where he made a statement, the first of twelve, as time would tell, outlining his movements the night before. After returning home shortly after midnight on Valentine's Day, Grommek had taken an antidepressant, after which he slept through without interruption until nine o'clock the next morning.

Grommek did not know Lynette White. In the weeks before her murder, he had heard muffled voices and the occasional door slam in the flat below and, although aware it was used sporadically by sex workers, he believed it was otherwise unoccupied.

Then on 22 November, after being picked up by detectives, he too made a volte-face. So many people suddenly deciding to 'tell the truth', independently of one another and at the exact same time: it was as if, one defence barrister jibed, some kind of spell had been broken.

Grommek, who was at the police station for over eleven hours that day, said that at one stage he asked if he could go home but was told he could not, as police suspected he knew more.

Officers had told him they had received a report of a man matching his description seen opening the door to his flat shortly before the murder, conceding that the report came from Angela Psaila.

Grommek told the court that after his doorbell had been rung repeatedly, he had eventually gone downstairs and opened the door to four strange men. Three of them he later came to know were Ronnie, Dullah and Martin Tucker. A fourth he had described as tall and black, with long dreadlocks and a goatee beard.

Tony Paris's defence counsel asked Tony to stand up in the dock. He was a whisker above five feet tall, with short hair and pebble glasses. The man you see – the barrister gestured towards Tony – was not one of the four men that night, Grommek was asked. No, he replied. And you did not see him on the premises at 7 James Street? Again, no. He had never heard the name Tony Paris before it was suggested to him by officers. John Actie was then asked to stand up. Once again, Grommek denied ever seeing him at the flat.

As with the previous two witnesses, the defence rattled through a plethora of statements, each signed after being held for long stints in police stations, each iteration revealing some suddenly remembered piece of the puzzle of the supposed final minutes of the young and tragic life of Lynette White.

Given that Grommek had claimed to have been too terrified to go to the police, had he been threatened at all over the preceding nine or ten months before coming clean? No, but he lived in fear of it. Why then had he chosen to stay at 7 James Street, at one stage moving to the top floor as it was a nicer flat, knowing these men could return at any time? He had simply not thought about moving out, Grommek said.

Even more surprisingly, in the autumn of that year Grommek had begun working five to seven nights a week as the resident DJ at the North Star, a bar frequented by Dullah and Ronnie. After complaints by regulars about the standard of Grommek's record collection, Dullah had lent him some reggae and Motown albums and, on occasion, Ronnie had bought him a drink.

To Grommek's claim that their apparent friendliness was laced with threatening glares, the defence shook their heads; that still did not explain why he had willingly entered the lion's den if what he claimed was true.

◆ ◆ ◆

For the five men in the dock, moments of levity during the trial were, unsurprisingly, few and far between. One of the rare moments they shook with laughter was during the testimony of the fourth and final chief witness, Paul Atkins.

Atkins was a small, comical character known to the police due to his record of over eighty offences for petty crime.

Previous to November 1988, Grommek, Vilday and Psaila had denied any knowledge of the murder. Not so Paul Atkins.

In the weeks following the murder, he had been pulled in by a detective whom he had known for many years, whereupon he proceeded to 'confess', fabricating four different scenarios: after hearing screams, he saw a man called 'Barry the homo' emerge from the flat; Grommek covered in blood, carrying a knife, saying he had killed her for £45; Grommek and he both did it and discarded the murder weapon in an alleyway; in the final version Atkins claimed he had acted alone, describing in detail furniture inside the flat that did not exist.

Paul Atkins was quickly ushered out of the doors of Butetown Police Station and did not return until he was brought back in November that same year.

While the others swore their accounts had been made without collusion or prompting, Atkins alleged that detectives put the men's names to him and had written accounts themselves, threatening to charge him with murder if he did not sign them.

Had he talked to Grommek in between breaks in questioning at the police station? Yes, Atkins said.

'Grommek told me "Just tell them you were there, make up a story" so that's what I did because I was scared,' he said. 'The police separated us for the interviews and they put words into my mouth.'

But such was the level of Atkins's suggestibility that he would instantly comply with whatever scenario was put to him in court, contradicting himself several times within the space of a single sentence and brazenly admitting he played games.

'I have played the fool since the day of the murder,' he said. 'I knew I was one of the chief suspects. I saw my way out as playing the fool so that no one would believe me.'

There was no denying it: the quality of the prosecution's chief witnesses was woeful. But regardless of its quality, their testimony was not sufficient to convict. Atkins's could not be taken seriously, while Grommek's only implicated Dullah and Ronnie, as he had not named the other three.

Vilday and Psaila, who had implicated all five men, had admitted, no matter the circumstances, that they used a knife to cut the victim and as such were accomplices. To convict on accomplice evidence alone would be unsafe.

In order to corroborate their horrifying accounts, the onus was on the prosecution to present further, independent evidence of the men's guilt.

Chapter Six

'Whether he did it or not, doesn't matter. He's got away with enough in the past and he's had it coming,' said Detective Superintendent Ken Davies.

During a lull in proceedings, Davies, the second-in-command of the murder investigation, a high-ranking senior detective in the South Wales force, bounced a squash ball off the oak-panelled walls of the court, killing time.

John Actie's guilt, he made clear to his lawyer as he passed by, was a moot point. Guilt specifically over the murder? Not really the point at all. The hunt for the killer of Lynette White appeared to have taken a back seat.

A twisted mindset might justify settling a score and bringing a thorn-in-the-side thug to heel by whatever means necessary as noble-cause corruption. A more realistic one might see it for what it was: a Faustian pact.

Sure, it would mean the police could wash their hands of a difficult case and release the city of its fetters to ramp up its bid for billions of cash to finance the dockland transformation. But setting the immorality of a wrongful conviction aside, the vexed question remained of exactly how noble it was to leave a killer walking the streets of Cardiff, or wherever it was the real murderer lived.

Approaching nearly five painfully long months since the start of the trial, the hostility of the police towards the defence teams had not abated. Far from it: it had intensified.

John, steeling himself to take to the witness box and give evidence, was still being goaded by some of the detectives in court.

Winking at him from the sidelines, gesturing a thumbs-down, mouthing 'you're going down', calling him a 'black bastard' and blowing mocking kisses to female friends and relatives in the public gallery, was unedifying even by playground standards. John could complain but with so much more at stake, it would not get him anywhere. Besides, who was going to believe him? The judge?

The febrility had spread like contagion around the court. John intuited a disquiet among defence QCs at what appeared to be the partisan persuasion of the trial judge.

All five accused men became increasingly riled by what they saw as a consistent bias towards the prosecution. In their view Mr Justice McNeill took a hard line with the defence while conceding to the whims of the Crown.

Maybe Mr Justice McNeill, with his slick of grey hair and heavy horn-rimmed glasses, had become addled, as a never-ending soap opera of witnesses, not far shy of one hundred in total, were wheeled out before him.

Aside from the four main testimonies, a conveyor belt of bit-part players who had overheard dubious-sounding pub conversations juddered along day after day. Some would break down in tears; others turned hostile witness, shouting from the dock that the police had made them lie, that they only signed their statement to get the hell out of the station and end unbearable harassment.

Opinion prompted by innuendo and leading questions, a sinister spin on meaningless observations – 'he looked worried', 'he scowled at me', 'he gave such and such a lift in his car' – raised suspicion at every turn. Each fragment of what amounted to a smear campaign, witch-hunt gossip about lifestyle or the prosaic churn of daily life, was placed under the microscope of a murder trial, to take apart the men's characters seam by seam.

The judge allowed previous convictions to be revealed after the defendants had attacked the character of some of the witnesses whom they accused of lying; according to law, it is deemed fair for the prosecution to have a chance to undermine their credibility to make such a claim. But it had been used outside those bounds by chief prosecutor Elfer, just one of many tactics defence counsel considered grossly prejudicial and improper.

Each defendant, apart from Tony Paris, had a record of violence. They held their hands up. The cold, typed record may not paint the full picture but, yes, they did it. But nothing, they implored, ever came remotely close to the attack on Lynette White. That is as may be, but criminal pasts, petty or otherwise, trowelled a further layer of fear and doubt in the jury's mind. These were bad guys, of course they are going to say they are innocent. No smoke without fire.

When it came to cross-examining the men, no one could expect the chief prosecutor to put them at ease. That was not Elfer's job; he was there to disprove alibis and undermine their accounts. But what everyone could expect of Elfer was that he did so professionally. But to the defendants and their legal teams, the style he adopted was viewed as oppressive, inviting argument and, at times, deliberately misleading the witness.

'It is evidence in this case, Mr Miller, that you knew Lynette used the flat to take clients,' he stated. That was not evidence. Stephen flat out denied any knowledge of the flat. Always had. No evidence to contradict that.

Elfer would interrupt midway through answers, and on the occasions the defendants did get a chance to reply fully, he would fire back with sarcasm, 'That's an honest answer, is it?' or 'Do you know how to answer a straight question?'

When one protested that he was trying to be cooperative, Elfer laughed out loud. 'Was that a serious remark?'

If they told him they could not remember something or they did not know the answer to a question, he would grasp it like a stick to beat them with, repeating it over and over and over again. At other times, grinning, he would say, 'Let's look at how evasive you can be when you really try.'

When the men said the four witnesses were lying, he would read aloud excerpts of their evidence and throw his hands in the air, incredulously. 'Are they wrong?' 'Are they all lying?' 'Are they talking rubbish?' 'It's all a tissue of lies? Is that what you're saying?'

◆　◆　◆

John Actie was the last of the five men to give evidence, on 14 February 1990, the second anniversary of the murder. Eager to get into the witness box and plead his case, he had coached himself mentally.

He caught McNeill's eye; the judge's look was one of disgust. Everyone's gaze was on John: the jury's, the press's, the public gallery's. He noticed his sister, Donna. She was ashen, visibly shocked. God, Donna thought, he looks like a corpse.

'Come on, John,' he thought to himself. 'Breathe . . . breathe.' But a voice inside his head wanted to scream, 'You know it wasn't us! Why have I got to go through this shit?'

John had only been in the witness box for a short time before Elfer rebuked him, ordering him not to look at the jury when he answered his questions, citing his demeanour as intimidating. But he is doing nothing wrong, his defence counsel jumped in.

Elfer repeatedly put it to John that he was the ringleader, the dominant force. He had called as witnesses twelve police officers who had guarded the men during the committal proceedings. Statements from them told how John and Ronnie had made verbal threats as well as gun and cut-throat gestures at Vilday and Psaila as they gave evidence. The allegations blindsided John and had only been submitted as evidence on the day the trial started.

It was wholly untrue, John insisted. Admittedly, he had repeatedly told them to tell the truth and to speak up but he had *never* threatened them.

Two solicitors, as well as Kenneth Spurlock, the magistrate who had presided over the committal, were called by Elfer. All strenuously denied the twelve officers' claims. Elfer asked Spurlock to recall how John's shouts had interrupted one of the witnesses taking her oath. He could not. As far as he was concerned, that had not happened. 'Really?' Elfer said, his tone arched. 'You say you can't remember.'

Maybe Spurlock, along with everyone else who had given evidence during the trial, felt frightened and intimidated when within John Actie's eyeline. Spurlock looked at him quizzically before reassuring him that as a survivor of a Japanese prisoner-of-war camp, he did not feel particularly fazed by John Actie.

But Elfer persisted with his smear campaign, making sneering remarks about how John leaned forward in the dock staring intently and was forever passing notes to his barrister.

His freedom was at stake: was it now a crime to pay attention? John found himself gripping the edge of the stand. His head pounding, his stomach gripped with spasms, he gasped for air as if his chest was caving in.

An adjournment was abruptly called before he was helped down to the cells. He collapsed on the floor, feeling the welcome cold of the polished concrete surface underneath his suit. Sweat poured from him as he writhed in pain. He thought he was dying. And, not for the first time, he wondered if that would really be such a bad thing.

As a doctor examined him, John Rogers QC, his chief counsel, stood over him, looking down coldly. 'Can you not just stand up?' he sighed, rattled by the inconvenience. 'We really need to get your evidence over with.'

John had never been a fan of Rogers. From that point on, he loathed him.

He could coach himself as much as he liked but, it seemed, his body had been keeping score. The stress of the trial, which neared its end, had overwhelmed his nervous system. The doctor, satisfied it was a panic attack and nothing more sinister, advised he rest and resume giving evidence the following day.

Elfer spent what seemed hours chewing over John's mix-up over weekends when he was first interviewed, claiming he had deliberately falsified his alibi. John vehemently denied doing so. With no reason to remember that weekend more than any other nearly a year before, he told him he was panicked and terrified at being arrested for something he knew nothing about and had made a genuine mistake by confusing it with the weekend before.

A full day's cross-examination, taking apart transcripts of John's interrogation, could be summed up with one, simple exchange.

Elfer: 'Having made this appalling mistake, were you trying to deliberately mislead police?'

John: 'No. I asked to check the house-to-house form I'd filled out soon after the murder but they wouldn't bring it to me. If they had done so, I would have realised I'd made a mistake.'

John's house-to-house inquiry form clearly stated he had been working at the Casablanca until 3 a.m. on the morning of the 14th. The police later admitted it would have been fair to show him a copy. Why had they not done so? They could not find it.

Elfer: 'You said you were nowhere near the Casablanca that night. Is that because you were trying to distance yourself from the men who had already been arrested?'

John: 'No, sir.'

Elfer: 'You cannot remember that night because you do not want to remember that night.'

John: 'I want to remember it, sir. I cannot remember it specifically as I go down there every weekend, sir.'

Elfer: 'And the anxiety which is worrying you at the moment is because you are covering things up.'

John: 'The anxiety which is worrying me is that I have not eaten for three days, sir.'

Apart from Stephen Miller's confession, during which once again John's name had been put to him by the police, the only other attempt to corroborate the witness evidence against him came from two other people.

The first, a distant relative, Gary George, worked as a security guard on the docks. He recalled driving to work late on Thursday night, 11 February. The lights at the junction of James Street were red. As he waited, he saw a man, clearly drunk, standing in the middle of the road shouting up to the James Street flats, shouting, 'Open the fucking door, you bitch.' It had only stuck in his mind because it was a 'comical scene', George recalled.

The man was 'half-caste', he told Elfer. When asked about the man's hair, George replied, 'Short, black hair like a wire brush. Not a wire brush . . . what do you call it? A Brillo Pad.'

Further away and totally separate from the shouting man, George said he saw a group of young men, standing talking on the street corner. He recognised one as his second cousin, John Actie, whom he had never actually met but had seen a few times around the docks. He was chatting and laughing with a couple of other 'half-caste' men, all of whom also had 'Brillo Pad hair', the jury was told.

It was a total lie, John insisted.

George had made his statement in late November 1988. Why so late? Well, it did not strike him as important. It happened on an entirely different night to the murder. He had simply recounted it to one or two people he met at work that night, one of whom must have much later mentioned it to the police, who contacted him nine months later.

Patrolling the docks in his security van, the court heard, George would check in on the yacht club from time to time. When asked if police officers drank in the club, he initially declined to comment but when pressed agreed that they did. Had one of the women who worked there, by the name of Violet Perriam, been among those to whom he had relayed the comical scene? Possibly, yes. He had once spoken to both her and Thomas Page, the docks police inspector, he told the court.

'Perriam's a busybody,' George told the court. 'She likes to stick her nose in and likes to be in on the action if anything is going on. I wouldn't tell her anything. She tells the world.'

Violet Perriam, it transpired, had all of a sudden nine months after the murder remembered seeing a group of men around 7 James Street late at night too. The details closely matched Gary George's account, although she claimed to have seen them between 1.30 and 1.45 a.m. on the 14th, matching the time and date of the murder.

The statement she subsequently made on 10 November 1988 was the ignition point of the entire case against the defendants. Among the group of men she saw in the vicinity of James Street were two familiar faces.

I work as a receptionist at the Butetown Health Centre, Docks, Cardiff. I am the secretary of the Cardiff Yacht Club which is situated on Cardiff Docks.

About 8pm on Saturday 13th February 1988 I went to the club to run the bar. I closed the club about 1.30 a.m. and began driving home . . .

I saw four coloured males standing in a semi-circle in the middle of James Street, just yards from the betting office.

They appeared to be arguing and jumping about. I drove slowly around them. I didn't hear anything that was said. This incident made me feel very nervous and I drove straight home. I would put the time sometime between 1.30 a.m. and 1.40 a.m. on Sunday 14th February 1988.

Because I work in the health centre, I am familiar with a lot of people from the docks area. Two of the persons were familiar to me. One was a Somali and another had long scruffy hair.

Why had it taken her nine months to come forward with her account? Fear, Perriam replied.

Six days later, Perriam made an amendment to her statement.

Because I work in the docks area, I have been concerned about my own safety. For this reason, I have not wanted to name persons I did recognise on this date.

> *One of the persons was Rashid Omar. I am almost certain*
> *that one of the men was John Actie. I didn't see his face*
> *but he is a very big person and he stands out because of his*
> *description. He was wearing a black leather jacket which*
> *he always wears . . .*

This is the first time John Actie's name is mentioned by witnesses within the inquiry.

A week later, the four witnesses pulled in for questioning were beginning to describe the accused men's role in a sickening gang murder.

Rashid Omar, a local man of Somali heritage, was among the nine men arrested in December 1988. Curiously, two things emerge from the evidence which coincide with Omar's subsequent release from custody.

In another room in another police station, his name was being drilled into Stephen Miller during his interrogation. Miller was having none of it. He had never heard of the guy. Omar was more widely known by his nickname 'Wibidi'. Try as they might, Stephen was not biting.

Coinciding with that, the jury was told, around this time Perriam was again contacted by detectives and asked to come into the station. Once there, she updated her statement to say that on reflection, she could not now be certain she had seen Omar that night on James Street but that she was surer of John Actie. Omar was released from custody and John was charged.

When asked about the changes, she said the statements contained mistakes, probably down to her. When pressed as to how she could be certain of John Actie given that she stated she did not see his face, she said that she did in fact see the side of his face. Maybe she forgot to mention it or the officer got it wrong. Either way, the statement was incorrect.

Perriam was asked about Gary George's recollection of seeing a group of men near the James Street flat. His recollection had, of course, been of events on 11 February, two days before the murder. Could she have been mistaken and seen men in James Street on the same day? No, it was definitely the Saturday night.

Her attention was drawn to the original typed version of her third statement. The date on it read 11 February 1988, the same night as Mr George's account.

That was a mistake too, she replied; it should have read 11 December.

Stephen Miller had been the first in the witness box. His confession had effectively sealed the case against the men.

While in his prison cell awaiting trial, John had made his way through a box of cassette recordings of Stephen's police interviews, listening to the entire nineteen tapes which had recorded thirteen hours of interrogation over five days.

During the first five interviews, Stephen was adamant: he knew nothing about the murder of his girlfriend. Then, gradually, over the ensuing interrogations, he began to break down and a story started to emerge of the events of Valentine's Day 1988.

By the end of the last cassette tape, John's mind was clear.

When Stephen was finally put in jail with the other four men, he made a point of seeking John out. 'John, man, I'm so sorry,' he said, clearly terrified. Holding out his hand, John said, 'Don't worry about it, Stephen. I've listened to the tapes and I know exactly what they did to you. We don't blame you for anything.' Stephen broke down and, by his own recollection, cried like a baby.

By the time the case came to court, during which his interrogation was played in full to the jury, Stephen Miller had recanted his confession. He insisted he had no idea who had killed Lynette.

Tortured by lack of sleep and the insistence by detectives that they would not stop until he confessed, he admitted he would have said anything just to make it stop. In the end, he agreed with whatever the police said.

'It seemed to me that they were blackmailing me,' Stephen told the court. 'If I didn't tell them, I'd be charged with it . . . They said there could be an "easy way out" for me. They said they would not stop, if I didn't agree with what they were saying I would be in the station forever. I had to agree with the police to make it stop . . . I didn't name my co-defendants. I was given their names by police. The truth is I lied; I wasn't there at all.'

The four detectives who had obtained Stephen's confession denied his accusations, insisting they had only been determined to get at the truth and had known the suspect was holding out on them.

The defence called a distinguished forensic psychologist, Gisli Gudjonsson, a pioneer in the field of coerced or false confessions. He had assessed Stephen and found him to be highly suggestible, and while appearing streetwise, his IQ was in fact equivalent to that of an eleven-year-old child, rendering him extremely ill-equipped to withstand such oppressive and sustained interview techniques.

Stopping short of making a circling screw-loose motion with his index finger at the side of his head, Elfer brayed in disbelief, dismissing him as living in 'cloud cuckoo land'.

In Stephen's 'confession', Tony Paris was cast as the central figure with an 'evil look in his eye', bossing everyone around and yelling at Stephen that if he could not do it, he would show him how to control his woman. He then proceeded to stab Lynette fifteen times, Stephen had told detectives, before ordering everyone else to join in.

Elfer had got his wires badly crossed when it came to the Tiger Bay dynamic, presenting Tony as a feared hoodlum capable of bringing the likes of John Actie to heel. This owing to a claim Tony had made in his interrogation that he had once told John to 'fuck off and wait his turn' when he demanded Tony serve him a drink quickly one night in the Casablanca. John had zero recollection of the incident. Maybe Tony had merely thought it or at a push muttered it under his breath.

After all, Elfer continued unswervingly, Tony was a judo aficionado with belts to prove it. Not exactly, Tony replied. As a teenager, he had enrolled in classes at the local community centre. He had been given a belt for turning up and the only other he had was used to hold his trousers up.

Staff at the Casablanca were called to swear that both Tony and John had been working constantly at the time of the murder, Tony standing out on account of his black check suit and dickie bow tie, and John on account of his size and position directly in front of the entrance. Well, you would say that, they are your friends, Elfer said, before accusing them of lying.

Elfer was demonstrably astonished when another of his accusations was met with genuine bemusement. Didn't these men know one another? Surely, they must have talked to each other about Stephen's missing girlfriend and speculated as to her whereabouts. Why would the men who barely spoke to one another spend time gossiping about an argument between a couple they barely knew?

So, the prosecution thought they had Tony's number: not only a gangland kingpin but a violent pimp to boot. Having temporarily split with his then girlfriend, later to be his wife, he had begun seeing a woman called Helen, who for a short time had worked around the Custom House while in between jobs.

Statements presented by police told how she was terrified of Tony, that he would beat her in 'fits of temper' and force her on to the street. Even after Tony left her and got married, he would hunt her down at her parents' and threaten her if she did not return to the street.

She had been in a local pub a short time after the murder when Tony walked in. They struck up conversation and the subject of Lynette came up.

'Tony turned around and said to me,' her statement read, '"I know who the person is who killed Lynette and you do as well." I asked him who it was. Tony wouldn't tell me but he did say to me I would know him. I asked how I would know him and he said "We've had drinks with them".'

When called to give evidence, she exploded in the witness box. It was all lies. She had never said any of that. She had been in love with Tony and was devastated when he left her. They had merely been chatting in the pub one night, wondering who had killed Lynette when he said something along the lines of, 'We might know the killer, for all we know we might have even sat down and had a drink with them.'

She told the court she had lost her job at a hotel after police constantly turned up there. They had also harassed her family and on one occasion after being ordered to attend the city's Central Police Station, she was locked in a 'room that stank' for five hours. The statements, she said, she signed in order to get the hell out and get them off her back.

Then there was the matter of Tony's cell confession.

◆ ◆ ◆

In 1987, Ian Albert Massey, a career criminal from Partington, Greater Manchester, pleaded not guilty to an armed robbery at a

120

Tesco superstore in Swansea, but was convicted and sentenced to fourteen years.

Serving part of his sentence in Cardiff Prison, Massey was a designated cleaner, a position that afforded him unrestricted movement around A wing, where the five men were held while they awaited trial.

If there was one thing above any other that John had advised a naive Tony it was this: 'Whatever you do, don't show anyone your papers, Tone. You don't know what they're going to do because people in here will say you confessed to them and stuff.'

Tony nodded in agreement but secretly thought, What's he on about?

Massey was a dab hand at calligraphy and agreed a cut rate to inscribe Tony's Christmas card to his mother in exchange for tobacco. The two men would talk regularly and with Massey purporting to be something of a 'legal eagle', Tony began to call on him for advice about his case, making the grave mistake of showing him detailed documentation that was arriving thick and fast from his lawyer.

Not long after that, Massey was transferred to HMP Long Lartin. Unbeknown to Tony, once there Massey had given a statement to South Wales Police. A section of it read:

> *In total I shared the prison wing with Tony Paris and the others for approximately six and a half months. In that period, I had many conversations with Tony Paris during which he admitted to me his involvement in the murder of Lynette White.*
>
> *He admitted stabbing her and the participation in the murder of Ronnie Actie, John Actie, Yusef Abdullahi and Miller. I cannot recall everything that was said in exact*

When giving evidence, Tony pointed to a damning inclusion in Massey's statement. It told of Tony's relief that nothing had been found on his clothes following forensic testing. But those results had not been confirmed until late June, by which time Massey had been moved from Cardiff jail. Tony could not have told him, so, he asked, who did?

Massey, who had been involved in a recent, unrelated super-grass case, had been visited six times by Detective Inspector Graham Mouncher, the officer in charge of the murder investigation, meetings during which no notes were taken.

Midway through the trial, armed police took up position on the roof of the Swansea courthouse, as another convicted armed robber, Cardiff-born Courtney Davies, arrived to give evidence.

Massey, Davies told the trial, had got involved in the other supergrass case, which related to a case in Manchester, against a man who turned out to be innocent. He had done it in the hope that it would help with his appeal.

Massey's deceit in that case, Davies said, had won him prison privileges, but his appeal had failed. So, Massey, bitterly disappointed, had been fishing around for an early parole deal ever since, telling Davies he was prepared to do anything to get out of prison early; he could either grovel or put someone's name in the frame.

Massey denied acting dishonestly, telling the court he reluctantly spoke with police only because Tony had told him someone was going to have a word with Vilday and Psaila to ensure they would not turn up to court. He feared the women were going to be harmed, he said, and he was only persuaded to cooperate when Mouncher said to him, 'It could have been my own wife and daughter.'

When asked if any inducement had been offered to Massey, Mouncher swore on oath that was not the case. No question of early parole. Ian Massey knew he was in effect risking his life by doing the honourable thing and had to be commended for putting himself at risk by helping to bring these men to justice.

To the defence, Massey, who had admitted giving perjured evidence many times in the past, was simply and wickedly feathering his own nest.

Another witness who had stepped up in the interests of justice, the prosecution held, was Ronnie Williams, married to Dullah's estranged partner's sister, called by Elfer to prove Dullah's alibi for the night of the murder was a manufactured one.

Dullah had been working with a number of men that night, carrying out conversion work on the bulkheads of a ship in Barry Docks called the *Coral Sea*. While a few rallied to his defence, a number of others remained out of reach. Dullah's solicitor was in a running battle with the Crown Prosecution Service over their tardy response to requests to disclose details of contact details the contractors in charge of work on the *Coral Sea* had passed to police.

But Ronnie Williams, effectively Dullah's brother-in-law, had also been working on the ship that weekend. He told the court he had returned to Cardiff on the Saturday night and that he and a friend had seen Dullah in the North Star, drink in hand, three hours before the murder took place.

Giving evidence, Dullah said Williams had always hated him and had admitted to working as an informer for Inspector Tommy Page in the past.

Another workmate recalled driving back to Cardiff with three others, Dullah among them, but over the passage of time could not be sure if that had been on the Saturday or Sunday night.

Dullah's estranged partner, Jackie Harris, told the court that he had drunkenly told her during an argument that he was in the room when Lynette White was killed. Knowing him of old, she brushed it off as another of his tall tales. She had mentioned it to her father, with whom Dullah had worked in Barry that weekend. He waved it away as nonsense. 'Ignore him, love,' he told her. 'You know what he's like. He was on the ship the entire time.'

Regardless, the obfuscation around Dullah's alibi had successfully undermined it.

As for Ronnie Actie, uneducated but razor sharp, he refused to play the game. There was no way he was taking the stand to have Elfer sneer over his private life. He had only been seeing Leanne Vilday off and on for a few weeks, but he knew for sure Elfer would make a meal of it.

The only other point against Ronnie was the claims his green Ford Cortina had been seen outside the murder scene. He insisted he had not bought that car until April 1988. Elfer turned himself inside out trying to prove him wrong. Leave him to it, was Ronnie's take.

Monday, 26 February 1990, began the same way the previous twenty-eight Mondays had. In what was now a familiar routine, John Actie arrived back in Swansea from Cardiff Prison, where he insisted on being held over the weekends, and the five men were transported to the cells underneath the courtroom. By now, a private-hire minibus had replaced the cavalcade of security.

Within a few minutes, John knew something was wrong. The barristers were usually down by 9 a.m. Where were they? he asked the prison guards. They shrugged. It was mid-morning when the solemn-faced legal teams finally filed in and asked the men to sit down.

'What's the problem, boss? What's the matter?' John asked, his heart rate quickening. 'My family. Is my mother OK?'

'Your mother's fine, John,' his lawyer assured him. 'But we've got some really bad news. It's the judge. He's dead.'

On the day he was due to begin summing up to the jury, Mr Justice McNeill, a sixty-eight-year-old father-of-four, had been found in the bathroom of the judges' residence, where he had suffered a heart attack.

Led upstairs to be further remanded in custody, the men were told they must now await the date of a new trial. The entire case would be reheard. From start to finish.

During a meeting of legal representatives that day, a question was raised by police regarding whether there were any suspicious circumstances surrounding the judge's death. The inference was clear: until they were convinced otherwise, they could not help themselves and wondered at the possibility that John Actie had had a hand in it.

Chapter Seven

In a cell on the first-floor landing of Cardiff Prison's A wing, a stinger cable, an illegally modified electricity cord, trailed from the ceiling light and into the charging port of John Actie's Sony Watchman pocket TV. The handheld device, the size of a small transistor radio, had been smuggled in by his brother during a visit shortly after his arrest.

It was a lifeline. For a news junkie with three months on his hands until the start of the second trial, a single fix of daily papers was never going to cut it for John.

The death throes of Margaret Thatcher's premiership, the Hillsborough disaster, IRA bombings, the fall of the Berlin Wall, civil war in Yugoslavia, Nelson Mandela's walk to freedom: John's life inside pivoted on the clockwork round of bulletins from breakfast TV to the evening news, the adrenalised orchestral intros administering a fleeting shot of relief from the pounding, mind-numbing monotony of nothingness, day after day after unrelenting day.

Sprawled on his bed, John's gaze was transfixed on the tiny screen.

'*This evening Strangeways was ablaze.*'

Flames jabbed through blown-out windows on the breaking ITN footage as dense clouds of smoke spewed into the sky, obscuring the afternoon sun and raining hot ash on to the streets below, where fleeing prison staff being marshalled to safety crossed paths with an advancing battalion of police in full riot gear.

The report continued:

'*The prisoners who had taken over the jail were now doing their best to destroy it completely.*

'*What had started as a disturbance during morning prayers in the chapel rapidly became a riot involving nearly 1,000 prisoners. They overcame prison officers, stole keys and opened as many cells as they could.*

'*Some smashed their way on to the roof and hurled missiles at the police gathering below. The tactic was containment and prisoners in areas of the jail not affected by the rioting were bussed to other prisons . . .*'

The biggest riot in the history of the UK Prison Service had erupted in Manchester on 1 April 1990.

Anger over squalid and overcrowded conditions and the prison system's misuse of Largactil, a sedative known as 'liquid cosh', had festered for months.

But the foreboding in Strangeways that morning was not isolated. It had whipped through the perimeter's barbed wire coils on the prevailing wind of tempestuous skies far beyond the prison gates.

In 1990, the UK was a nation in turmoil.

Crime soared and Margaret Thatcher's Conservative government nosedived. The Iron Lady's galvanisation of the police and hammering hard line on law and order had been a mis-strike. An embattled criminal justice system struggled to cope with heaving courtrooms and its ageing prisons were stretched to breaking point.

Just a day before, on the last day of March, London had been rocked by one of the most infamous civil uprisings in recent history – the poll tax riot. Fissures of unrest around the country had built to convulsion on the streets of Westminster as factions of two hundred thousand-plus demonstrators came to blows with police and exploded into full-blown rebellion.

History would assign the 'poll tax' – named after a fourteenth-century levy which sparked a bloody peasants' revolt – as Thatcher's biggest political misjudgement. Officially called the community charge, the tax replaced the centuries-old rates system for filling local government coffers.

The new levy would no longer be based on the value of a house but would be a fixed rate on the head of every adult living inside it. It was more lucrative, Thatcher opined, and fairer too. A 'loadsamoney' yuppie banker paying less than a bin man's family? Enough was enough.

At the close of Thatcher's rule and the 1980s, a decade that cleaved a nation, economically, politically and culturally, Britain, red hot with conflict, had laid waste to the post-war societal landscape. From its rubble, a new order, predicated on materialistic individualism, would rise. Love it or loathe it, change was a-coming.

Within hours, news reached John that two coach-loads of evacuated Strangeways inmates were headed to Cardiff Prison to begin the laborious, snail-pace process through the prison reception.

Any hope of improved conditions in South Wales would soon be crushed. Some months later, an inspection of the site – built in 1827 and one of the oldest jails in operation – condemned it as one of Britain's worst. In the 'bang-ups' league table, Cardiff Prison left Strangeways standing. Staff sickness and overcrowding at double capacity saw lockdowns hit twenty-seven hours at a stretch.

Inspectors condemned 'gross' conditions akin to a hell-hole. Inmates issued with a single piece of underwear, unable to shower from one week to the other, shuffled around the landings in rotting socks, dodging trails of rats' droppings. Kitchens bristled with cockroach infestations and bacteria strains swirled around washing-up sinks butting queues for the slopping-out sluices.

Agreed, incarceration was not meant to be a pleasure cruise but, prison reformers countered, if curtailing recidivism was society's mutually beneficial aim, surely basic humanity was a must? Calls for the jail's closure were shouts into the wind.

For John Actie, though, things were slightly different. The 'old boy network' was far from exclusive to elite public schools and Oxbridge universities. John's version of Eton had been a detention centre, and with a 'double first' from borstal, he knew the prison ropes.

His cell door was the first to be opened and every morning he would step through it with a rolled-up towel under his arm. A daily shower was his non-negotiable. That and the bucket latrine; that was strictly a no-go for him and the other two sharing his cell. A bludgeon kick to his door would alert one of the screws – Billy Bang-up, Prince Charles, Biffy, King Eddie, depending who was on duty – of any bathroom requirements.

During the day, he would politely knock on the door of an office inside the centre, a tungsten steel-gated rotunda hub from which prison staff had full visibility of the two galleried wings stretching out like the spokes of a wheel.

'OK if I quickly call my mum, Mr Dicks?'

Mr Dicks was a senior officer and one of the jail's most uncompromising. He lived next door but one to John's mother and, back in the day, would while away a Sunday afternoon with John's father, tinkering away on their Ford Zephyr saloons.

Like Mr Dicks, many of the staff had known John man and boy; his first foray in detention had been at the jail's young offenders' wing in the mid-1970s. No doubt about it, Actie could be troublesome, but he was a known quantity and, perhaps above that, they had been around him long enough to detect flashes of likeability beyond the coal-black eyeballing menace of his trademark stare.

'Go ahead, John,' Mr Dicks would say, nodding at the rotary dial phone on his desk.

Others noting John's privilege would chance their arm, replicating the same diffident approach to the office door.

'Back to your cell,' Dicks would bark before they had a chance to even open their mouths.

Any apparent mollification of 'Big John' was less down to favouritism, more a calculated investment in the day-to-day greasing of the prison wheel. Regardless of its motivation, amid the high drama about to descend on Cardiff Prison, it would pay rich dividends.

What John wanted, within reason, John made sure he got. In the afternoon, he would tap up a contact in the kitchen to sort him out a toasted cheese sandwich for later. He would see them OK for some draw.

An almost endless supply of cannabis, a valuable trading commodity, would filter through the visit hall. Every day without fail, his quotient of three visitors would be met.

Like a surrogate father, John's elder brother Stephen would juggle the demands of family life and running a business to race around collecting containers of home-cooked food from his mother, a selection of chocolate bars, cling-film wraps of weed, Upjohn's (Xanax) and temazepam. John's once sound sleeping routine had been shot ever since his arrest.

A merry-go-round of family and friends from the Bay would be gathered each afternoon around a table in the visit room. At times, cans would be cracked and spirit bottles twisted open out of sight under the table and decanted into prison-issue plastic cups.

John would emerge falling-down drunk, acting out over the confiscation of a Twix during the post-visit pat-down, knowing full well he would be swiftly ushered back to his cell, cling-film wraps safely wedged in his underwear.

There was a sufficient group of the guys inside to form a united front of Tiger Bay. The only reason John agreed to share a cell was because he could do so with friends from the docks.

The safety in numbers would normally have been a comfort for Tony Paris, but it had, by now, become painfully clear that not even the might of Tiger Bay could save him from this particular fight.

Like a babe in the woods, he endured each day on a stomach-churning high alert. During lockdowns, he would stare endlessly out of the window towards his father's flat just beyond the bridge perched high in the Bay's tower blocks, so close he felt he could almost reach out and tap the window, and scan for the fleeting consolation of a blurry shadow of movement or the flickering blue light of the TV at night.

Moving about the landing, Tony would tuck himself behind his cell-mate Ronnie, shielded by Ronnie's phosphorescent forcefield of fury at their predicament.

Ronnie, the oldest of the Actie grandchildren, lacked the physical heft and sheer presence or the love-him-or-loathe-him character of his cousin; running with his own, outside crowd, he may not have been so invested in his black heritage or the diehard all-for-one-and-one-for-all credo of Tiger Bay, but as a wide-eyed Tony would attest, Ronnie's blood ran hot with the intractable do-not-fuck-with-me entitlement and blitzkrieg aggression of the Actie DNA.

Tony rubbed along with Dullah, who, for the majority of the time, drifted in a mind-numbing haze of whatever drugs he had secured during visits, often by means of the studied kiss of a former girlfriend.

Existing, as had long been the case, in the parallel universe of the hospital wing, Stephen Miller attempted to ameliorate an eviscerating mix of guilt and trauma by writing long, anguished letters home.

> Dear Mummy,
>
> I am writing a few lines to let you know that we are back in court next month for the new trial. I just don't know what to say. I feel very depressed. I hate it in here so much. I hope I can hang on a little longer.
>
> I am innocent, Mum, and should not be in prison. As you said before and I am telling you, I have not got it in me to do anything like that. Believe me, please, because if no one believes me, I might as well be dead. I loved Lynette and I just want the truth to come out so she can rest. I think about her very much and sometimes cry in my sleep.
>
> I pray every night for everyone I love, Mum. Please tell the family to pray for me. I need all the prayers I can get.
>
> I feel so hurt. I hope it will all be over soon.
>
> Your Stephen Wayne

At 8.40 a.m. on Sunday, 8 April 1990, after slop-out, as the last of the landings filed down the balcony stairs for breakfast, a fight broke out between a group of prisoners on Cardiff Prison's A wing.

Throughout the week, the latest outrage of the ongoing drama at Strangeways, a siege that would endure for twenty-five days, had dominated the news, as headlines, incorrectly it would turn out, screamed '20 DEAD'.

A carnival-like public horde gathered outside Strangeways; children licked ice creams as adults slugged beers, spreading picnic blankets with snacks, as they revelled in the day-trip spectacle of the rooftop show.

In a phantasmagoria of psychological warfare, police lobbed grenades of potatoes laced with firework bangers over the walls as the deafening judder of low-flying helicopters beamed searchlights on to the swivelling arcs of water cannons tracking dancing, face-painted inmates streaking butt-naked amid a flurry of broken roof tiles raining down like ticker tape.

Deafening music pounded from gigantic speakers to drown out the invective of the rioters. One song, a questionable choice given its upbeat vibe, played on repeat: ELO's 'Mr Blue Sky'.

Weaponised irony was, it seemed, a component part of the armoury of state control.

The unprecedented media glare had helped ratchet up tensions that would blow in a domino-effect across the nation's entire prison system.

The fight that morning during breakfast in Cardiff was accurately detected by sceptical staff as 'pretend'. Seconds after they intervened, the alarms wailed. A protective scrum of prison officers closed around a colleague bleeding heavily from a head wound, and swept into the cover of the centre.

The riot in Cardiff, one of five of the more serious 'copycat' disturbances in jails around the UK, had begun.

All hell broke loose as the ringleaders ran amok, unlocking cell doors one by one with keys wrenched from the belt of the bludgeoned officer.

Scores of panicked wardens charged along the landings, zigzagging and barging through the tackles of rampaging inmates, hurling themselves down flights of stairs in a single leap in a mass, mad-dash withdrawal.

His staff all accounted for, the principal officer – Buttons, John called him, on account of his uniform epaulettes – ordered the double locking of the centre's layers of barred gates.

Toxic fumes and smoke from burning mattresses billowed inside the jail. Doors ripped from their hinges, lockers, flaming papers and clothes, you name it, were hurled over balconies as prisoner animus descended into brawls.

John, arms folded, stood outside his cell near to the centre, where he overheard Buttons negotiate terms with inmates for fire crews to come in to douse the flames. Prisoners, it was agreed, would leave them alone providing their only role was to protect lives.

For three hours, John surveyed the madness. Tony, as usual, stuck close to him and Ronnie, his asthma inhaler whistling at the force of his panicked gulps.

'Fucking hell, what are we going to do?' Tony asked.

'We do nothing,' John replied, laughing. 'Stay here, Tone. No one's going to trouble you.'

Had John been wrongly convicted of murder by that stage, his next move might have been very different. But the fact burned in his mind that the start of the second trial was just five weeks away. The rest of his life was at stake.

As the madness spiralled around him, trouble of a different sort had unravelled east of the Welsh border in Worcestershire. John had arranged for a copy of Ian Massey's statement to police, detailing the confession he claimed Tony Paris had made, to reach a contingent of Cardiff prisoners being held at HMP Long Lartin. It was the same prison Massey had been moved to.

'Ian, what's all this about?' one of them had asked, confronting him with the paperwork.

'Load of rubbish. Load of nonsense,' Massey blustered in reply. 'Police said they'll help me out. Take no notice of it.'

'Did Tony say something like this to you?'

'No.'

After a momentary pause, Massey flew into a rage, clawing at the statement but failing to tear it away.

Snitches tend not to fare too well in jail. Within an hour, he had been spirited away. His life, the second trial would subsequently hear, would become a living hell, confined to solitary confinement ever since for his own protection.

Back in Cardiff, a rioting prisoner walked past John, swearing at and taunting officers, dangling the stolen jail keys beyond Buttons' reach at the centre gates.

'Give me the fucking keys,' John told him. The inmate, taken aback, looked askance at him. 'I said give me the fucking keys.'

Strolling over to the centre, John handed them to Buttons.

The riot was over.

The official report into what happened stated it was well contained and eventually quelled by the prudent actions of prison staff.

In part, that was true. But only in part.

'You have been found guilty of taking part in a horrible and most frightening murder.'

Mr Justice Leonard rose from the bench at the Guildhall, Swansea, for the final time on Friday, 23 November 1990. Any hope that the second trial would be shorter than the five interminable months of the first, had long since dwindled as the slow-motion turn of calendar pages dragged it into legal history as the longest-running trial to date.

In Kafkaesque scenes, the men, as if caught in a time loop, had returned to the unwelcome familiarity of the holding cells in the basement of the court. It was mid-May, four months since the death of the first trial judge, when the players reconvened and the Crown Prosecution Service clapperboard snapped on 'take two'.

The new judge, Sir Hamilton John Leonard, a former army captain who had helped nail the Kray Twins, ran his court with a rigour matching his predecessor, but the accused men intuited a sense of equity and human fallibility they had, unfairly or otherwise, found wanting in McNeill.

As the knock-out rigmarole rounds of jury selection played out, the first of a series of heatwaves that would parch the verdant folds of the surrounding countryside a sickly yellow took hold. Fanning the black cloth of their gowns under the broiling heat of the glass ceiling windows of the court, rivulets of sweat trickled from the scratchy curled edges of the barristers' horsehair wigs.

Over the summer, the mercury swelled to near one hundred degrees Fahrenheit on the thermometer, rendering the complexion of prosecutor David Elfer QC, which flashed at beacon levels in the depths of winter, a disconcerting hue of livid before the judge relented to the sun's fervour and permitted the removal of headdresses.

Imbuing the wearer with status, the judicial wigs simultaneously signal uniformity and anonymity, a personal distancing and emotional detachment from the drama of proceedings at hand. Maybe it was the result of the heat, as Elfer's hostility, at least outside of formal proceedings, appeared to have softened.

'Good morning, Mr Actie,' he would nod theatrically, as he bustled into court at the start of another seemingly endless day. John, momentarily amused, would respond cordially. Elfer was only doing his job, John reasoned, his equanimity never lasting long as he endured another week, another month, of what he considered to be a show trial.

By late September, the cooler air of the autumn equinox did little to assuage the pressure-cooker stress levels which threatened to blow the top off Court Number Two for a second time.

On a midweek evening, Mr Justice Leonard, in his early sixties, had retired to his judge's chambers, the same rooms in which his predecessor had succumbed to a fatal coronary, when he was gripped by chest pains.

Sweating profusely, he gasped sufficient breath to summon help.

'This thing is cursed,' John sighed the following morning as the clerk solemnly announced an adjournment. The judge was undergoing emergency treatment for a heart problem.

Apologising for the inconvenience on his return a week later, the legal cavorting rolled on into November, the marathon trial's seventh month, when, finally, the end was in sight as the closing speeches began.

Laying out no clear motive, and with a dearth of anything remotely resembling cogent evidence, Elfer, in reference to John Actie, cut to the crux of the entire prosecution.

'John Actie's reputation,' Elfer announced to the jury, pausing to let his words resound for dramatic effect.

'He acknowledged before you that he was a well-known character in the docks. He accepted the police suggestion during interrogation by not denying that he was the "big bad man" . . .

'The fact is he had such a reputation. The fact is he held Leanne Vilday's hand when she cut Lynette White. He is the "big bad man".'

Seizing on this, John's barrister, John Charles Rees, a Cardiff boy who had worked on the docks before graduating with a first from Cambridge, where he was awarded a Blue for boxing, weighed in.

'Reputation,' he countered, 'is a dangerous concept.

'It is often based on gossip and hearsay rather than fact. It is often wrong. Once a man has a reputation it sticks forever. "Give a dog a bad name" . . .

'In his final address to you I was appalled when Mr Elfer suggested that you should, in effect, convict him because of his reputation.

'This is a wholly improper way to use reputation. Reputation or character goes only to the question of credibility. It does not go to the question of propensity to commit a crime. It would be unfair, unjust and simply wrong of you to accept the invitation given to you by Mr Elfer to convict John Actie because of "his reputation" whatever that is.'

Highlighting witness evidence attesting to John's 'polite and friendly' character, there had never been so much as a suggestion, he continued, that he carried a knife, beat up women, was involved with prostitution, supplied drugs to Stephen Miller, threatened any prosecution witness, or did anything other than carry on his life as normal after Lynette White's death.

'Two days after the murder he was at the birth of his child and had to look the other way when the child was born,' Rees continued. 'So much for "big bad John".'

As for the prosecution's sinister code-of-silence theory, John, he said, had cooperated fully with house-to-house inquiries, putting forward the name of Lynette's boyfriend, Stephen Miller. Similarly, Ronnie Actie put the police on to Leanne Vilday. So much for the code of silence.

Drawing his argument to a close, he asked two burning questions that would come back to haunt all assembled in the court-house and far beyond it that day.

'Whose palm print was found on the chimney breast? Whose blood is on the wall in the vicinity of the window?'

In a caveat to his summing-up, Judge Leonard, an experienced judge, said this case had been the longest and most complex over which he had presided. Above any instruction he had given the jury during the many hours of his summing-up, he was resolute in one thing in particular: keep evidence against each man in separate compartments.

If, for example, they were convinced Stephen Miller's confession was true, its contents could only be used to decide *his* guilt and could not be applied to any of the other men.

◆　◆　◆

On Monday, 19 November, the jury of eight men and four women retired to consider their verdicts. Shortly before 5 p.m. the following day, the five men were summoned to the dock. Unanimous verdicts had been reached on two of them.

All except Stephen Miller should leave the dock, Tony Paris being ordered to stand by. The patter of rain on the ceiling windows was the only sound to break the bated-breath silence of the heaving courtroom.

'How do you find against the defendant on a charge of murder – guilty or not guilty?'

'Guilty.'

Stephen Miller lowered his head. As he was led out, Tony was ushered in.

Convinced he would be found not guilty after the nonsense of the past seven months, not for the first time Tony's naivety got the better of him.

Guilty.

He froze, gripping the brass railing of the dock.

'I'm haven't done anything. I'm innocent,' he said.

'Yes, alright, Mr Paris,' the judge snapped back.

Sobbing in the public gallery. 'Oh God, no,' a woman cried out. His sister, Rosie. The sound of someone falling. Eyes wide with fear, still clenching the handrail, Tony craned his head back to see what was going on. His brothers stooped, soothing Rosie and they helped her off the floor.

And then there were three.

By Wednesday lunchtime, the judge signalled he would now accept a majority verdict, on which at least ten members of the jury were agreed.

In a repeat of the day before, the three remaining defendants were called into the dock shortly before 5 p.m. Had the jury agreed on any further verdicts? Yes. Ronnie Actie.

In a ghastly charade of 'musical chairs', John and Dullah, relegated to round three, were led back downstairs.

From the cell, John strained to hear. Uproar. His heart pounded as he filtered through the noise to detect the guttural jubilance of his brothers. Not guilty.

'I'm innocent,' Ronnie shouted at the prosecution. 'I told you and you never believed me!'

A tumultuous, amorphous scrum spilled out of the court into the dark, wintry night, Ronnie emerging from the clamour, his face ashen, fighting for breath, wincing at the harsh glare of the awaiting TV crew's lights.

'I have been put in jail for two years for a crime I did not commit, I don't know anything about,' he raged on the verge of nervous collapse.

'I don't know nothing. Why pick on me? And John Actie is innocent. John Actie is innocent! They're all innocent! All of them are innocent!'

Ushered away towards an awaiting car by weeping family and friends, Ronnie broke away, rushing at the cameras trailing behind him.

'God knows, justice has been done today and all those people have committed perjury against me and the other defendants. Perjury!

'The person or persons who killed Lynette White are out on the streets. They're walking the streets. There are innocent men in there. Innocent men!'

In his cell in Swansea jail, John Actie, frozen in a brown study, lay motionless, sleepless, unable even to contemplate undressing.

In the same suit as the day before, an anathema in normal life, he rose the next morning to board the prison bus for the final time. He and Dullah, handcuffed, sat in silence, a far cry from the fury of the early-days-siren-blazing convoys.

Minutes before 2.30 p.m. on 22 November, Dullah climbed the stairs to the dock as John waited at the bottom, straining to hear. When he heard a woman from the public gallery shriek 'no', he realised Dullah had been found guilty.

'I wasn't even in Cardiff,' he said pleadingly, scanning the court. 'You took my life away from me. You took my life away from me. I'm innocent. You took my life away from me.'

'Let him go downstairs,' the judge said. 'Put up Mr John Actie, please.'

Unable to walk unaided, John, his nerves lacerated with fear, ushered by a prison officer, shuffled to the foot of the narrow wooden stairs leading up to the court. If there was one person, besides Charlie, his father, that John would think of on his deathbed, it would be his guard that day, Mr Maitland.

'It's OK, John, I've got you, John,' he whispered, bolstering his arm hold around his back. 'I'm going to help you. It's going to be OK, John. I'm going to phone Taryn and your mum and let them know what's happened. It's going to be OK. Come on, John, it's going to be OK . . .'

The distorted stretch of the wooden staircase, its treads bevelled by the myriad guilty and innocent footsteps before him, yawned like an unscalable mountain as his heart bludgeoned against his ribs. Grinding his leg into action to meet the first step, his foot juddered violently, snapping back like an elastic band.

After what seemed an eternity, his hands gripping the wooden rail, his legs faltering with every step, John's body gyrated with terror as he stood in the dock one final time.

'Would the foreman please stand,' the clerk said. John fixed his gaze on him as if to distract from the agony of the impending verdict on his life. Gordon Jones. Small, calm, grey-haired, anodyne Mr Jones. He would never forget him.

'In respect of the defendant John Arthur Actie, on a charge of murder, has the jury reached a verdict upon which at least ten of you have agreed?'

'Yes, my Lord.'

'Would you please answer guilty or not guilty. How do you find against John Arthur Actie?'

'Not guilty, my Lord.'

Not guilty, not guilty, not guilty, not guilty: the words reverberated in John's head. As he struggled to comprehend them, a muffled roar behind him grew louder. He shouted to the jury that he loved them as police tried in vain to prevent a crowd vaulting the wooden barricade of the court-level public gallery to lift him from the dock.

Reporters raced outside to take up their positions. Above a distant roar, a high-pitched, animalistic howl grew clearer, louder, finally erupting through the entrance doors into the winter sun. John, his face twisted with anguish, his trembling hands held aloft, faltered as he was swept along by a clamouring, roaring crowd.

'Justice! Justice!' he shouted, his voice breaking.

'This is what they do to the Acties,' his brother Stephen yelled. 'This is what they do to us all the time.'

'Tony Paris and Yusef Abdullahi,' John cried, 'they are innocent, innocent! They just wanted to put anyone inside.'

What are your feelings? a reporter asked.

'My feelings? I am bitter, I am broke. I want to go home to my family.'

Blasting their horns in jubilation, the cavalcade from Tiger Bay drove like a bat out of hell out of Swansea to begin the forty-five miles of motorway to Cardiff.

Now retired, former Detective Chief Superintendent John Williams, reacting to the three convictions, told reporters that 'an evil root has been taken out of the Cardiff Docks area' and God forbid the day ever comes when they are returned to society.

In what was to be the final case of his distinguished career, he said he had always been optimistic he would get to the truth and as in every inquiry, things did not always run smoothly, but the path had always led back to the docks' community, he said.

Asked why it had taken the witnesses ten months to come forward, John Williams replied, 'They realised that the police were not going to be moved away from the docks until they came to the truth and I think they came to trust us in certain respects and decided to tell the truth.'

Later that afternoon, the judge sentenced the three convicted men to life terms with a minimum tariff of fifteen years for their part in a 'horrible and most frightening murder'. As Stephen was led away, he called out, 'I haven't done anything wrong, sir. I'm innocent.'

Dullah shook his head and Tony Paris initially resisted before calling out, 'But members of the jury, I haven't done anything. I've never been in the building. I'll be out soon anyway.'

The judge commended the police for an 'obviously very thorough' investigation, but said that due to the number of officers involved it would be wrong to pick out individuals for special praise. To the jury, some of whom were in tears, he said they would be exempt from jury service for life.

Elfer then said the reference in his opening remarks to 'an upside-down world in which people carry knives' had offended some people but, he insisted, his words had been taken out of context and he wanted to make it clear that it was never meant to refer to the 'ordinary, industrious and good citizens of Butetown'.

John Actie in 1983.
(Courtesy Simon Campbell)

John with Taryn eighteen months after his acquittal.
(Courtesy of the authors)

The burned-out remains of the Casablanca nightclub before it was razed.
(© Paul Rose / Western Mail Archive / Mirrorpix)

Lynette White (centre), Stephen Miller in a prison van (left), freedom campaign poster (right), artist's impression of the man seen bleeding outside 7 James Street (bottom right).
(© Richard Swingler / Western Mail Archive / Mirrorpix)

The communal entrance (left door) and the bedroom of Flat One, 7 James Street, directly above the betting shop.
(© Staff / Western Mail Archive / Mirrorpix)

Police search wasteland at the back of James Street, towards the dock front.
(© Staff / Western Mail Archive / Mirrorpix)

Detective Chief Superintendent John Williams.
(© Staff / Western Mail Archive / Mirrorpix)

Robinson John Actie, a seaman from St Lucia known as 'the gentle giant'.
(Courtesy of the Actie family)

Charlie and Maria on their wedding day, with
Ronnie Actie Snr and John's auntie, Marie Actie.
(Courtesy of the Actie family)

Charlie before he fell ill, with Maria, John and sister Donna.
(Courtesy of the Actie family)

Stephen Actie and John with sisters Clare and Natalie.
(Courtesy of the Actie family)

The North Star.
(© Media Wales/Reach plc)

The Custom House pub.
(© DW Collection / Alamy Stock Photo)

Tony Paris in 1982.
(Courtesy Simon Campbell)

John Actie leaving court a free man, embraced by cousin Ronnie Actie, with brother Carl
between them and Stephen standing behind.
(© Staff / Western Mail Archive / Mirrorpix)

Lloydy Paris leads a freedom march with a campaign banner
made from bedsheets by supporter Andy Marshall.
(© Staff / Western Mail Archive / Mirrorpix)

*The Reverend Al Sharpton protected by bodyguards on a protest march
from the docks through the city centre.*
(© Staff / Western Mail Archive / Mirrorpix)

Yusef Abdullahi campaigning against miscarriages of justice after his release.
(© Staff / Western Mail Archive / Mirrorpix)

Malik Abdullahi leading one of many freedom campaigns in Cardiff.
(© Staff / Western Mail Archive / Mirrorpix)

John with daughter Remi outside their home in Bute Street.
(Courtesy of the Actie family)

John at his mother Maria's house in Llanrumney, with his niece and nephew.
(Courtesy of the Actie family)

Yusef Abdullahi and Tony Paris arrive at a welcome home party at The Bosun pub, Loudoun Square.
(© Staff / Western Mail Archive / Mirrorpix)

Yusef Abdullahi and Stephen Miller emerge as free men from the Court of Appeal.
(© PA Images / Alamy Stock Photo)

Jeffrey Gafoor being led into Cardiff Crown Court for sentencing.
(© Andrew James / Western Mail Archive / Mirrorpix)

Ronnie Actie with sister, Michelle.
(Courtesy of the Actie family)

Joseph Abdullahi Harris shortly before his death in 2022.
(Courtesy Tiffany Abdullahi Harris)

Chapter Eight

In late November 1991, a year and a day since his acquittal, life, through the lens of the hovering TV crews and newspaper photographers at least, appeared to be going OK for John Actie.

Sunglasses shielding his eyes from the bright winter sun high in a cloudless sky over the docks, he appeared in cheerful, sociable form, jumping on the spot and flexing a banner held in both hands in a bid to keep warm. Organisers corralled the press away as he limbered up to help marshal a jostling crowd on a protest march through a Saturday-busy Cardiff city centre.

He looked in good spirits. Why wouldn't he? He was home and dry after all. But then many things at a cursory glance, perhaps especially in Tiger Bay, are not always as they seem.

The day before John had watched news reports about the arrival at Heathrow Airport of American civil rights leader the Reverend Al Sharpton.

After his flight from New York cleared customs, Sharpton emerged into the arrivals hall, where he was quickly surrounded. A battery of reporters and TV crews closed in amid a salvo of camera flashes, his expression one of sangfroid as he returned fire on rhetoric camouflaged as questions.

'What would you say to claims that your visit to the UK will incite racial violence?' one reporter asked.

'If anything,' he replied, righteously, 'my visit will incite justice.'

A slew of hostile newspaper headlines branding Sharpton 'odious' and 'dangerous' had fired early-warning shots. Sharpton had made a powerful opponent in the British media.

'Anytime you start to shake the root of a system,' he reasoned, 'then you're going to have a discredit campaign.

'I think this whole psychology of not questioning the police and assuming that a policeman's word is true just because it is the police, is dangerous and borders on totalitarianism.'

A barrage of epithets – impresario of hatred, demagogue, hate monger, racist clown, pudgy exhibitionist, rabble-rouser, publicity seeker – ricocheted off his trademark shell suit, shiny and taut around his twenty-stone heft like a thick, neon-emblazoned nylon skin.

Sharpton's mien, derided by some as 'small-time ghetto hustler', had been thoughtfully curated, a composite of traits borrowed from the potent line-up of masters who had fired his life's mission.

His self-assured, authoritative demeanour in homage to assassinated black empowerment activist Malcolm X was crowned by a conk, chemically straightened hair, styled into a lustrous James Brown-style pompadour, his Zapata moustache a nod to civil rights leader, politician and fellow Baptist minister Jesse Jackson.

A gold medallion depicting Martin Luther King Jr hung around his neck in glinting fealty to King's non-violent, Nobel Peace Prize-winning struggle against the segregation of African Americans, which led to the creation of the Civil Rights Act of 1964 and, four years later, his assassination aged thirty-nine.

As for Sharpton's shell suit, it was likely dual-purpose. Comfort was a priority when it came to street-pounding marches and, of course, it tipped a collective nod to hip hop, rap and the hood. The same street-style two-piece conjured a different vibe in the UK, mocked as scouser style and synonymous with the unravelling, recession-fuelled inner-city dole queues.

Sharpton's flamboyance was turbo-charged by a precocious, God-given ability to make a noise, preaching his first sermon aged four from the pulpit of his neighbourhood Pentecostal church.

The 'fiery black preacher from Brooklyn' with his adopted 'no justice, no peace' rallying cry, had erupted in a blaze of controversy after picking up the cudgels for civil rights during the 1980s.

Sharpton's profile had attracted the attention of activists from Britain's urban black communities. Among them, the newly formed National Black Caucus, who had issued a distress call.

In the arrivals hall, Sharpton had hooked up with awaiting bodyguards who escorted him as he stopped and started to answer more questions from reporters.

'I'm trying to raise the issue of injustice,' he explained. 'You cannot have a healing without an operation. Until we can cut out the cancer of injustice there can be no healing.

'Everybody wants everyone to grab hands and sing "We Shall Overcome" but you've got to first distribute the justice fairly. Until you can give justice to people like the Cardiff Three then you cannot have a serious discussion about healing the wounds when you are constantly inflicting wounds on me.'

With the Acties' acquittals, the Cardiff Five had become the Cardiff Three. The fiery preacher from Brooklyn was bound for Butetown.

The Reverend Sharpton had rolled along Bute Street early the next morning in the back seat of a chauffeur-driven stretch limo. He was primed to lead a protest march from Butetown through the city centre after holding a press conference in one of the oldest surviving dock-side pubs, the Big Windsor Hotel, where final preparations were underway.

In step with the area's inexorable dilapidation, the former grandeur of the Big Windsor's stuccoed cake-layer storeys, carved arch windows and columned portico entrance was now faded and ghostly.

Overhead in the near distance, crane jibs gyred in the skyline to the hammer of pneumatic drills and digger buckets gouging up the old. Banners depicting smiling, happy people hung from fenced building sites, proclaiming, 'Cardiff Bay Development Corporation – Creating Opportunities for the Community'.

Promotional videos of power-dressing executives rushing round the city in a whirr of mobile phones and leather briefcases, glamorous young couples strolling home in black-tie dress wistfully surveying the sunrise up over the bay, shilled 'The Emerging Vision' for Cardiff in corporate London boardrooms, to ensure the private investment millions kept rolling in.

In the Big Windsor, where once the post-war rich and famous had pulled back chairs to savour the gastronomic wizardry of internationally acclaimed chef and restauranteur Abel 'Papa' Magneron, a decorator's pasting table had been set up for Sharpton, behind it a display of home-made campaign posters, in front of it, a bank of eager journalists.

Sharpton, in his chosen shell suit for the day, bright blue with neon-green flashes, strode in, leading Pauline Abdullahi, Dullah's mother, by the hand.

Pauline, a smart, grey-haired, kind-natured woman, who used to be regularly seen riding a pushbike to the shops or to visit elderly Somali seamen to help write letters and fill in various forms, had barely left her house over the past year.

For Tony Paris's father, Arthur, each shop that fell quiet as he entered, each unmet smile, ignored 'good morning', every gossipy nudge and no-smoke-without-fire raised eyebrow, would tug at an open wound.

Fissures had begun to appear in the once adamantine 'all-for-one' defences of Tiger Bay.

'What's going to happen to Tony?' Arthur would ask his daughter, crying. 'The police don't just make things up, Rosie.' Arthur Paris was old-school. Tony's mother, the knowing matriarch, had issued a clear directive to her children: 'Get your brother out of jail.'

Arthur's health had begun to deteriorate. He was both too weak and stressed to take centre stage alongside Sharpton. Rosie, a blistering force behind her brother's freedom campaign, disliked the media spotlight and had opted, as usual, to blend into the crowd.

Mrs Abdullahi, her trembling hands adjusting her 80s-style oversize, turquoise-frame glasses, took her seat beside Sharpton, flanked by Tony Paris's brother Lloydy and her youngest son, Malik.

Lloydy and Malik had grown close during shared journeys in an old blue Ford Fiesta driving west along the motorway to support their brothers during the unrelenting days of the trials at Swansea.

On the day of the final verdicts, Lloydy, a popular, tranquil character and a noted reggae singer, had erupted with uncharacteristic anger at TV crews outside court, swearing and warning reporters to back off. Malik, in contrast, had broken down as he passed the press, beseeching someone, anyone, to see sense.

Within hours of arriving back in Cardiff, both had come to terms with the reality that their lives, just like their brothers', had been changed irrevocably. Something had to be done and the onus was on them.

A handful of contacts from the city beyond the bridge, experienced in the knotty mechanics of both the legal bear pit and public sector, rallied to offer guidance on setting up a publicity campaign.

Malik and Lloydy duly called a public meeting at Butetown's community centre. Around a hundred and fifty attended, a passionate crowd of lawyers, students, campaigning groups and political parties. Many locals showed up. Many others stayed away.

Lloydy, who had joined the merchant navy after school, had since made a living singing and picking up work here and there. Being an enthusiastic supporter of a successful campaign against plans to build a road through Butetown a few years before, and championing community arts projects, was the extent of his experience in civic matters.

Small and wiry, his cute-as-a-button face framed with fronds of dreadlocks, Lloydy had always sidestepped trouble in favour of a peaceful, fun-loving existence.

From a young age, he had excelled at karate. More interested in the spiritual cultivation aspect than combat, he had been sufficiently fortified by the discipline to move about his day-to-day business assuredly in a tough area. It had also taught him to think, instilling the *dojo* wisdom of always moving according to your opponent.

Instinctively, he knew that had to be their approach. Fighting fire with fire had long been denied the community of Tiger Bay, but the strategy of the 'Cardiff Three Campaign' would move precisely in accordance with the system it was taking on: investigative, adversarial and constitutional.

More pragmatic and assertive, Malik, rangy, doe-eyed, with a tousle of curly black hair and a straggly chevron moustache, was also well-liked, less attention-seeking than his eldest brother, Dullah.

Leaving school at sixteen, Malik had worked in a bookmaker's for a time among other off-and-on positions within the limited job market availability of his neighbourhood's CF10 postcode.

He could think on his feet and had discovered a newfound confidence and articulacy as spokesman. The campaign had burgeoned an interest in the dynamics of evidence gathering and advocacy. Cardboard box towers of case files collected from solicitors' offices lined the walls of the campaign's HQ, a back room in Malik's family home.

Each morning after their children were dropped at school, he and Lloydy would open up another box, each one a different rabbit hole of dossiers, statements, depositions, interviews, forensic reports, crime scene photographs, court transcriptions and unused material.

Long days were spent on the road – London, Manchester, Birmingham, Leeds, Sheffield – addressing student unions, political party meetings, workers' unions and church groups. The details of the case were retold on a constant, never-ending loop. The one aspect many appeared to find most shocking was the fact that black people actually lived in Wales.

Then there was the administration, writing and responding to letters, arranging meetings, revising action plans and strategies, travel arrangements, fundraising; the relentless demands consumed their lives.

It was during a campaign committee meeting in the summer of 1991 that the subject of Reverend Al Sharpton was raised by one member, a young freelance campaigning and investigative journalist, Satish Sekar, an uncompromising Londoner of Indian heritage, who in the early days of the freedom fight had jumped on a train to Cardiff, where he sofa-surfed as he helped drive the campaign from one victory to another.

Some members had blanched at the suggestion that they invite Sharpton to Cardiff.

'Why don't you want this?' Lloydy had asked them.

'Oh, we need to be careful,' they said. 'He's divisive and deals with the "black thing" too much.'

'Well, this is a black thing,' Lloydy rounded. 'Are you blind?'

Lloydy was adamant. The campaign, like the history of Tiger Bay, had always been firmly rooted in the unity of black and white. Regardless of anyone's opinion, he knew Sharpton would stir things up and project his brother's wrongful conviction on to a global stage.

As the chairman of the campaign, he was clear: Al Sharpton was coming to the UK and he would speak on behalf of the Cardiff Three Campaign, end of story.

◆　◆　◆

'I come today to support the efforts to free these three men because I have a firm belief in their innocence,' Sharpton announced to the rapt press pack crowded into the Big Windsor.

Holding aloft the original poster circulated by detectives depicting both Lynette and the composite of the man seen bleeding outside the James Street flat, he said that the fact police had stopped pursuing this man after his image had been shown on national television was deeply suspicious.

Referencing the trials held in Swansea, a city with only a relative handful of people of colour, mostly students, he drove home a wider political point.

'I think that it is incumbent upon us to deal with the reality that an all-white jury anywhere in the western world is outdated and archaic,' he said.

'Multi-racial juries must happen, especially in multi-racial communities. And it is this basis of an all-white and people of colour exclusion that leads to these types of unfair verdicts.

'I commend the families of these three people for continuing the fight and not get intimidated into trying to butt-dance and kowtow to get justice but to stand up with freedom fighters to fight for freedom and not ask for favours by denouncing those who would try to help them. We will be campaigning for the Cardiff Three wherever we go around the world.

'I think the incarceration of people unjustly leads to the breakdown of society. Any time in a city like this, that you have this amount of people waiting to march, certainly the leaders of the justice system here ought to look at this again and they ought to deal with the fact that there's no forensic, there's no other evidence to hold these guys, that there's a miscarriage of justice, a mis-selection of a jury and that these young men are being held wrongly.'

Was Sharpton saying that the conviction of these three men was racist? a BBC journalist asked.

Fearing it unpalatable and likely to alienate public support, the racism issue underlying the case had been consistently skirted around. Sharpton had no such qualms.

'I'm saying that an all-white jury is racist anywhere in the western world,' he said. 'People should be judged by their peers, the peers in this town, or in any other place, should not be all white.'

'The jury's colour made a difference?' the journalist persisted.

'I'm saying that it's much easier to put people of colour in jail than put whites in jail. And it is very strange to go from one white man with blood on his hands to three people of colour that have no blood or any forensic evidence that would even suggest they committed this beastly act of murder on this young lady.'

The trial was the longest in British legal history and the police were convinced of the men's guilt. What did he say to that? asked another reporter.

'I say that they didn't go long enough,' Sharpton shot back. 'I don't think length leads to conviction. I think evidence does. Having the longest trial in British history does not mean you came to the right result.

'It's not the first time the police have tried to cover up a lack of investigation and a lack of good police work by hanging it on three young men of colour that happen to be available and hope that society will not come to their rescue.'

Did he think his reputation for controversy was detrimental to this campaign? Sharpton was asked.

'The fact of the matter is that most freedom fights are won by freedom fighters,' he replied. 'All freedom fighters are controversial. The only way the state acts is when there's pressure put on it. And I'm one of the best pressure cookers in the western world!'

The police presence around the march was heavy. Fear had been simmering in the news. This was Tiger Bay after all. The authorities were braced for civil unrest.

Gwilym Jones, a Conservative Cardiff MP and Welsh Office bigwig at the time, vibrated with fury when interviewed the previous day.

'If there is any claim there is something wrong with the verdicts the evidence ought to go to the police and to the courts,' he said, his eyes narrowing under a deeply furrowed brow.

'British justice will resolve this, not crude emotions causing problems on the streets of Cardiff.'

The reporter chimed in, 'But Reverend Al Sharpton was saying the police are actually part of the problem.'

Jones's jaw clenched.

'Well, I suggest comments like that are distinctly unhelpful and will do nothing to achieve any progress.'

Pointedly, the crowd had assembled to begin the march outside 7 James Street, where Malik and Lloydy laid flowers in memory of Lynette.

Led by the megaphone chants of Kermit, a Bay FM DJ and sound system MC, the three-hundred-strong protest began the mile-long walk, which would take them under the bridge, through the heaving shopping thoroughfares and on to the city's civic centre, under a cacophonous, unyielding shrill of whistles.

Still holding Mrs Abdullahi's hand, Sharpton, who had been recently stabbed during a rally in Brooklyn and had received threats to his safety while in the UK, embedded himself at the forefront of the mass, barricaded by bodyguards.

By pure happenstance, Tony and Dullah, in Cardiff jail for weekend visits from their respective prisons of Wormwood Scrubs and Gartree, were alerted by fellow inmates that the march was approaching.

As the chanting grew louder, they could hear their names being repeated, and were both shouting from the barred windows and scanning the gathering for people they recognised.

Reverend Sharpton signalled for the procession to stop. Moving forward to the prison gates surrounded by photographers, he huddled for full dramatic effect with family members.

'The family had a private prayer to ask God to show mercy on a cruel and wicked system that has unfairly incarcerated a member of their family,' he explained.

One reporter fired back, 'What do you say that this presence is inflammatory outside a prison?'

'Well,' Sharpton rounded, 'I think if prayer is inflammatory then you'll have to take that up with Jesus not me!'

As the procession neared the city centre, a uniformed officer with a megaphone bellowed at a man behind the metal cordon lining the route. The man was shouting over at John Actie, goading and gesticulating that he was guilty.

John was ready to fly at him; Kermit, still leading with the bullhorn, signalled for help and a group of friends swiftly surrounded and placated John. The mobilisation of riot squads had been averted, much to the disappointment, there is little doubt, of many who would have relished the resulting mass arrests.

Thereafter, John's exuberance at the front of the march, supported by his ever-attendant brother, Stephen, appeared to go offline.

As the crowd descended on Cardiff Crown Court, and the final speeches began, John sat on the stone steps and slumped forward, staring at his hands.

'I'm happy to be here today to enjoy people of all races and colour to talk about the injustice that has happened to these three brothers. It is clear that it is only because of their social, economic and racial status that they are in jail,' Sharpton said, bringing the march to a rousing close.

The real killer remained at large. Three black men had been penalised because police felt they were available to be penalised, he added. Calling for mass mobilisation, he warned that the same thing was happening all over the UK and all over the western world.

'We must not be intimidated to stop fighting. I don't care what names they call us, how bad they write about us. We're fighting for our very lives. We're fighting for justice. It doesn't matter what they call us, what matters is what we call ourselves.

'And let me say this . . . when I got into Cardiff the media wanted to know whether our presence would incite problems. The problems were incited by police that will not arrest criminals, not by those who come to fight for justice.

'We marched through the streets and the shopping district – not one stone thrown, not one brick hurled, nobody was hurt so how can we be inflammatory when we're being redemptive? We're going to save the British soul from the wicked people at the top.

'So, I salute the families of the Cardiff Three that have had the guts to stand up and you, black and white, that have not gone for the hype but have gone for justice and to stand together across racial and class lines to demand justice.

'Stand up for justice! Stand up for freedom! In the end we will win cos in the end right is stronger than might!'

The crowd cheered in support. John Actie remained seated, motionless, lost in thought.

A letter written by Dullah on behalf of the three imprisoned men was read out by Malik.

'We are now coming up to our fourth year of being held as hostages in Her Majesty's penal dustbins for a crime we didn't and couldn't commit,' Dullah had written.

'I feel a great relief that injustices have finally come to light such as the Birmingham Six, the Guildford Four . . . The Irish have had their day, their trials and their successes. Now is the time for all innocent, black and white, miscarriages of justice to have their days.'

I was kidnapped from my bed by soldiers with grease paint on their faces, dragged from my bed, handcuffed and taken to a police station and tortured. I was then hooded and handcuffed and flown to a foreign country, England, and tortured again . . . And I mean torture; to be held naked, to have Alsatian dogs set upon you, to be taken out naked to country lanes, hooded, handcuffed, the hood taken off and told to open your mouth. And when I shook my head, they hit me in the head with a revolver . . . they stuck a gun in my mouth, pulled the hammer back and pulled the trigger . . .

And then we were taken before a judge and the outcome was already decided . . . innocent Irish people and they wanted to hang us. But I knew, I always knew I was going to get released because I shouldn't have been there. I didn't deserve to be there. I'd done nothing wrong except be Irish.

—An excerpt from Gerry Conlon's speech at a 2013 event held at Trinity College Dublin, in support of whistle-blowers, organised by Afri: Action from Ireland — a non-profit organisation working for peace, justice, human rights and sustainability

Tiger Bay had been viewed by many living outside of it as a suspect community ever since its rows of stone terraces had sprung up around the burgeoning trade of Cardiff's docklands.

Over the course of its lifespan, other groups of people around the UK had been slotted in and out of the same scapegoat category depending on the public mood of the day, shaped by conflicts and politics and, crucially, their portrayal in news media.

Maybe that goes some way to explaining member of the so-called Guildford Four Gerry Conlon's affinity with Butetown and his vociferous support of the Cardiff Three campaign, which, many hold, blazed its trail more brightly within a key circle of influence than the fireworks of Al Sharpton.

Conlon had been sent information about the Cardiff case by members of the campaign committee. After reading it, he immediately agreed to help.

For decades, particularly around the time of the Troubles – a period of sectarian conflict in Northern Ireland beginning in the late 1960s between Protestant Unionists who wanted to remain part of the UK and Catholic Nationalists who wanted to become part of the Republic of Ireland – another immigrant community had emerged across large swathes of mainland UK: the Irish.

In the aftermath of coordinated bombings in England by the Provisional IRA (Irish Republican Army) the mere sound of an Irish accent could be incendiary enough to spark a guilty-by-association street attack on an innocent person. It certainly happened after the atrocity in Guildford.

On a Saturday night in October 1974 in the country town within the southern commuter belt of London, surrounded by the Surrey Hills Area of Outstanding National Beauty, the pubs were packed with off-duty servicemen and women from the nearby Pirbright army barracks.

At 8.30 p.m., the first of two bombs, planted under the table of a dimly lit fireside seating alcove, exploded. The second detonated in a nearby pub thirty minutes later. Five young people, three men and two women, were dead and sixty-five others injured.

Weeks later, twenty-year-old Gerard Conlon from Belfast, in London looking for work at the time of the bombing, was arrested, along with three others, two men and a woman. All four were subsequently charged.

They were found guilty and sentenced to life in prison, the sentencing judge declaring, 'If hanging were still an option you would have been executed.'

Conlon's aunt, Annie Maguire, who had moved to London where she brought up her family, was also arrested, along with other family members, including Conlon's father, Patrick 'Guiseppe'. Known as the Maguire Seven, among them two boys aged fourteen and seventeen, they were jailed for possession of explosives.

In October 1989, Gerry Conlon, having watched his father die in jail, stormed out of the entrance of the Old Bailey, his conviction quashed by the Court of Appeal, in scenes so extraordinarily dramatic they captivated the attention of a nation.

Like an animal released from captivity, he charged on to the street punching the air. Confused and overwhelmed, he ran down the road the wrong way. Weeping family members, who were grasping and kissing him, turned him round and walked back with him to the media pen.

'I've been in prison for fifteen years for something I didn't do, for something I didn't know anything about,' he said, his face contorted with pain. 'I'm a totally innocent man. I watched my father die in a British prison for something he didn't do.

'He was innocent. The Maguires are innocent. Let's hope the Birmingham Six are next to be freed!'

Just weeks before Gerry Conlon arrived in Cardiff, to hold a press conference in support of the Cardiff Three freedom campaign, the Maguire Seven's names were cleared. And a few months before that, another landmark miscarriage of justice had been exposed.

The convictions of six Irishmen known as the Birmingham Six, serving life for pub bombings in the West Midlands, a month after Guildford, had been declared unsafe.

Sticking his head above the parapet, Chris Mullin, a journalist and later an MP, who led a lengthy campaign for the men's release, had endured the inevitable flak. At one stage 'Loony MP backs bomb gang' was splashed across the *Sun*'s front page. Mullin framed it and hung it on the wall of his study.

But there was more to come.

In the days following Conlon's visit to Cardiff, the convictions of the so-called Tottenham Three – jailed for the murder of PC Keith Blakelock during the Broadwater Farm race riot in north London in 1985 – were also quashed.

Something was rotten in the state of Denmark.

The press conference at Butetown Community Centre in November 1991 was, unsurprisingly given Gerry Conlon's profile, well attended by journalists. The *South Wales Echo*, however, Malik had highlighted, had consistently failed to send a reporter to any of the campaign's events.

Sitting towards the back of the hall, one hand holding his head as he gnawed at the fingernails of the other, was John Actie. His partner, Taryn, sat alone on the far side of the room.

'This case is very similar to the Guildford Four, Birmingham Six, Tottenham Three . . . uncorroborated confessions,' said Conlon, resting his chin on his raised, clenched hands, in a softly spoken, understated delivery, in stark contrast to Sharpton's holler.

The unreliability of Stephen Miller's confession was one of the four points on which the campaign rested, that along with a lack of forensic evidence, unreliable courtroom witnesses and new alibi evidence.

'If you get young vulnerable men in police stations, they're being accused of something they know nothing about and you've got policemen who are being pressured from the top, sometimes there's a lot of malpractice,' Conlon continued.

'The police are put under pressure by the press and local communities. And the police's attitude has always been "it's better to get someone than no one".

'There are certain elements in the police who will go to any extreme to clear up a crime. I'm not saying all but I think every police force has its share of them and I don't think South Wales would be any different from Surrey or West Midlands or Manchester.'

Conlon had already been to visit Tony and Stephen at HMP Wormwood Scrubs.

Stephen, he said, was baffled and traumatised. Tony, well, in line with his personality, he was bubbly, strong-hearted and optimistic about an appeal.

John Actie had also visited Tony not long after he began his sentence in the lifers' wing at the Scrubs. Tony always tried to be upbeat, smiling, joking, not wanting to worry his family, knowing the toll already exacted on them. But John, his prison radar finely tuned, saw through it. Tony was terrified.

'Just be yourself, Tone, and you'll be OK,' a Cardiff Prison officer had reassured him as he left his home city for London.

'Are you having a fucking laugh?' Tony shot back. 'I'm small, black and Welsh and going to an English jail!'

By that stage, Tony had told his wife to divorce him and get on with her life. Take control now, he reasoned to himself, rather than risk opening a 'Dear John' letter in a weak moment in jail. That really would send him over the edge.

Every morning as the keys rattled to open his cell door, for a split second he would think, 'Maybe they've found who killed Lynette and I can go home.' But it was never the case. Instead, he would run through a mental checklist: 'Chest out, deep voice, chin up, no eye contact, don't look at no one, Tone.' Like a boxer preparing for the ring, he would psych himself up, not over the top but enough to be left alone.

Necrophiliacs, terrorists, double, triple murderers, 175 of every kind of maniac under the sun. The thought would replay in his mind. One wrong look and you could get your throat cut or be thrown over the balcony. They were already doing life, what did they have to lose?

Tony became friendly with a young inmate from Bridgend. He later found him hanging from the door of his cell.

Thoughts of doing the same had crossed his mind, he later recalled. 'Looking at the bars, laying on my bed in the evening, the moonlight coming through the window, the bars shining on the wall.

'And you're looking at the bars, thinking "if I fucking kill myself now, it's done, no more pain". But then you come back into reality, and start thinking "nah". The police will say "see he couldn't handle the guilt". I ain't doing that, make their lives easy. No, no, no. I'm fighting. I'm coming out. Can't keep me in. I ain't done nothing. They picked on the wrrrroooong family. The Parises would fight 'til doomsday to get me out.'

At regular intervals, a group of campaign supporters mobilised to the gates of Wormwood Scrubs, holding banners and dancing to the rhyming chant of 'Cardiff Three, set them free'. As darkness fell, they would peel off as Tony retired to his cell, waiting for the clank of the lock-up keys. No one could hurt him now. Breathing a sigh of relief, he would mutter under his breath, 'Another fucking day over.'

In the early days, Dullah was demonstrably broken up. Along with two friends, John had driven to see him in Winston Green, Birmingham, the first jail he was sent to after the end of the trials.

Adamant of his status as a hostage, Dullah refused to comply with the prison regime. Regularly thrown into a strip cell, a bare room with only a concrete bedding area and a toilet, he found it difficult to eat, his body as wasted as his 'jack the lad' cockiness.

Breaking down in the visit hall, he had pleaded with John to get him out of there. 'You'll be alright, you'll be out soon,' John reassured him. Expressing sentiment or any emotion outside of anger had never been John's strong point. There had never been much love lost between him and Dullah, but seeing him in that state haunted John.

In time Dullah, buoyed by the campaign efforts and the support of other inmates in similar positions, focussed his attention on prolific letter writing, addressing envelopes to anyone and everyone he thought might help, deliberately fixing the stamp upside down in treasonous defiance.

'The area where we all came from,' he wrote in one, 'had taken the brunt of these racist attacks . . . I have seen now that these things happen to young people from ethnic and working-class backgrounds every week in every city, all around this country.

'I know I am no angel but I am not a monster and it takes a monster to commit a crime like this. I said to my QC the day we were convicted, the person who did this has got to be a psychopath and will strike again.'

A year into his sentence he, like Tony, was granted leave to appeal. Stephen had been refused. On that score, Gerry Conlon's support of the campaign would prove to be pivotal as would become apparent.

A few hours before the press conference, Conlon, knowing only too well the impact of a wrongful accusation, had called by John Actie's home to ask how he was doing.

Yeah, he was doing OK, John shrugged and inwardly squirmed, unable to acknowledge let alone access the trauma flaying his nervous system.

Conlon talked about his own raw, unfolding sensation. The devastating crash after the initial wave of euphoria into a twilight world between imprisonment and freedom, the burden of being recognised in the street, the need to shrink back and hide from the outside world.

'Well, I don't think I'm ever going to get over the experience of spending nearly half my life in prison for something I knew nothing about,' Conlon had told the press conference when asked about the impact of his own experience.

'If you go into prison for fifteen days or fifteen years, you're still scarred mentally by the experience.

'It's unfortunate that they don't allow journalists to go in and see prisons how they really are instead of taking them to see a nice little show piece. That's why I'm getting involved in this case because I know what it's like to lie in a prison cell when you shouldn't be there.

'You can inflict no more cruelty upon a person than send them to prison when they haven't done anything. I don't think that anyone who hasn't suffered the experience of prison can fully understand the anguish and torment you go through.'

When John had arrived back in the Bay a free man, his brother, who had driven him home, screeched his car to a halt on spotting Taryn walking her daughters back home from school. John had asked her to stay away from court that day in case he was convicted. As he had promised, the prison officer who had helped John up the stairs to the dock had telephoned Taryn to pass on the good news.

The couple's house was jammed with friends and family, and a TV crew captured his homecoming for the evening news. During an interview, Taryn's arms wrapped around him protectively, John caught sight of the first in a steady stream of police cars driving up and down Bute Street, slowing down and pointedly stopping outside the house before moving off.

The high he had felt on being found not guilty rapidly transmuted into a suffocating fog. As the party rolled on into the early hours, he had retired upstairs early, panicked by the crowd.

The next morning, Taryn found him sitting on the edge of the bed with his head in his hands, crying. He asked to be left alone. Naively perhaps, she had thought he would just be happy to be back home, that they would simply pick up where they had left off. But that morning she knew instantly something had broken inside him.

The police had ransacked his bedroom and taken his clothes on the morning of his arrest. He rifled through Taryn's wardrobe, picking out an over-size tracksuit, which he struggled to get inside, and took General, his dog, for a walk. Engulfed by a crippling sense of guilt for the three convicted men, and gripped by paranoia about the world around him, he retreated back to the house.

Unable to work, he had gone to sign on at the benefits office. The clerk had asked his name. 'Ah! The famous John Actie,' the clerk announced to the packed room. John cringed.

His heavy addiction to temazepam soon become painfully clear to Taryn. Unable to function or sleep without it, and even then only ever fitfully and for a few hours, he would grow anxious about not having enough and harangue his GP daily for more, telling him his previous prescription had been stolen.

After a few weeks, in the lead-up to Christmas, he and Taryn had walked up to town for an evening out. John winced at the crowds, burrowing his face in his coat as people stared and nudged. He felt as if he had been away for twenty years. Suddenly everything closed around him like a vice.

The festive streetlights swirled around his head as he rasped for breath, shaking as Taryn struggled to steady him. In the throes of a full-blown panic attack, he pleaded with her to take him back home.

The mundanity of supermarket shopping would descend into a nightmare. Spotting an off-duty police officer, John would become frantic, convinced the officer had come to arrest him. Demons beset every minute of his waking and sleeping life. Watching TV in the safety of his living room, a sound, a voice, an image, a scene, would trigger a nerve-shredding emotional meltdown.

The couple had always enjoyed a healthy independence. John was ever the extrovert, out and about, while Taryn was more reserved, happy to spend time alone recharging. Now terrified of being left, he was stiflingly clingy, phoning Taryn incessantly while she was at work, crying and pleading with her to promise she would never leave him.

Once she had reassured him that she would stay around him for the day, he would retreat into silence for hours on end, staring into space as if in a daze. Where once he had been affectionate and loving, he was now unfeeling and cold.

Whenever she broached the subject about him getting help, he would close it down. The stigma around therapy for men at that time, particularly in the macho industrial strongholds of South Wales, was fervent.

Taking care of the night feeds for Remi as a baby and taking his stepdaughter to and from school had always been a pleasure for John. Indulgent as he was towards the girls, it had always been left to Taryn to impose discipline. Now they recoiled from him, frightened by his fly-off-the-handle temper and the dark, pervasive cloud of his mood.

Early on during the first trial, John had become disillusioned and depressed by the bias of the judge. 'They want me gone,' he would repeat to Taryn during prison visits. Maybe he knew all along how prescient his fear would turn out to be. The John Actie everyone close to him had known and loved really did appear to have gone.

As Gerry Conlon's press conference in the community centre drew to a close, the newly installed head of South Wales Police CID, Phil Jones, was preparing a statement to be wired to newsrooms.

'The trial jury had the benefit of hearing all the evidence in court,' he wrote. 'It's easy for one who was never present there to claim injustice.

'In the current climate of celebrated miscarriages of justice there is always a danger of a bandwagon effect. It's always easy for persons with a variety of motives who have little or no knowledge of a particular case to espouse the belief that there's been a miscarriage of justice.'

But Gerry Conlon's last thoughts that day, an unwitting rebuttal to Mr Jones's disparagement, were sobering to say the least.

'It's still very much the situation that the police use the media when they arrest someone,' he said. 'It's the old nod and wink, "we got the right people". And the press goes along with it.'

Chapter Nine

'There are some people who would say privately, perhaps not publicly, that the only injustice of this case was that you and Ronnie were found innocent.'

John Actie appeared unfazed.

It was December 1991, a year since his acquittal and three since his arrest.

The relentless drive for publicity around the case had continued unabated. Now the campaign had manoeuvred itself under a spotlight beam that flashed directly into the heart of the British polity.

A doyen of investigative journalism, Tom Mangold of BBC current affairs programme *Panorama* had rolled into town from London, his production team boldly turning over every stone of the Lynette White murder inquiry. Word had spread around the city. They were clearly on to something.

Campaigners rubbed their hands eagerly, braced for a bandwagon effect.

On this occasion, though, it was a film crew from BBC Wales's own current affairs programme, *Week In Week Out*, that had set up for an interview in the living room of John's home.

'Yeah, well they can think and say and do what they want,' John replied coolly, a picture of thirty-year-old sturdiness, casually resting his head against the back cushion of a grey leather sofa.

But the camera-ready shrug belied his daily fulmination against a shackle of stigma and suspicion. In reality, John was unravelling. Obsessive and intrusive rumination trammelled his mind, his nervous system shredded by the incessant, impending fear of the police and another arrest.

People will talk, John told the TV journalist, appearing unperturbed; he did not lose any sleep over it.

His protestations were untrue. His sleep was shot: erratic and toxic with nightmares. Lying awake in silence was intolerable. He would do anything to bludgeon the void, to hold back the flood of psychic vituperation, images and voices, baying and hissing like static in his mind.

Soon after his release from jail, family members had sat John down to tell him that his mother, Maria, had been diagnosed with breast cancer and was scheduled for a mastectomy. They had not wanted to tell him before the end of the trial. John was convinced stress had been the cause of it. He knew how much she had suffered. No one could tell him any different.

The drone of the television, its blue shadows flickering around his bedroom like a child's night light, was a comfort against the monsters raging in his head. Its volume, turned up loud, was an early morning lifeline amid the loosening grip of temazepam on the floodgates of heaving, engulfing waves of consciousness.

Every night, he would chew a fistful of rugby ball-shaped capsules, the bitter liquid squirting on to his tongue, staining it green. On the day of a new prescription, he would empty the bottle, two weeks' worth, each time wondering to himself, in no way wistfully – he was not suicidal – but certainly fatalistically, if he would wake up the following morning.

Bounced from one GP practice to another, successively removed from the patient register for terrifying surgery waiting rooms with constant meltdown demands for more and more sedatives, he would pivot between a clutch of black-market dealers.

At times his body seemed to revolt against their soporific effect. Instead, his brain would race, flashbacks careering around his mind like out-of-control missiles. And when the dopamine stone of cannabis failed to land, there was always the ephemeral oblivion of crack cocaine.

John continued the interview in defiant form. He was proud, he insisted, he kept his head held high. He could never do that to anyone, let alone a defenceless woman. People thought he had done it and got away with it? Did they think he did not know that? But to focus on that every day, he said, well, that would send him mad.

In reality, he feared he was going mad. And he did think about it every day. All day, every day. He may as well have been physically branded. Going out, simple things like a walk into the city centre, meant running a gauntlet of ignominy, his hyper-vigilant scan zooming in on the side-eye of passers-by, stares, whispers, nudges, points.

That and the unceasing running battle with the police.

But then John did have a reputation, the interviewer reminded him.

That was only down to the police, he retorted. They would have rather he went to jail and the other four men be acquitted. He would walk into town, he said, and officers would swear at him, telling him they were going to get him while squad cars would drive past his house and on seeing him walking out the gate would turn on their blue lights and sirens to taunt him.

What about the women who had given evidence in court? he was asked. They were still around in the area. Did he ever speak to them?

No, John said, he had no time to speak to anyone who had given evidence against him. Besides, he did not blame them. In his mind, they were just puppets being pulled on a string. He blamed the police for terrorising them. One of them, he went on, was a junkie who they had locked in a cell and told her that if she did not side with them, she would not see her baby again.

His feelings about having spent twenty-three months of his life in prison?

John's jaw hardened. Oh, he was bitter. How could he not be? The police had destroyed his life.

Behind the façade, in the daily churn of John's life, there was no escape. Walking through the door of a pub outside the cordon of the docks would be enough to bring the curtain down. Heads snapped in his direction, the chatter and din of drinkers fading to a charged diminuendo.

Routinely, someone drunk enough or brave enough, buttressed by a gang of friends, would fix their stare provocatively. John would ask them what their fucking problem was. 'What you did to that poor girl,' the reply.

And so, another story of that lunatic Actie in another brawl spun around town. The same for Ronnie but in the different areas of the city he hung out in.

Unable to go about his daily life unhindered, finding work with a bad name relegated to crazed murderer was impossible. So, John figured, or rather others around him did, that he may as well capitalise on his one asset: his notoriety.

Someone had bought a dodgy car, had a deal reneged on, or a debt defaulted on – they would seek John out and negotiate a fee for his services of intimidation. Usually, a simple call would suffice. He really did not want to have to come down in person to make his position clear, he would sigh down the line, but if that is what it would take.

Back in John's living room, immaculate and tastefully furnished with muted colours and tall, waxy-leaved plants, the interviewer broached the subject of his innocence. Lynette White's murder had been vicious: could he ever be roused to something like that?

Impossible, John said. Just because his name was John Actie did not mean he could go and murder someone. After all he had only been to jail for stupid crimes when he was younger. It was an horrendous murder and whoever did it was a lunatic who deserved to go to jail for the rest of his life. Plus, it had been proved in court that he was not guilty.

Continually driven to prove his innocence in daily life, John would make a defiant point of calling at bars in the neighbouring area of Splott, known hang-outs of Lynette's father, Terry, and his associates. Why should he crawl under a rock? He had nothing to hide.

At the post office or the local shop, he would look up to find other members of Lynette's family, some of whom still lived in the Bay, glaring at him. Her grandfather George would hold eye contact longer than the others. A war of attrition. John always won. Why should he look away? He was innocent. But beneath it all, the stand-off would wound him.

All of it, he told the documentary crews, the entire case against them, was down to the Bay development and the pressure on the police to get a conviction. It was better to get someone than no one.

That theory was regarded with circumspection by certain camps within the docks. The murder investigation had terrified many and caused bitter divides. Some readily accepted the men's guilt. The police had made it all up? All those witnesses had been forced to lie? Come on now, there had to be some truth to it. Where there is smoke, there is fire.

Besides, many held, John Actie had not been the only one spinning out of control. They rued the demise of the old due order of Tiger Bay, when the older generation of men would have summarily yanked the insubordinate back into line.

Some influential political figures in the community refused to put their weight behind the campaign, feeling resentful over the conduct of a section of the younger male generation in the area over recent years.

While leaders spent their free time tirelessly jumping through the hoops of local government, fighting for their community, for desperately needed investment, better living conditions, job opportunities, what had these men contributed? The area had been fighting for its life and they been running around partying, fighting and dealing drugs.

One or two bitterly remembered how some of those now involved in the campaign had been members of an anti-establishment political faction of young men in the area. Amid bitter power struggles, they had been seen to be throwing their weight around, disrupting public meetings and intimidating well-meaning liaison officers appointed by the Cardiff Bay Development Corporation, to the point they refused to work in the area.

Now they wanted to unite and look at the bigger picture? The due order of Tiger Bay may well have been in its death throes but vestiges of it remained and they were prepared to hold the line.

They would continue to put their energy into the fight for children sleeping against damp walls, families on the breadline, and against the empty promises of well-paid jobs for locals from the Bay developers.

John had involved himself only in some elements of the campaign. Sure, he would attend press conferences, give interviews and make an appearance at events regularly organised to further corral support.

He would join in a run of street-party-style family fundraising events, food stalls, live music, bouncy castles, stoking energy before, once again, a crowd, white and black, young and old, congregated for another march from 7 James Street, the procession walking behind a huge, impressively designed banner, fashioned out of a white bedsheet and two broom handles by a campaign supporter.

But the case sickened him, and whether or not it was unlikely to win him any respect, the thought of sitting through more meetings after the torture of two trials was too much.

As the BBC Wales interview in John's living room drew to a close, he repeated that he had nothing to do with Lynette White's murder. As far as he was concerned, he added, the burning question was around the photofit of the white man seen outside the flat with a bleeding hand.

Where is he? John asked. Why did they not catch him? And whose blood was found in the flat?

◆　◆　◆

The exact same questions burned in Stephen Miller's mind, in everyone's mind for that matter.

Caught up in the web of prison life in Wormwood Scrubs, its petty politics and prison officer conflicts, Stephen's body became more emaciated and his mental health deteriorated.

While Tony and Dullah had been given leave to appeal, Stephen had been refused. New information had emerged around the prosecution of the other two, whereas precious little had been successfully proffered on his behalf.

One afternoon Stephen was unexpectedly led from his cell to attend a legal meeting he knew nothing about.

Moments later, a diminutive, middle-aged woman, her delicate facial features encased by a helmet of thick, bobbed, russet-brown hair, approached, grappling a large bag with one hand and clutching a wad of papers to her chest with the other.

She smiled, her tone soft and placid as she introduced herself. Her name was Gareth Peirce.

Stephen looked at her in bewilderment. Confused not only by her unusual name but by what on earth she, a caring and concerned stranger around the same age as his mother, was doing visiting him in jail.

Many years later, he would remark about that day, 'The most shining beacon came into my life. My goodness gracious me. Oh, what a woman. The most fantastic woman.'

'Stephen, I promise you,' Stephen remembered the woman saying, 'you're going to be out of here within eighteen months.'

'That's impossible,' he replied, shaking his head.

'I'm going to get you out within eighteen months. And furthermore, I have good news. Have you heard of a barrister called Michael Mansfield?'

'No,' Stephen said. 'Is he any good?'

At that point, he recalled, Peirce looked at him. She explained that she knew him well and that she had briefed him on Stephen's case. There was no doubt in her mind, she reiterated, the two of them were going to secure his freedom.

Returning to his cell, Stephen lay down on his mattress and curled into a foetal position. After three and a half years of false starts and shattered hope, he struggled to process why something about this strange woman's unshakable conviction had suddenly renewed it.

But there was far more to it than merely a gut feeling. No one was more adept at navigating a Byzantine and capricious legal system than Gareth Peirce.

On the face of it, after re-examining the facts about Lynette White's murder and applying a bit of logic, an appeal hearing, one would presume, would have been easily achieved.

Quite apart from the more complex matters that were beginning to be unearthed behind the scenes, the campaign had principally pointed to the white man seen bleeding outside the murder flat, and the fact that blood had been found on Lynette White's clothing, smears on the hem of her jeans and socks.

Early DNA profiling proved it did not belong to any of the accused. Blood from an unidentified male, sharing features with that on the clothing, had also flicked on to the wall beneath the window under which Lynette's dying body had been dragged.

On the chimney breast directly above the spot where her throat had been cut was the clear outline of a palm print. Blood spatter patterns around it and, more notably, an absence of any within it, proved it belonged to someone who had leant against the wall during the attack.

Once again, its features eliminated any of the suspects.

Such incontestable facts would have led any layperson, unversed in the law, forensic science or police investigation, to scratch their heads and point to a glaring hole in the entire premise of the police's case.

Ah, but rest assured, the lofty voice of a legal expert would interject, no need to fret. Built into the criminal justice system were firewalls, stages when the alarm would be sounded on a suspect prosecution.

Firstly, the Criminal Prosecution Service, set up as a fair, objective, independent body in 1986, dispensing justice under the Director of Public Prosecutions.

No alarm raised there, however. It had been fully satisfied with the evidence put forward by detectives, readily ticking the box marked 'a realistic prospect of conviction'.

Still, no need to worry unduly.

The next safeguard, at least as things had stood in 1988, was the magistrates' court, where an old-style committal would convene. The bench's role here was to adjudicate witness testimony, heard either in person or via written statements, to assess if there was a prima facie case against the accused. Despite the absence of any cogent evidence, the case was rubber-stamped 'sufficient' and dispatched for trial.

At each of these buffer phases, the men had been convinced common sense would prevail and all charges would be dismissed out of hand. Their last hope at the advanced stage had been the red-robe Crown Court judges. They had the ultimate sanction and could refuse to hear a case on the grounds of unsound evidence. Both trials went ahead without delay.

In theory, checks and balances may well have been in place. In practice, they simply did not work.

At several junctures in the first trial of the Cardiff Five, protests and objections made by the defendants had been waved away by the judge. If they felt they had been treated unjustly, he had repeatedly informed them, 'then there is always the redress of the Court of Appeal'.

Another safeguard of the legal system; another major spoke in the wheel of justice.

Faith in the system had been progressively eroded by a slew of recent unsound convictions spilling out of the Court of Appeal. The sitting Lord Chief Justice at the time, the most senior judge in England and Wales, ruled in some of them that the police had been 'less than honest'.

That could be seen as laughably euphemistic given the scandals raging around policing at the time. 'Plastic bagging', for instance, where suspects were partially suffocated in interrogation rooms in order to extract a 'verbal', an untaped coerced confession, was only the tip of the iceberg of a Wild West methodology that eventually led to West Midlands Serious Crime Squad being disbanded in 1989.

While some wrung their hands and bewailed the breakdown of the pillars of justice, others rubbed theirs with glee, seeing the wider controversy for what it really was: a painful and long overdue evolutionary *breakthrough* in the system.

It had been a long time coming. During the 1970s and 80s, a pitched battle played out over the question of oppression and police brutality and the Court of Appeal's refusal to look at fresh evidence that emerged post-conviction. Regardless of its exculpatory weight, a jury's verdict must be respected, it opined.

Put simply, any lawyer dedicated to the cause of undoing the wrongful convictions of the innocent was faced with the challenge of scaling a labyrinthine range of legal and political mountains.

Take the case of the Guildford Four. Backed by compelling evidence, a group of men had held their hands up, declaring they had in fact planted the pub bombs and that the men in jail were innocent. The response from the Court of Appeal went something along the lines of, 'OK, perhaps you were there, but we think the others are guilty too!'

The only option at this point was another mountaineering expedition to the Home Office and the hope of a belay en route from a robust and influential Member of Parliament.

And even if successful at that point, there were yet further obstacles in the way. The Court of Appeal was unwilling to embrace emerging expert evidence.

World leaders in forensic psychology, along with more embryonic forms such as forensic linguistics – the tell-tale signs of formulaic, stylistic language, police speak, discordant vernacular – were met by those heralded as the most brilliant and revered legal minds in the land with mockery, ranging from reductive derision to schoolboy snickering.

Undeterred, a small rope-team of indefatigable lawyers ventured into glacial terrain determined to overcome a frozen-in-time legal system. Over years, decades, the routes they had pickaxed inch by inch in the investigative quest of miscarriages of justice, were beginning to coalesce into a viable route to the summit.

The team's undoubted leader? Gareth Peirce. Woe betide anyone who underestimated her composed, diffident demeanour, or raised a doubtful eyebrow at her upper-class hallmarks of Cheltenham Ladies College and Oxford University.

The one-time journalist, who worked in the USA in the 1960s with the civil rights movement, had returned to the UK, retrained and joined a radical law firm from which, her peers described, she would 'transform the criminal justice system in this country almost single-handedly'.

The stars had aligned for Stephen Miller and, as time would tell, his co-accused.

The evidence of forensic psychologists, generating empirical evidence of the crucial factors of suggestibility and compliance in the rendering of coerced, uncorroborated confessions, was beginning to break through. Their testimony had proved crucial in the high-profile overturned convictions of the Tottenham Three a few months before.

It was this crucial factor that paved the way for Stephen.

Gareth Peirce was true to her word. A short time after their meeting, a letter was delivered to Stephen's prison cell. In it was the date of his appeal hearing at the Royal Courts of Justice alongside Tony and Dullah.

The well-oiled machinery of the campaign had won through yet again, thanks to Satish Sekar, who had been responsible for sounding the SOS to Peirce.

The Reverend Al Sharpton, Gerry Conlon and now Gareth Peirce: few would disagree that the door-ramming, anorak-wearing Sekar had proven himself to be a priceless asset. But he was not done quite yet.

◆ ◆ ◆

In February 1992, Tom Mangold, a colossus of investigative journalism, a reporter who had cut his teeth on the Profumo scandal – a constitutional crisis triggered by the exposé of the love triangle of a teenage showgirl, Christine Keeler, the Secretary of State for War John Profumo and Soviet spy Eugene Ivanov, at the zenith of the Cold War – positioned himself outside the front door of 7 James Street.

Wrapped up against the cold in a long camel coat, Mangold awaited his cue. Early evening traffic whisked by, the wan glow of streetlamps stretching out in the distance beyond the edge of the camera's opening shot.

'Four years ago, a young prostitute was savagely murdered inside this house. After the longest murder trial in British history three men were sentenced to life imprisonment. But growing controversy surrounds the case fuelled by persistent allegations that the police investigation may have been flawed.

'Tonight, *Panorama* examines disturbing new evidence and asks if this could be the latest in a series of unsafe convictions . . .'

The theme tune that followed was one of the most recognisable of all TV theme tunes, a drum-roll clarion call resounding from television sets from suburban living rooms to the corridors of power and everywhere else in between.

At a time when the media landscape consisted of four national television channels, heavyweight current affairs series – *Panorama*, *Rough Justice*, *World In Action*, *Dispatches* – had elbowed their way on to weekly prime-time slots of commercial and public service networks alike, their might bolstered by a teeming schedule of robust BBC radio documentary.

As radical lawyers pummelled away from the inside, compelling, respected and, crucially, influential reporting on the outside had stepped into the breach of a not-fit-for-purpose system, pulling its weight as the indispensable fourth estate, the ultimate court of appeal.

For Mangold, a grammar school boy on the *Croydon Advertiser*, the upper-crust of the BBC with its fabled first from Oxbridge entry requirement had always seemed beyond reach. For the ambitious likes of him, the beaten track to the bear pits of Fleet Street's ubiquitous Sunday and daily newspapers beckoned.

In the anti-establishment, disruptive grip of the counterculture of the mid-1960s, the climate of opportunity had shifted more equitably as ITN's new-look and red-hot approach to journalism upped the competitive ante.

The entrance of BBC Broadcasting House creaked open for a single intake of Fleet Street thugs, Mangold once recalled, to spice things up and redress the balance. His foot in the door, Mangold's documentary on notorious East End gangsters the Krays blazed the trail for the BBC, at a peak time in its authority and credibility, for boots-on-the-ground investigation and fired his rise to national prominence.

As he rose through the ranks, a clutch of campaigning journalists, broadcast and print, shirked off the knee-jerk censure habitually fired at whistle-blowers, ragging, terrier-like, at alleged injustices and holding authority to nowhere-to-hide account.

Panorama's intercession had been set in motion ten months previously as, once again, the campaign's redoubtable Satish Sekar, dossiers, unremitting self-belief and duffle bag in hand, had beckoned a new programme strand at Channel Four, *The Black Bag*, an investigative series highlighting all too often overlooked issues pertinent to a young black generation.

The undemocratic absence of their voice in the national media conversation was one of many themes to emerge in the aftermath of the race riots of the 1980s. The onus on public-service channels to promote platforms for the under-represented was underlined.

Some saw it as a sop, others a step in the right direction for multiculturalism. For the freedom campaign, however, *The Black Bag* offered the first rigorous examination of the case on mainstream television screens.

'Butetown, the Bridge and the Boys' served its viewers thirty minutes of an all too familiar story – its opening refrain was: 'Some people believed that justice had been done. Others believed the men had been done by justice.'

Interviews with solicitors working on appeals for the men showed that the evidence from twenty-two witness statements, crucial to the defence and the men's alibis, had been, they claimed, deliberately withheld as part of the Crown Prosecution Service's 'dirty tricks campaign'.

The statements, which only came to light from the CPS three months after the convictions, attested that the men never left the Casablanca the entire evening. These accounts, defence solicitors insisted, could well have impacted the verdicts.

Detective Superintendent Ken Davies swore on oath at the trial that police had fulfilled their legal obligation to pass on all material to the CPS before trial.

Added to that, they cited redactions in evidence it had disclosed: Leanne Vilday's enforced hypnosis by detectives; the video shown to the jury cut off before the acclaimed expert conducting it turned to detectives to say emphatically that Leanne knew nothing of the murder, a detective heard agreeing with her.

More emerged regarding the notorious supergrass Ian Massey, a villain with a long criminal record, who had signed a detailed statement claiming Tony had confessed to him in his prison cell.

Not that long before doing so, Massey, desperate for a concession on a fourteen-year sentence for armed robbery, had signed another statement helping to secure a Manchester police officer's seventeen-year jail term for supplying firearms to criminals.

The officer's conviction, described as a 'travesty of justice fuelled by fabricated evidence', was quashed two months before the start of the Cardiff Five's second trial in Swansea. Despite this, Massey's evidence was waved through.

'There's a good chance that this man is not telling the truth,' said Peter Jackson, the former Greater Manchester Police inspector who had led the inquiry into allegations against the vindicated officer.

In his mind, he said, he could not separate the false allegations in that case from the Cardiff one.

'And I find it very difficult to believe the police and the director of public prosecutions have allowed Mr Massey to give evidence as a credible witness.'

For a reporter who had worked internationally – North America, Africa, the Middle East, Vietnam – immersing himself in lengthy, complex investigations, following leads, digging for information, dead ends, clutching at straws, painstakingly peeling back layers to get at the truth, Tom Mangold's experience in Cardiff had shocked him.

His first question: Where was the motive? How can you have a murder without a motive?

Panorama's money-no-object budgets bankrolled high-class investigative journalism. These sorts of things took time and did not come cheap. But this? This was child's play. Dead easy. The theory that five people would come together to kill Lynette White? It was the most blatant miscarriage of justice he had ever come across.

Everything he tested came apart in his hands.

During an extensive inquiry in Cardiff, not one person, Mangold noted, came to him and said, 'I'm telling you, those guys were involved'. If they had, he would have rocked back on his feet and been cautious, examining their evidence. But it never happened.

It was clear to him from the off, before any interviews had been filmed, that the men were innocent.

Fuelled by a conviction that anyone who frames someone for murder, commits murder themselves – not only sentencing an innocent man to a lifetime in prison but, far worse than that, allowing the real murderer to go free – Mangold delved into the barrel of the case. Every apple he pulled from it was rotten. Without exception, every piece of evidence he examined: rotten.

The screams Leanne Vilday and Angela Psaila claimed had alerted them to Lynette's plight? Within two days he proved via the expertise of a specialist sound team and a screaming actress that they were lying. The screams could not be heard in their flat.

He spoke to men who had been working on the *Coral Sea* in Barry Docks with Dullah on the night of the murder, the testimony that had never reached defence teams until long after the trials had ended.

Oh yes, no doubt in their minds, they had seen him aboard the ship at intervals that night, one speaking to him fifteen minutes before the murder took place eight miles away in Cardiff. Another labourer had seen him an hour after the time of the murder.

Did he look like a man who had legged it to Cardiff in the pouring rain, committed a brutal murder and pelted back to Barry in record time? No, not at all. Dullah was as 'cool as you please', making small talk about football over tea in the galley.

Delving into the barrel again, another rotten apple.

Dullah's chief and singular alibi rebuttal witness, Ronnie Williams, was his brother-in-law. He too had been working on the

Coral Sea but went against the testimony of colleagues and friends who had seen Dullah on the ship around the time of Lynette's death.

'Absolutely positive, no doubt in my mind,' he recalled, he had run into Dullah that night, in a pub, the North Star, a stone's throw from the murder scene.

Williams, the defence had asserted, was an informant of one of the inspectors on the investigation. No, no, the inspector had argued from the witness box, Williams would just phone him from time to time, volunteering information about the goings-on around the docks.

But now Williams admitted he had made a mistake.

'I stand by everything I said except for the date,' he told Mangold.

'But I've always said the same thing in court or on one or two occasions that I could be mistaken about the day. I could also be mistaken about the time. It's going to be roughly around that time. But the date is obviously very important. What that date was I can't be 100 per cent sure of but what I can be sure of is that I did speak to Dullah in the club. Could have been a day earlier, could have been a day later. In actual fact it could have been anytime.'

It turned out, just as Dullah had insisted all along, that Ronnie Williams, a brother-in-law who had denied claims by the defence of having a vendetta, was wrong.

Next in the barrel, Dullah's estranged partner, Jackie Harris.

She divulged that in the lead-up to the first trial, several questionable meetings had been arranged by police between her and Leanne Vilday. Two prosecution witnesses meeting in this way went strictly against protocol. The two of them, she told, were left alone on four occasions as if to prevent any doubt in her mind and to coach her testimony in court.

'They would come to me and bring Leanne with them,' Jackie said, breaking down in tears. 'She would go into [detail about] the stabbing and she would tell me where Yusef stood, where this one was stood, where that one was stood.

'Four times I was allowed to meet that woman. And you tell me there is no police malpractice? There is no police malpractice? There was police malpractice from the day they arrested them five guys.'

When she retracted evidence she was due to give in court, she said officers threatened her children would be taken away from her if she did not play ball.

'This can't be allowed to happen again,' she sobbed. 'They put me through torment. Four years later I've got to go to a drug clinic and I'm under a psychiatrist. I'm taking tranquilisers to sleep and keep the nightmares away because they left me with nightmares, scarred me for the rest of my life.

'I would not have given evidence at all had that blood not belonged to him. And I was told over and over and over again that it did belong to him.

'There's a lot of lies that have gone on from the prosecution witnesses. Me, myself, I elaborated a bit because I wanted him to suffer, I really wanted to hurt him. I didn't lie I just exaggerated and elaborated a bit. I really believe had I not given evidence he would not be serving a life sentence today.'

Into the barrel once more and multiple other witnesses told of having a 'really rough time', signing statements they disagreed with only to get away from the harassment of police who had lied to them, insisting that all five men had confessed in detail to the murder.

As for the case against Tony Paris, the thorny subject of Ian Massey emerged again.

'He's a manipulator,' a former inmate on the same prison wing as Tony and Massey told *Panorama*.

In line with other convicts who had testified in court, Massey, he said, wanted his fourteen-year sentence reduced and, in his view, if framing Tony was a means to that end, then so be it.

'Right from day one, he knew what he was doing . . . in short, he is a liar, he'll do anything.'

Did he really think Massey would frame a man for a murder he did not commit? Mangold asked.

'Yeah,' the former inmate replied. 'You've got to see him to know him.'

Perhaps the one thing that stood out in Mangold's mind was the refusal of Angela Psaila and Leanne Vilday to engage with him. He had worked with sex workers on occasion during investigations, notably in the Profumo scandal.

There was a symbiotic relationship between the women and journalists, he held, one based on how much money they could get. The fact that neither Vilday or Psaila so much as inquired what he might be willing to pay strengthened his suspicion that they either had something to hide or had been threatened not to talk, or both.

Mangold had door-stepped Mark Grommek in his new flat, north of Cardiff in the South Wales Valleys.

When questioned, Grommek stuck by his story about letting the men into 7 James Street. When asked why his account had changed so dramatically before the arrests, Grommek shrugged. 'I don't have a reason, I suppose,' he said before shutting his front door.

All this before even getting to the issue of Stephen Miller's confession.

Forensic psychologist Dr Eric Shepherd, a former army intelligence corps interrogation expert who trained police forces across the UK in ethical interviewing techniques, had been drafted on to Stephen's appeal team.

He had hired a gymnasium, where he laid out in sequence Psaila's and Vilday's forty statements and Stephen Miller's interrogation to produce a pictorial dimension of the police techniques used.

He mapped out the oppressive, highly manipulative good cop-bad cop interrogation of Stephen, a man with an IQ of an eleven-year-old and assessed as highly suggestible, interviews that totalled thirteen hours over a five-day period. Dr Shepherd noted that once the bad cops had chastened him, the good guys had come to his rescue, offering a get-out clause, an apparently safe option.

Gaslighting him, the detectives suggest Stephen, a known user of cocaine, could have been 'completely out of his head on something stupid'. It is possible he may not have remembered what happened. Stephen rejects what the detectives propose but, regardless, the seed is sown.

The bridge of a web is spun.

As Stephen's will is sapped by a lack of sleep compounded by unceasing, oppressive interviewing, his once vehement denials begin to wane.

At this point, detectives further strengthen the web by weaving radial threads, suggesting scenarios of what happened, details of other witness accounts, drawing diagrams of the murder scene and filling any gaps in his knowledge.

He was an innocent bystander, they propose; he did nothing wrong. If only he would agree, this would all be over for him. Desperate for the torture to end, he acquiesces, now complicit in further binding the web around himself.

At a point when Stephen will submit to anything to stop the torture of interrogation, this enables him to be led into giving a statement detailing a fictional account.

Any backtracking on his behalf is robustly shut down with threats, detectives at this stage still reassuring him that he did nothing wrong.

At his weakest point, they go in for the kill. They accuse him of stabbing Lynette along with the other men. He is in too deep. His denials are futile. The damage is done.

With a dearth of forensic evidence, Miller's shortcut-to-justice confession, backed by the witness testimony, was enough to charge all five men.

Tony Paris vividly recalled the night *Panorama* aired. A prison officer who used to bully him walked into his cell and said, 'Paris, what are you doing in here?'

For the first time since arriving at Wormwood Scrubs, Tony allowed himself to cry. With his appeal due later in the year, he knew it was only a matter of time before he was freed.

Mangold had ended his investigation with the words of Ronnie Actie, who had given a rare interview.

'I'm not that bad,' Ronnie said. 'I'm not a bad person. Do you understand what I'm saying? Why they want me off the street for the rest of my life? I don't know. I'd love to know why. One day it will come out and everybody will know.'

What none of the documentaries knew at the time was just how much more was beginning to come out.

As well as the twenty-two witness statements, South Wales Police had also failed to disclose another key piece of evidence: details of a prime suspect that had dominated their investigation.

The man, a former client of Lynette White's, a known sex offender, had been described by his own doctor as a psychopath. He shared the same blood groupings as samples found at the murder scene and had been under intense surveillance up until a few weeks before the five men's arrests.

Chapter Ten

Stretched out on the sofa, John Actie turned the volume on the TV down a couple of notches. It was late, gone 11 p.m. on a Wednesday evening in late September 1995.

'Jo-hn . . . ? Jo-hn . . . ?'

The call had followed light knocking on the small window of frosted glass on John's front door.

Any of his friends would have rapped loudly, yanking the door handle and shouting one of his nicknames: 'Yo, Arth!' 'Yo, Luca!' – Arth, a shortening of his middle name, Arthur, and Luca after Luca Brasi, Don Corleone's mobster enforcer in *The Godfather*.

'Jo-hn . . . ? Jo-hn . . . ?' came the voice again.

His dog grumbled. John snapped his fingers to quieten her.

Propping himself up on his elbows, he narrowed his eyes, straining to recognise the voice. It was friendly but forcedly so, an edginess to its cadence.

Knocking . . . calling . . . knocking . . . calling . . . a persistent, rhythmic round. It must have been going on for over a minute by now.

Alarm tightened in John's stomach. Something was off.

Crouching down, he crept through to the kitchen at the front of the house and raised his head slowly in the darkness to peer through the edge of the net curtains. He instantly snapped it back.

It was Terry White, Lynette's father. His eyes were wide and fixed straight ahead, both hands gripping a sawn-off shotgun.

If John had answered the door, he would have been blasted backwards on to the staircase.

The door, he remembered. It was unlocked. All White had to do was try the handle.

Frantic and barely able to breathe, John ran into the back room, his dog following as he opened the patio doors and escaped through the backyard gate, running to a nearby pub.

White had warned him it was coming. It must have been about eighteen months before when John had returned home to find a rambling handwritten note taped to his front door, vowing vengeance for the murder of White's daughter.

John had scanned the letter, crumpled it up and thrown it away. White was probably drunk, he thought. Besides, he had more pressing things on his mind than to worry about empty threats. For the past few years, the burden of stigma had taken its toll on every element of John's life: his relationship, fatherhood, his mental health, his addiction to crack cocaine. And at that particular time an eviscerating grief had compounded the chaos.

But the warning from White had never been an empty threat. Earlier that Wednesday night, White had been in a pub in the nearby area of Splott, where he had asked a fellow drinker for a lift to Bute Street on the back of his motorbike. He was going to shoot Actie, he told him. The man laughed it off and walked away, dismissing the talk as pub bravado.

Undeterred, White had walked, a couple of passers-by doing double takes at the sight of him striding up Bute Street, like a Wild West gunslinger, the barrel protruding from the front of his sheepskin coat.

When the police arrived, White was nowhere to be found. A short time later, reports came in of gunshots being fired in an empty marketplace close by.

The next morning, officers continued to search the area around John's house, and later that day, he was informed that White had been arrested.

In late September 1995, appearing before the city's magistrates, White was remanded in custody. His wife, Carol, Lynette's stepmother, had broken down in the public gallery and had to be helped from the building.

How much more could her family take? The continuing anguish, made even worse over the past three years, had finally pushed her husband over the edge.

Reacting to the ruling, her son, twenty-two-year-old Terrence, Lynette's half-brother, had lost it, pulling a knife on a court security guard and smashing the windows of a police car parked on the street outside.

Regularly for the next ten weeks, the torturous scenario played out. White would appear in the dock, the family hopeful of bail, only for him to be further incarcerated. It was only towards the end of the first week of December that the *South Wales Echo* ran with the story: 'Christmas bail for father of Lynette'.

In the New Year, White was given a suspended jail sentence after pleading guilty to all charges.

'I've been abused and laughed at for the last seven years after these men were freed for my daughter's murder which in my mind they undoubtedly committed,' he said. 'I had had enough and just exploded.'

Even if White had not fallen on his sword and had been sent for trial, John had made it clear he was not prepared to testify against him. White's actions had terrified him and almost certainly had he answered the door that night, another innocent life would have been lost.

There may have been no love lost between the two men, but beyond the bedlam of his own existence, John recognised that White, like him, was broken, a man haunted by the brutal fate of his daughter.

Convinced that White had been provoked into such drastic action, John held responsible those, many of them police officers, who pointed to him, more so than to any of the other four men, insisting that John had got away with murder.

No, the blame, John was adamant, did not lie with Terry White. The blame, no mistake in his mind, could be traced back to the reaction by some to the tumultuous scenes that had played out almost exactly three years before.

In the darkness before sunrise on Monday, 7 December 1992, a minibus pulled out of the docks and headed east along the rain-soaked streets of the city towards the motorway.

Lloydy and Malik had planned to allow plenty of time to clear the M4, navigate the stop-start of London's commuter jams, park up and be calmly waiting in the court lobby for the opening for-malities of the Cardiff Three's appeal.

But as with the best-laid plans, things soon went awry. As the campaign team set off in the vehicle borrowed from the local school, they were running late. The driver was told to put his foot down. Haring across the Severn Bridge into England in near-record time, they were gaining ground. Until the bus, wobbling under the strain, put its own foot down and ground to a halt.

For the past two years, the campaign had achieved the seem-ingly impossible, and now on the verge of victory in one of the biggest legal battlegrounds in Europe, they were stranded on a hard shoulder in the middle of the West Country.

A small group huddled under the open bonnet, poking and prodding at the gasping engine. Ruling out the disaster of a blown head gasket, they concluded that the engine had simply overheated.

After waiting what seemed like an eternity for the engine to cool down, Lloydy cupped his face with his hands in anguished prayer as the keys turned in the ignition. The engine juddered into action and the bus rejoined the motorway, the driver, now even more fired up to make up for lost time, revving and crunching through the gears.

Miraculously, as the school bus from Tiger Bay rolled under the clear skies over Westminster, and the cathedral-like gothic façade of the sprawling Law Courts hove into view, they were running ahead of schedule.

Once inside, as if entering the Emerald City's Palace of Oz, the group felt a mixture of awe and fear as they surveyed the mosaic marble floors, sweeping stone staircases and soaring arches of its grand halls, all bathed in colourful pools of light streaming from stained glass windows.

The morning chill of the court building seemed to intensify their already bristling nerves. The Cardiff crew had found their way to a cafe when a towering fifty-one-year-old man with a crop of silvery-grey hair swept through in black robes and starched white cotton jabot. He introduced himself as Michael Mansfield QC.

As he talked through his strategy with Lloydy and Malik, the rest of the group were transfixed. His manner was effortless, seeming perfectly at home in what to them was such a daunting, hostile place: the heart of the British justice system. Urbane and unfazed, Mansfield was the embodiment of confidence. The wizard at the end of the yellow brick road. For the first time, they allowed themselves to feel a glimmer of hope.

In truth, Mansfield was not that confident. He too had arrived at court that morning in the grip of pre-fight nerves. The legal system was only just emerging from an era when the police were regarded as beyond reproach. This appeal did not hang securely on something as tangible as forensic science, but rather dangled on the hit-or-miss of a subjective interpretation. There was simply no calling it. Trepidatious he may well have been, but, as with any opponent worth their salt, there was no way he was going to show it.

It has been said of Mansfield that had he been an American, his public profile would have given Johnnie Cochran, O.J. Simpson's showbiz lawyer and fierce advocate for victims of police brutality, a run for his money.

But even without the televised high drama of the US courts, Mansfield, handsome, radical, anti-establishment, regularly spotted cutting a dash on his bicycle around the byways of the Old Bailey, had come closer to being a household name than any other barrister in the UK.

But the civil rights crusader, champion of the underdog, ardent voice of the scapegoat, an avowed 'meat is murder' vegetarian, at a time when the sentiment was fringe, was unsurprisingly not without his detractors. To some, he was nothing more than a flouncing agitator, a champagne socialist, a dangerous subversive.

Loathed by right-of-centre newspapers, he was nicknamed 'Moneybags Mansfield' by the *Daily Mail* on account of his high-earning status. The majority of his billable hours, Mansfield would counter, came via legal aid, with levels being set by the Treasury.

His CV read like a *Who's Who* of British miscarriages of justice, the conquests of a stellar career forged by a seemingly prosaic incident he had witnessed as a young schoolboy.

Born into the leafy north London Tory stronghold of Finchley, he was raised by unfailingly polite parents, arch supporters of local

MP Margaret Thatcher, who, like almost all middle-class couples of their time, had placed an unstinting faith in the integrity of the police.

But during a run-of-the-mill outing to the local supermarket that faith was shaken to its core when Mansfield's mother was mortified at being wrongly accused of a parking violation.

Infuriated by the officer's dishonesty, she later defended herself in court Perry Mason-style, calling her disabled husband, a railway worker, as a witness. The officer had overlooked the fact that her husband had been in the passenger seat at the time and was able to give evidence refuting the charge. Mrs Mansfield won hands down, the tale of her plucky fight for justice making headlines in the local newspaper.

'Well, there you are, Michael,' she had told her son. 'Don't automatically believe authority just because it wears a uniform. If they can do this to me, God knows what they're doing to everyone else!'

After being rejected by Oxbridge, Mansfield eventually graduated from Keele University in Staffordshire, and despite being warned it would be difficult without the right connections, he set his sights on the law.

Called to the bar on his third attempt aged twenty-six, at a time of immense judicial support for the police, the path of a young maverick lawyer hell-bent on, in his own words, 'defending the indefensible', was not one for the faint-hearted.

His 'unspeakable' allegations against the police – corruption, brutality, oppressive questioning, fabricated confessions – frequently left judges spitting feathers and summarily ordering a line of cruelly maligned officers to file into court during the case's summing-up.

'Members of the jury,' the judge would opine, 'do you really believe this fine group of men have put their heads together to fabricate evidence and indulge in the kind of malfeasance Mr Mansfield alleges?'

Juries always found that one difficult.

But with an unremitting self-belief that far outweighed any desire to be agreeable or popular, Mansfield, undeterred, continued to shine a light on all things 'difficult'.

The appeal of the Cardiff Three was a case in point.

After Gareth Peirce had contacted him about Stephen Miller's case, she had dispatched a box containing all nineteen cassette tapes, the full word-by-word recordings of his thirteen-hour inter-rogation, each interview lasting approximately forty-five minutes and conducted over a five-day period.

Such recordings were a relatively new feature. Previously the accepted police practice was to compress any number of interviews, conducted in or out of the station, into a selectively edited final statement purporting, more often than not wrongly, to be an accu-rate summary of what had been said. This was known as 'verbals' and at the more extreme end, they had no basis in truth and had been simply fabricated.

This, among many other things, had been criticised by the Royal Commission on Criminal Procedure. In answer to the out-rage levelled at a discredited justice system, in 1978 the government had set up the Commission to undertake a rigorous three-year examination focussing on the balance between police powers and the rights of the individual citizen.

The Commission, on the back of wide-ranging and in-depth research, was asked to examine its findings for any necessary reca-libration of the system. What was found necessitated not so much recalibration as significant overhaul.

As well as the establishment of the Crown Prosecution Service and the Police Complaints Authority, the Commission's find-ings paved the way for a sweeping and game-changing piece of legislation: the Police and Criminal Evidence Act 1984, commonly referred to by the acronym PACE.

PACE set out an A–Z of police powers along with a unified code of conduct for forces across England and Wales, a safeguard against any further embarrassing miscarriages of justice.

And within it, technology had an important role to play.

To ensure transparency from behind the closed doors of police stations and to act as a deterrent against any misconduct by officers, PACE mandated that all interviews with suspects be tape recorded and, importantly, done so in the presence of the solicitor representing them.

This signalled a big change and in line with the vagaries of human nature, the shift was met with fierce resistance. Nevertheless, it had been slowly and, in many cases, reluctantly adopted. Progress nonetheless. But, yet again, a problem emerged.

Hours of neatly labelled tape recordings might well be available, but who had the time to sit and listen to them? Time was money, and even if a jobbing solicitor had found the resources necessary to set aside long days to delve into them, it did not stop there. Any red flags would require further scrutiny by an expert, a forensic psychologist, which, of course, meant even more time and more money.

On the occasions the tapes were admitted as evidence during trials, often only damning, inculpatory sections were played to the jury, who were never made aware of the full, exculpatory context of the interviews.

That was not the case for Stephen Miller. The full unabridged versions were played in open court during both trials. No one but his defence took exception to their tenor.

Mansfield had always insisted on examining evidence for himself. Taking the box of tapes into a small, back bedroom of his terraced home in south London, he removed the first cassette from its plastic case, slipped it into the machine and pressed play.

Alongside the tapes, he had access to fine-grain analyses from two world-leading, pioneering forensic psychologists.

The first, Dr Gisli Gudjonsson, had been contacted by Stephen Miller's defence team soon after his arrest and Gudjonsson had visited him in jail to conduct psychological assessments.

In comparison with the general public, Stephen was found to be highly suggestible and highly acquiescent. He also scored significantly for neuroticism, worry and anxiety, and social desirability, an eagerness to please. In addition, he had a poor ability to communicate and low self-confidence. His IQ, at 75, showed a significant impairment, aligning with him being educated at a special school.

PACE made provision for special protection when interviewing vulnerable people, advocating an 'appropriate adult' be present in addition to a lawyer. Stephen had not been assessed and as such was flying solo.

Gudjonsson's evidence that Stephen's confession had been coerced was, of course, ruled as inadmissible by the judge in the first trial. Even when admitted in the second, the prosecution bullied him, marginalising him professionally and personally.

The derision had horrified Gudjonsson, who, during other trials, had contended with the implication that he, a foreigner, was out to destroy the British criminal justice system. In another, his scientific assessments were, one judge witheringly remarked, like a party game.

But his scientific quest had been sparked by real boots-on-the-ground experience as a detective with the Reykjavik police in his native Iceland, during which time one particular investigation changed the course of his life.

A woman alleged that a man she had met in a bar and who had visited her flat for a drink, had stolen her purse. After questioning and being accused by Gudjonsson, the suspect finally admitted he must have taken it but really had no memory of doing so. Not long after he was charged, the woman apologised. She had found her purse. It had been in her apartment all along.

The ease with which the false confession had been elicited appalled Gudjonsson. He abandoned his career with the police, a decision that led him to King's College London's Institute of Psychiatry, Psychology and Neuroscience, where he and a colleague developed the concept of memory distrust syndrome.

A feature in many high-profile miscarriages of justice, the syndrome shows how an individual develops a profound distrust of their own memory and believes instead what the police are presenting, adopting it into their mind in some cases for many years to come.

But for Gudjonsson, gaining a run-of-the-mill coerced confession did not require a master manipulator. If you can identify vulnerabilities and apply certain psychological tactics or triggers, he insists most people will eventually fold under the pressure and admit to something they have not done, even a serious crime.

The second expert was Dr Eric Shepherd. A former Royal Marine and Intelligence Corps officer, he specialised in interrogation and ethical interviewing predicated on a discipline of checkable facts.

For him, the premise was again simple: human beings respond to fear, and faced with threat to their integrity, psychological, physical or sexual, they will confess to almost anything to stop it happening.

Shepherd regarded Stephen Miller's case as iconic, symptomatic of a mindset of expediency, a shortcut to justice that had greased the wheels of criminal prosecution for decades but that had more recently threatened to derail it. How to solve a crime in four easy steps: come up with a hunch, create the narrative, get a confession and move on.

Shepherd had seen it all before. Pressure builds on a high-profile murder investigation and a hazy case theory based on an emotional and spurious suspicion, often fuelled by a cognitive bias, begins to take shape. Tunnel-visioned officers lock down on it, convinced of a suspect's guilt.

Their belief gathers momentum until it hurtles out of control, hell-bent on a self-fulfilling prophesy. The detectives operate mindlessly, blind to reason or objectivity and quite literally lose the plot.

A suspect is arrested and they go at it hammer and tongs to build, bend and shape a guilty narrative around the suspect. If something does not fit, such as a lack of forensic evidence? Ignore it. A confession will contaminate that inconvenient truth along with any other.

Stephen's case followed a well-worn path, but what made it stand out was the fact that the entire process had been recorded verbatim on tape. And this interrogation was by no means the worst Shepherd had heard.

So what exactly was the detectives' case theory? Stephen, furious at Lynette's disappearance and his loss of income, was out of his head on drugs and could not remember murdering her.

Mansfield listened to the first two tapes, conducted without the presence of a solicitor, and learned that police ascertained two basic facts to lay the foundations of their case: Stephen was taking money from Lynette and he took drugs.

Five interviews on, the age-old manipulation technique of good cop, bad cop was playing out in full force.

A group of four detectives was split into two factions. The bad guys go hard on him and ratchet up the hostility; they are unreasonable, intimidating, bullying, aggressive, shouting, accusing, hectoring him for the truth, their truth, the truth that he is guilty.

The threats begin as he is told he is stuck, nowhere to run, no escape until he gives them what they want. Other people have told them he was there. Why would they make it up?

Stephen insists he was not there.

They lie to him. His alibi has been blown away. There are all these people who have seen him at the murder scene. Everything that they have put to him is the truth. The facts will not change. There is nothing he can do.

He was not there.

Listen Stephen, they reassure him disingenuously, we know you did not kill her, we only want to eliminate you. You did not participate in it; if only you would just say you were there in the room when the others attacked her.

The names are rammed home again: John Actie, Ronnie Actie. Cannot blame you for being scared of those two, Stephen. Tony Paris, the little shit, you do not like him much, do you, Stephen? Dullah. Violent to women. He hated Lynette. These Cardiff boys are going to turn on you and make a laughing stock out of a big London man. You happy to sit by and serve a life sentence to protect the likes of them?

He was not there.

If they were in his shoes, they would be petrified. He is looking at a life sentence. His fate is in his own hands. He has the power to put an end to all this now. He can save himself if only he will comply with the truth.

He was not there.

Lynette's death, they remind him relentlessly, was ferocious and malicious, he saw her in that room with her damn head hanging off, her arms cut, the state she was in, mutilated, hacked to death. The poor girl must be allowed to rest in peace, they bellow.

Stephen breaks down and rages with anger. Do they think he does not want the same? Do they think he is not haunted by how she died? That he has not been able to sleep at night for thinking about it? That he went with his mother to the family doctor to try to get some help?

HE WAS NOT THERE!

They taunt him, wind him up, rubbish him, psychologically erode his sense of integrity, his self-belief. The woman he was supposed to love? They get in his face and scream that he did not care a tuppenny for Lynette. She was nothing but a damn workhorse for him.

The guilt and shame had plagued him but he did love her. He breaks down crying. The thought of her alone, fighting for her life tormented him.

They can lock him up for fifty billion years but he was not there.

More threats. They have warned him, they are not going to stop. They will keep going until they 'got it right', until he submits to their version of the truth.

Stephen feels like he is drowning, like he cannot breathe, as if he is going mad. Make it stop! Please, someone help me.

The more Mansfield listened, the more he felt the confines of his own room close around him. Feeling the full force of Stephen's ordeal, he waited for his solicitor to intervene, growing more incensed when he did not.

The hectoring continues. Stephen is so tired and pleads for some water, for a rest. He cries out and sobs. There is no respite. The siren of cortisol rampages through his bloodstream, his heart rate hammering in alarm. Danger engulfs his brain. Fight back? Run away? Make a choice, it screeches, we have to get out of here! But the response is blocked; he can do neither.

HE WAS NOT THERE! HE WAS NOT THERE! HE WAS NOT THERE!

Then, the good cops come to his rescue.

Calling him by his first name, the officers speak softly. No matter how much you cry, no matter how you feel, and you must be in turmoil right now, the facts have not changed. You cannot have a snort or a spliff, you cannot do anything, you are knackered, Stephen. We have seen the anguish you have gone through. What can we do? You have a little cry, got yourself in a right old knot. It is you against five, six, seven, God knows how many we are interviewing right now. All we want to do is help.

Do not let the other two back, Stephen pleads. The good cops reassure him that as long as they make progress, they will protect him.

It was at this point, Gudjonsson's and Shepherd's analyses outline, that something crucial happens.

As if handing him a lifeline, a possible way out, the good cops gently suggest maybe he was stoned out of his head on drugs that night and he could not remember.

No, Stephen says, he had only had a bit of coke, a bit of weed and hardly anything to drink. He was not there.

Could it have been the case, though? You might well have been blocked up. It was the weekend; you might have taken a bit too much or something like that? Finally, they reveal a chink in his armour.

It is a possibility, he says, but he was not there.

The bad cops return, haranguing, browbeating, taunting, barbing, ramming home doubt into his frantic mind. Now he is saying it is a possibility he was there!

He was not there.

But it is a possibility! They goad, mock and reactively abuse him. Look at you, getting all het up! You were there. People saw you there. Come on, we want the truth. You hold the key! We are not going to stop until we have the truth!

He was not there.

Mansfield has been keeping a running tally of Stephen's denials. It is now in the hundreds. Not that the number would have made the slightest difference at the time.

In the 1980s, Shepherd knew only too well, an insidious belief had gained great currency that the more you deny something, the more it proves your guilt. Like a witch trial, damned if you do, damned if you do not.

To add to his ordeal, Stephen, shackled and barefoot in the December cold, is bussed to the magistrates' court for an application to extend his detention.

Alone in his cell, he cannot sleep, stress and fear lurch in his stomach. They wanted answers he could not give them. He can barely eat, a cup of tea, then the door clanks open and it starts all over again.

With each day, with each fightback, his resources are ebbing away. His body ramps up its defence, surging stronger hormones, corticosteroids, into his bloodstream, his mood lurching from positivity to crashing depression.

He is broken. His head feels like cotton wool; he cannot think straight.

We feel for you, Stephen, this is not easy, we can see that, the good cops say. Do not interrupt, let me show you what happened all the way through. It is the weekend, you might have been on a buzz that night, maybe taken a bit too much. You don't know, do you? You could have been somewhere that night and not remembered, seen some horrendous things. Your mind has blocked them out. It has happened before, to other people.

I could have been there but I know I was not, I know I was not, I am certain I was not there.

You are in the Casablanca looking for Lynette. The guys are laughing at you. Suddenly someone says they know where she is, you all go over. You teach her a lesson, a few slaps and it goes wrong, it all goes terribly wrong . . . No wonder you've got a hazy recollection of that night, I would not have known what planet I was on! You were off your box. Do you think that's what happened, Stephen?

He does not know, it . . . it could have happened like that.

The anger has drained, Gudjonsson noted, Stephen appears more comfortable, he breaks down but he has come to accept that what the police are saying actually happened. Now in a state of despair, he concedes to a version of events that are slowly but firmly drip-fed to him.

As the rest of the tapes play out, more doubt is sown into Stephen's mind. Stay with us, Stephen. We are finally getting somewhere, the detectives say. We have almost corroborated Vilday's account here. This could be the most important two minutes of your life. We have got to get these guys who murdered your girlfriend in this picture somehow. Here, let me draw you a diagram. How well do you read, Stephen? Here, let me read Leanne Vilday's statement to you.

It seems the detectives were aware to some extent by then, Gudjonsson points out, of Stephen's intellectual limitations. How well do you read? was not a question likely to be asked of a twenty-two-year-old of average intelligence.

In each interview, Gudjonsson also notes, a powerful pressure comes with the constant reminder that the interviews will continue until the police get the information they want.

On the final day, Stephen fleetingly regains some strength. It is all lies, none of this happened, it's all bullshit, he says. What? The good cops become threatening. He falls back into line. They are so close to the finish line, Stephen, just a little longer and all this will be over.

Naively, Gudjonsson notes, Stephen believes he is not being viewed as a potential suspect, that he is being treated as a useful prosecution witness. But then . . .

As for his role in all of this, the police ask, he just stood back and let it happen? He was out of his head. How did he know he did not stab her too? Even if you cannot say either way, you were so blocked up you did not know what you were doing.

Stephen's passive solicitor, by his side since interview three, finally intervenes. He is fobbed off by the detectives, who refused to interrupt the interview.

On tape nineteen, the last interview, Stephen is blathering and says he just stabbed her, not stabbed, he did not mean to say he stabbed her, just thumped her in the face.

Sorry, Stephen, but you just said you stabbed her. And just so we are clear, you were stoned but you knew exactly what you were doing, right? You knew exactly what was going on, right?

Tormented to the point he can barely speak, Stephen's harrowed words, like those of an agonised child, render into howls as he sobs and gasps for breath, his mind and body convulsed by the heaving, thrashing waves of despair.

The interrogation is over but the nightmare has only just begun. At no point will twenty-two-year-old Stephen Miller ever recover from this moment.

Mansfield looked at his tally, the number of times Stephen had told the police he was not there. It totalled 303.

My God, Mansfield thought to himself, in words reminiscent of his mother's warning to him over forty years before. If they're doing this on tape, God knows what they are doing off it.

◆ ◆ ◆

Four years to the day since the arrest of Stephen Miller, Lord Chief Justice Taylor took his seat at the bench of the Court of Appeal, flanked by his two accompanying judges.

Dressed in a suit, Tony Paris darted his gaze over the rammed public gallery before he leant back to survey the vast courtroom. Never before had he seen anything like this in his life. Carved panelling, burnished oak benches, red velvet swags, shelves teeming with gilded leather books, the backdrop for a cast of bewigged players shuffling their scripts in readiness for curtain-up. Like something out of Shakespeare, Tony thought to himself.

Dullah, tugging at the constraints of his shirt and tie, squirmed and jittered with contempt. For him, it was another grotesque masquerade but, at least, now, finally, the mask would be ripped from the true villains of the piece. Or so he believed.

Stephen, in jeans and a green blazer, was more subdued, scarcely glancing at the gallery, fearing its collective, burning glare. This was all his fault. If it had not been for him, they would never have been dragged into this snake pit in the first place. Sitting between Tony and Dullah in the appellants' dock close to the bench, he looked up and as he did so, caught Taylor's eye.

For a few seconds, the two men stared at one another, the prelude to a reckoning that would impact far beyond the individual burdens of their wildly divergent worlds.

For Stephen, this was the man in whose hands his fate lay. As for Taylor, one can only imagine the thoughts that crossed his mind.

Newly appointed at the helm of the judiciary of England and Wales, Taylor's selection had followed 102 Members of Parliament demanding his out-of-touch predecessor be sacked.

In an attempt to ameliorate the odium of a 'disgraceful and discredited' justice system, the opprobrium inflamed by economic meltdown, soaring crime rates and rising unemployment, Taylor had been heralded as the great redeemer.

The provincial lad whose Geordie grit assured a common touch had risen to prominence over his public inquiry into the Hillsborough disaster in which ninety-six football fans were killed in 1989. His final report laid much of the blame on a failure of police control.

Starting his tenure as he meant to go on, Taylor broke with cloistered tradition and took the unprecedented step of calling a press conference, during which he promised a sea change.

'Of course, the public are anxious,' he had said. 'Indeed, the judiciary are anxious about the cases that have gone wrong. We've all got a job to do to restore faith in the system.'

Unpropitiously, the reassurance coincided with headlines quick to remind him of his own hand, no matter how unwitting, in that eroded faith.

In May 1992, eighteen years after her arrest as a twenty-five-year-old suffering from mental illness, Judith Ward was acquitted of IRA bombings when the Court of Appeal heard that parts of her confession had been fabricated and that government forensic scientists had withheld evidence from her defence team. Taylor, albeit unaware of this, had helped prosecute her.

The *Daily Mirror* hailed her freedom as the 'latest in a series of cases to rock the justice system'.

'Dodgy forensic tests,' it fumed, 'concocted evidence and forced statements have resulted in 38 people having convictions quashed since the Guildford Four were released in October 1989.'

That rising total included another notorious and tragic miscarriage of justice, a case in which Taylor had been the chief prosecutor.

In 1975, the remains of eleven-year-old Lesley Anderson, who had been stabbed and sexually assaulted, were found on moorland in Yorkshire. Stefan Kiszko, a twenty-three-year-old with a learning disability, was picked up by police in the home he shared with his widowed mother.

Kiszko later claimed that when he arrived at the police station a confession had already been written out for him. He signed it, fearing he was about to be beaten.

Sentencing him to life, the judge asked that the police be specially commended for 'their great skill, dedication and duty'.

Sixteen years later, in February 1992 – the day before Taylor's appointment as Lord Chief Justice was announced – it was accepted that forensic evidence proving Kiszko's innocence had been not been disclosed by the same commended officers to either the prosecution or defence at his trial.

Kiszko's mother, who had devoted her life to campaigning for the release of her son, who was transferred to a prison psychiatric hospital after a series of attacks by inmates, was bereft when he died shortly after his release.

Minutes before Taylor took his seat to begin the Cardiff Three appeal proceedings, Tony, Dullah and Stephen had nudged one another on spotting the familiar if not welcome face of David Elfer QC. The prosecutor from the Swansea trials had beetled into court, his arms laden with files and his face like thunder.

He was alone, Tony had noted – not a single police detective in sight. Maybe, he thought to himself, they knew which way the wind was blowing.

Any loathing they might have once felt for Elfer had long since dissipated into an acceptance that he had merely been cast in a leading role of a macabre pantomime of justice.

Dullah's legal team's dossier revealed a raft of exculpatory material not disclosed to the defence during the trials, including accounts crucial to his alibi. A clutch of signed affidavits told how witnesses had been terrified by threats into giving unsound evidence, while others had been deliberately misled into signing key statements.

All that before the intrigue of a chief suspect who had been under surveillance right up until the five men's arrests, details of whom had been edited out of an overarching statement by the second-in-command of the investigation and not mentioned in sworn testimony.

This evidence from the defence, which should have been disclosed in advance of proceedings, had only been handed to Elfer that morning.

Taylor demanded an explanation.

Following hand-wringing apologies to his lordship, Dullah's counsel, Roger Backhouse QC, expounded with ill-disguised relish that its short notice was on account of witness intimidation compounded by the wholesale corruption swirling around his client's conviction by the investigating police and the Crown Prosecution Service.

Elfer, furious, requested an immediate twenty-eight-day adjournment. Taylor told him he had until after lunch.

With the confession of Stephen Miller central to the three men's convictions, it made sense that Taylor directed Stephen's barrister, Michael Mansfield, to be the first to take to the stage.

Beyond Mansfield's eloquence, the core of his case was as stark as it was, to many, deeply uncomfortable. PACE, hailed as a ring of steel around an embattled system, simply did not work.

If the investigation into the murder of Lynette White had, so far, done nothing else, it had brought to light every problem that had beset British justice.

PACE bound judges as a matter of law to exclude any confession evidence elicited by oppression. On this basis Stephen Miller's defence had wanted his 'confession' ruled as inadmissible as evidence in both the original trials. Special hearings had been convened in the absence of the jury, known as a voir dire, or a 'trial within a trial' during which the judges examined its admissibility. In each case, defence claims that his interrogation amounted to a verbal beating over the head, were rejected and his confession was ruled admissible.

PACE mandated tape recording to safeguard against oppressive practices. It seemed that far from changing an entrenched police mindset, in this case it had only ensured that detectives had been hoist by their own petard.

PACE decreed a solicitor be present to protect a suspect. What use was that to Stephen Miller when his had been 'gravely at fault for sitting passively through this travesty of an interview'?

But, in Mansfield's mind, the burning question at the heart of Stephen's case was the word 'oppression' and what constituted it.

Picking up cassette number one, he once again slotted it into a tape machine and pressed play.

As he picked his way through the tapes, playing each in open court, he nervously waited for something to give, a sign, a chink in Taylor's armour of inscrutability but, so far, nothing. Everything still hung in the balance. Until, that was, he inserted tape number seven.

As the full-force tyranny of Stephen Miller's ordeal jounced around the courtroom's panelled walls, a horrified realisation swept through the public gallery, with many attendees mirroring Stephen's own recoil at having to relive it, slumped head in hands and crying.

Mansfield intuited a flinch, a change in Taylor's expression. Tony Paris had seen it too, noting succinctly that he looked 'vexed'.

'It just shows how important it is to hear the tape,' Taylor told the court. 'One could read the transcript where they are talking and shouting together without getting any flavour at all.'

Horrified by the police's 'sledgehammer' tactics, which flew in the face of PACE regulations, Taylor told the court: 'It is almost beyond belief that officers could conduct and interview like that knowing it was going to be recorded . . . a mixture of bullying and seduction by sophisticated officers.

'It is not right that relentless questioning should continue when the interview has reached a stage where a person is reduced to a state of crying . . . If you go on asking somebody questions, even if he is not particularly susceptible, and tell him he is going to sit there until he says what you want, there will come a time when most people will crack.'

Taylor said he was at a loss to see how the convictions were justified.

The writing was on the wall.

But that was not all from Mansfield.

Two other facts remained. One, that a prime suspect, identified only as Mr X, had been under surveillance running up to the five men's arrests. And two, that he matched an offender profile of the possible killer. Both were significant facts, but neither was disclosed during the trials.

The detailed profile, commissioned by the police and drawn up by experts at the University of Surrey, surmised that the killer likely held a grudge against prostitutes and his revenge had been a symbolic act of mutilation. Injuries to Mr X sustained in 1985 during a revenge machete attack by a woman he had assaulted, the court was told, matched those inflicted upon Lynette's body.

A convicted rapist and paedophile, who had spent time in a psychiatric hospital, where a doctor treating him described him as a psychopath, he had been a client of Lynette White's and had told police he had been swindled by sex workers in the past.

Police had also noted that Mr X had at one point looked close to confessing and that his rare blood grouping matched specimens found at the murder scene.

No, no, quite untrue, Elfer argued. Mr X had been excluded when laboratory DNA tests showed his blood did not match. It was a logic, however, that had not been applied when it came to charging the Cardiff Five.

'We do not accept this,' Mansfield rounded, 'and have asked to see the laboratory notebooks. The only test was on blood found on wallpaper, not on the victim's jeans.'

As Mansfield rested his case, the overturning of Stephen Miller's conviction was a foregone conclusion and along with it, surely the quashing of convictions against his co-accused?

With Vilday's and Psaila's testimony shot through, it was evident the jury had wrongly predicated all verdicts on Stephen's confession, including the acquittal of the Acties. This had gone against clear direction from the judge that the confession could only ever be used in deciding Stephen's guilt.

Ah but, Elfer persisted, refusing to give up the ghost, other corroborating evidence remained; he still had a case against Tony and Dullah.

The two men looked at one another incredulously.

Lord Justice Popplewell, sitting to Taylor's right, clearly thinking the same, leant forward over the bench to peer down at Elfer.

'With regard to Paris,' he said disdainfully, 'are you referring to the disputed evidence from Ian Albert Massey, the armed robber jailed for fourteen years?'

Tony turned to Elfer. His face beetroot red, Elfer tugged peevishly at his gown before sitting down in high dudgeon. He conceded.

'I think you have adopted a very sensible position,' Taylor responded to Elfer's actions.

Just four days into a hearing scheduled to last two weeks, all three appellants were free to go. The Lord Chief Justice would give his formal judgement in due course.

The increasingly familiar scenes of uproar and ensuing media scrum unravelled in front of the Royal Courts of Justice; another shunt at the system, another angry backlash, another excoriation at another hastily convened press conference and another three tally marks chalked up on the *Daily Mirror*'s shameful total of wrongful convictions in the past three years.

Around the time Tony and Dullah arrived back in Tiger Bay for a homecoming party at a local pub, the BBC and newspaper reporters had caught up with the man, now retired, who had led the investigation into the murder of Lynette White.

'The police are not the only persons involved in this,' former Chief Detective Superintendent John Williams said.

'There are Crown Prosecution Service and all sorts of barristers and lawyers; we're not the only agency involved. And I think it unfair to criticise the police at this stage.

'Regrettably, I think that the criminal justice system at the present time is hell-bent on leaving victims suffer and letting villains tread all over them! It's a sorry state of affairs and I feel very sorry for the British public at large at the present time.'

But of all the invective that had been spun into the ether that day, Tony Paris had got the last word when interviewed at the homecoming party at his local pub.

'This has been a stigma on our community,' he said. 'With the authorities trying to say that we done something we never . . . they don't know who done it, killed Lynette White. Anybody will do. And they thought we were just "anybody" but they made a big mistake down here because we are somebodies, we're not anybodies.'

Tony had painted on a smile for long enough and left the party early, drained and exhausted.

Being among so many people felt unsafe. My God, he thought to himself, the old Tony would have danced 'til dawn. Whatever happened to 'Pockets Paris', the chirpy, fancies himself, girl-mad party boy? He was dead and buried, just like his cheerleading but ultimately heartbroken father.

The world for him had shifted from glorious Technicolor to black and white.

Tony P went home that night and thereafter, for the rest of his days, rarely left it.

◆ ◆ ◆

Within a week, the release of Lord Chief Justice Taylor's formal judgement put the cat among the pigeons.

'Short of physical violence,' he had written, 'it is hard to conceive of a more hostile and intimidating approach by officers to a suspect. It is impossible to convey on the printed page the pace, force and menace of the officers' delivery.'

'But,' he added, placatingly, 'this is not to instigate a witch-hunt but to provide an example of what we hope we shall never hear again in this court.'

But hang on a minute, the force's Chief Constable Robert Lawrence countered, the same interview had been put under a microscope and admitted into two trials; indeed, the second judge, who had heard the entire contents of the tapes played out loud in court, had commended all officers involved. Now, two years later, the same evidence is inadmissible? All a matter of opinion.

It was met with a political backlash.

Retired detective-in-chief John Williams was having none of it, and stepped back in the ring, fists rolling.

'Well, what are the police to do?' he told a BBC news crew. 'We're living in strange times. We are there to get at the truth. And that is what my officers were doing at the time . . .

'Some people have to be shouted at; some people have to be spoken to quietly. That is the way interviews go, that is the way personalities get at each other, that is life, that is street life! I don't know how differently you can conduct such interviews.'

What of Taylor sending Stephen Miller's interview to the Chief Inspector of the Constabulary, the Director of Public Prosecutions and the Royal Commission on Criminal Justice, a body set up a year before to investigate the epidemic of wrongful convictions, as an example of how not to do it?

'Yes, well,' he snapped, arms folded, 'if we can get guidelines to police officers or even take away from police officers the right to interview and let them who think they know better take over! I'm afraid that at this time it's very difficult for the police; they just don't know now which way to turn.'

Guidelines? Taylor's judgement had covered that one. PACE clearly stated no confession should be obtained using 'oppression' and it had been clarified by his predecessor five years before that, who said the *Oxford English Dictionary* definition more than covered it – the use of authority in a harsh, burdensome manner, unjust or cruel treatment.

South Wales Police made its position abundantly clear. Yes, it took pride in the Lynette White murder investigation. No, there will not be a new inquiry. And no, there will be no disciplinary action against any officers.

The inference was clear: they had got the right men all along. The Court of Appeal had found the convictions unsafe, but that did not equate to innocence.

Terry White, beside himself, vented his anger at the men's release by smashing eighteen windows at the offices of the *South Wales Echo*. 'Everybody is more concerned with the people who did it,' he had said. 'Nobody is interested in the way my family and I have suffered and are still suffering. I just can't get justice.'

Not long after, he had written his warning letter to John Actie.

In the years leading up to the attempt on John's life, the case had been in and out of the news, with repeated calls for an inquiry and reinvestigation as well as John's continuing pitched battle with the police.

On that score, there was no end to the drama.

In 1992, a prominent local politician, one who had refused to lend her support to the freedom campaign, had stepped in to remonstrate with officers who, armed with batons, had surrounded John after seeing him walking through a local music festival holding the hand of his four-year-old daughter.

Two years later, in 1994, the High Court ordered the publisher of a book to pay one of the murder investigation detectives, Detective Constable Thomas Mitchell, now retired, 'substantial damages' over an allegation by John that he had fitted him up for the murder. Accepting there was no truth in the claim, the court also ruled that thousands of copies of the book be destroyed and a half-page apology be printed in the *South Wales Echo*.

John was not alone. Dullah, now a zealous justice campaigner with speaking engagements around the UK and Europe, made a formal complaint about a vendetta by the force against the men, claiming he had been strangled and beaten after being accused of smashing a window at Butetown Police Station, a crime he denied.

An editorial in the *South Wales Echo*, perhaps the biggest signal of a shift in public mood, opined that while it was no surprise the men were not favoured by a force they had exposed as a laughing stock in front of the nation, it smelt a rat.

'If Abdullahi's allegations of a police vendetta are even partly true,' the editorial read, 'it will constitute a major scandal. There needs to be a full independent investigation into all aspects of this worrying case.'

John, more than any of the men, felt haunted by the police. But as his abuse of crack cocaine hit rock bottom, any blame for his snowballing criminal record – shoplifting, affray, going equipped to cheat, using abusive or insulting words, blackmail, assault on a police officer, affray, wounding – could be laid nowhere but at his own screwed-up hand.

The nosedive of his family life was perhaps best encapsulated during frequent visits to the local builder's merchant's, so frequent that each time he walked in the guy behind the counter would automatically say, 'New front door, John?'

Taryn, a smart, beautiful woman who at one time would have done almost anything for him, had reached breaking point. She had never doubted his innocence, endured ignominy to stand by him, traipsed to a train station platform in the freezing rain to shout over to his jail cell that she loved him, and gripped his hand during his countless breakdowns during the darkest moments of the trials, soothing him with the reassurance that she was there for him.

But she had watched the home she had taken so much pride and care in making beautiful being wrecked too many times. One too many holes kicked in the front door, one too many screaming rows and tearful apologies. She had lost count of the nights she had been woken by her bedroom windows rattling from the bass of the car stereo outside, John sitting motionless on the car's bonnet.

The man she had fallen in love with was sinking fast. She had held on for long enough and now it was time to bail.

But there was even more heartache to come for John.

It was a few months later that he picked up the phone to his close friend Mark Harris, who was known as 'Max'. When it came to trouble, it would have been a close call as to who between the two of them it followed around more. But skulduggery aside, Max had always been there for John and he had just called to check in to see if he was OK, telling John he was heading to a rave in Bristol; he would back home in the morning and he would call round later in the day.

The following morning there was a knock on John's front door. It was Max's wife. She was crying. Max was dead. After being pulled over by police, he had been arrested after a fierce struggle when a stolen cheque book and credit cards were found under the front passenger car mat.

Three hours later, just before 11.30 p.m., he was found hanging by a belt attached to a grille in the wall of his cell.

Frantic efforts were made to revive him, but he was dead on arrival at hospital, to where John had driven to see him for the final time.

An inquest into his death heard that he had no history of depression or suicidal tendencies, that he had been in a 'happy-go-lucky' mood that night, keen to be released so he could meet friends at the rave. An open verdict was recorded, although the coroner stressed there was no evidence anyone else had been involved in his death.

And so, another crusade started up in Butetown. The Mark Harris Truth and Justice Campaign organised public meetings and demonstrations and monitored the case lodged with the Police Complaints Authority, but for John, they were screaming into the abyss.

A year later, in September 1995, Terry White would be knocking on the door and a few months after that, Cardiff Bay planners would be given the go-ahead to demolish the Casablanca, deeming the 136-year-old listed building unsafe.

But Cardiff Bay Development Corporation, locals were assured, had promised to cough up for the cost of salvaging the former chapel, one of Tiger Bay's best-known landmarks situated in Mount Stuart Square, site of the once world-famous Coal Exchange, and incorporate its classic architecture into any new building on the site.

'This is a very significant milestone on the way to re-establishing [the square] as one of Cardiff's principal business districts,' the Corporation's chief executive said.

A year later, before any salvage work was done, the building was gutted by a fire started, it was reported, by arsonists.

Like dominos, all the other pubs and clubs emblematic of the docks and Tiger Bay had shut one after the other.

But still, plenty of new wine bars and restaurants were popping up in their place, purpose-built to cater for the business community,

Entrepreneur magazine gushed, opening and closing to suit their needs and providing the right kind of food, drink and atmosphere for the latest conversation piece: the prestige of a proposed £60m Cardiff Bay opera house.

Plans for a five-star hotel and a surge of interest from leading luxury housebuilders promised to expand on the two thousand completed new homes, which buyers could be confident would rocket in price once the Cardiff Bay barrage was complete.

The jewel in the development's crown, plans for a barrage that would control the tide and impound the flow of two nearby rivers to form a freshwater lagoon, had overcome fierce political and environmental opposition.

Due for completion in 1999, the barrage would flood, cover up and eradicate from view what some saw as the filthy eyesore of the silty, undulant mudflats, exposed twice daily by the ebbing tide, the wetlands of wading birds for so long emblematic and evocative of the old docks around Tiger Bay.

But as illustrated by the old story of King Canute – how the English monarch sat on his throne on the foreshore and forbade the tide to come in only to end up getting wet – man, no matter how powerful his regard, will always be humbled by an inexorable force far greater than his own.

A barrage there may well be, but outside it the tide around Tiger Bay was turning and in its wake came the stirrings of an ill wind.

Chapter Eleven

The *Guardian* newspaper's introduction to the latest article high-lighting mounting pressure on the government for a public inquiry into the scandal of the Cardiff Five, read: 'Britain's worst case of institutional corruption involving a single police force'.

In the intervening years since the appeal, the region's police, battered by a bombardment of criticism from the local and national media denouncing its failings and alleged corruption over the Lynette White murder investigation, was deeply conflicted.

The fourteen unsolved murders on its books, a number boosted by a growing legacy of exposed miscarriages of justices, including that of the so-called Cardiff Newsagent Three, hung like a reputa-tional albatross around the force's neck.

In 1987, three white men had been convicted of the murder of a newsagent, Phillip Saunders, who ran a well-known kiosk close to the city's train and bus station. Struck on the head five times with a shovel on returning with the day's takings to the backyard of his home in the Canton suburb of the city, he died five days later from his injuries.

Three hapless teenagers – Michael O'Brien, Ellis Sherwood and Darren Hall, from a nearby council estate in Ely – had been arrested for stealing a car when they were ushered into the frame. One of them, Hall, another vulnerable young man, confessed all to police in a written statement, tape-recorded interviews yet to be operational.

Bearing many of the damning hallmarks of the Lynette White case, the Court of Appeal quashed their convictions twelve years later.

One of the men told how he was made to sit on the floor while chained to a hot radiator, denied food, water and a solicitor for long periods and mocked over an indecent assault he had suffered as a teenager. 'You enjoyed it, didn't you?' the officers taunted.

'I am going to become South Wales Police's worst nightmare,' one of the three, Michael O'Brien, vowed on his vindication. He was proving true to his word.

Then in July 1993, there was the mystery behind the bodies of a couple in their sixties, Harry and Megan Tooze, found shot in the head at point-blank range and rolled in carpet hidden under hay bales in an outbuilding of their remote smallholding near the rural village of Llanharry, eighteen miles west of Cardiff.

Chillingly, inside the farmhouse, where there was no evidence of intrusion, the kitchen table was laid with the Toozes' best China tea-set. Whoever had killed the couple had likely been expected as a guest.

On later meeting the Toozes' prospective son-in-law, Jonathan Jones, who had travelled to the scene from his home in Kent, where he lived with the Toozes' only daughter, detectives had a hunch. They could see straight through the descriptions of Jones as a loving man with no history of violence who had enjoyed a good relationship with the Toozes.

A smudge of his fingerprint was found on one of the tea cups at the crime scene, which, Jones protested, had been unsecured, and into which he had freely walked. Convinced he had committed the murders for the life insurance pay-out, detectives charged him. A year after his conviction, he was freed by the Court of Appeal amid criticism of the police investigation and subsequent trial and the emergence of fresh evidence which could have backed Jones's alibi that he was in Orpington, Kent, over 180 miles away, at the time of the killings.

All the while, disquiet around a clutch of other high-profile cases in the region gathered momentum.

Newly appointed as head of the force's CID, Detective Chief Superintendent Wynne Phillips, known for his mild manner and intelligence, determined something had to be done. The Lynette White murder inquiry, around which swirled slurs of racism in addition to corruption, was undoubtedly the biggest scar on the force's reputation. It was the only place to start making amends.

The lightning-fast expansion of science and technology had yielded a sensitive and powerful DNA profiling system called SGM Plus, capable of re-examining evidence from the James Street crime scene. After years of rumblings and heckling pressure, notably from the Cardiff Three freedom campaign's antagonistic Satish Sekar, the bit still firmly between his teeth, South Wales Police finally called a press conference to announce a cold case review in the summer of 1999.

Led by two experienced senior detectives retired from Lancashire Police with no connection to South Wales, the review would scrutinise the original inquiry for issues of integrity and objectivity and determine any prospect of a full-scale reinvestigation.

In preparation for its outcome, Phillips assembled a small team of Major Crime Squad prodigies to be based in a Portakabin at the back of police headquarters.

For his deputy Kevin O'Neill, freshly promoted to detective superintendent and in overall control, it was a hospital pass. Factions within the force were angry, denouncing the review as a waste of time and money. What was the point? They had got the right guys all along.

In the minds of many, the erstwhile CID chief John Williams had got it right. In yet another interview, he had insisted to the press that Lynette White murder hunt had been a 'tremendous inquiry'.

'I can tell you in amongst that time so many people were seen and interviewed,' he said, figuratively tapping his nose, 'so much evidence was gathered at the end of the day, the persons who were taken to court was the only thing that the police could do.'

But O'Neill, the son of a staunch trade unionist and grandson of a prize-winning boxer, had never been shy of fighting his corner. Galvanised as a schoolboy in the legendary boxing gyms of Merthyr Tydfil, the 'iron capital of the world' and powerhouse of the Industrial Revolution, a tough, post-industrial town twenty-four miles north of Cardiff, he had joined the police as a feisty eighteen-year-old, setting aside ambitions to become a surveyor, figuring it beyond his reach.

Resisting the clubbable, bar-room culture of the rank and file, he would go his own way, regularly showing up for shifts with eyes blackened and teeth missing, the fallout of another black belt tournament with the British karate squad or Welsh team, which he captained. What he lacked in flexibility and high kicks, O'Neill more than made up for with resilience and a prevailing counter-punch.

On joining Major Crime, he had looked up to its battle-scarred ranks of detectives. In return, they had little time for the likes of him, a new breed of upstarts drifting in on the hot air of bloody PACE training courses.

O'Neill had no truck with the old trope of the mastermind detective's sixth sense or hunch. It was, to him, 'a load of bollocks'. In the same way he adhered to the rules of karate's *dojo kun*, he would stick to the rigour of his training, to the drills, check and double-check. It was not a case of what he *thought* he knew but what he *did* know, in black and white, and even then, he needed to corroborate it.

Under him but in operational control was Detective Chief Inspector Brent Parry, the son of a miner from the coal village of Tondu in the Garw Valley, who had scaled the ranks after joining the police cadets at sixteen, thriving in an army-like environment of mountain camping and physical endurance.

Settling into married life in a police house – homes specifically built for officers within the community – Parry, known as the 'Tondu flyer', the try-scoring wing who would find space on the field where nobody else could, bolstered South Wales Police's formidable rugby side, whose line-ups had boasted a coterie of international players.

But his likability far outstretched the camaraderie of team sports. Parry had the sort of equanimity that ensured that policing the pickets during the year-long miners' strike had no bearing on the long-standing friendships with those fighting for livelihoods in the struggle.

Brought up to treat everyone the same and step in to help when needed, on the flip side Parry had the never-to-be-underestimated drive to make damned sure to nail those not playing by the rules.

Both O'Neill and Parry had joined a force that had reflected society's customs and norms at the time, but they had come of age professionally in a very different world. Both promoted thanks to a more equitable, less nepotistic selection process, they had been immersed in the *Murder Investigation Manual*, a strict code of focus and standards first published in the late 1990s amid the unabating storm of Stephen Lawrence's murder in 1993.

A public inquiry into the scandalously bungled investigation into the killing of black teenager Lawrence – a well-loved and popular school student, talented athlete and church volunteer, stabbed to death by a gang of white men in a racially motivated attack as he waited at a bus stop – impacted British society like a meteor strike.

The inquiry's outcome, The Macpherson Report, published in 1999, concluded the investigation had been 'marred by a combination of professional incompetence, institutional racism and a failure of leadership'.

The report was a milestone in British history. The then Prime Minister Tony Blair responded in the House of Commons, saying, 'We should confront as a nation honestly the racism that still exists in our society.'

The aftershocks swept through police forces around the UK. The timing of the reinvestigation into Lynette White's murder was surely no coincidence.

As O'Neill and Parry, along with a small team of officers carefully selected for the diversity of their geographic, ethnic backgrounds and sexuality, braced themselves for a mammoth trawl of some six thousand statements from the original inquiry, William Hacking and John Thornley, the retired Lancashire detectives, arranged to meet with each of the Cardiff Five.

With characteristic directness, John Actie told them straight: he had been fitted up. While his vehemence might well have been convincing, the state of his head – resembling Frankenstein's monster, riven as it was by the tracks of eighty-seven stitches following a six-hour maxillofacial surgery to sew his nose back on after being set upon by a gang in Bristol – hardly screamed innocence.

John's apparent death-wish extended way beyond the prescription and illegal drugs he continued to pump into his system.

His mother, Maria, had broken down on first seeing his injuries. Plagued by a misplaced but enduring guilt that she had failed him when he was taken from her and sent to reform school, she never stopped trying to compensate, always going the extra mile for him. John, his siblings were painfully aware, had always remained

Maria's baby. They would regularly comfort her as she sat crying over what the case had done to him, maybe reminded of a similar affliction and vulnerability she had witnessed in her dying husband.

John would reassure her he was OK, his elder brother Stephen, as always, on hand to smooth things over, responding at the drop of a hat to yet another plaintive phone call, yet another vain attempt to protect John from himself. Even if his brother did seem to have nine lives, Stephen worried John was running low on chances to land on his feet.

But then the lives of all five men had become terminally diseased.

An embattled Stephen Miller, desperate for redemption and obsessed that Lynette would not rest in peace until the real killer was caught, publicly gave the new inquiry his full support.

Tony, who had experienced people spitting on the pavement as he passed, ventured outdoors rarely, shopping only in the dim light of early morning. One time he had summoned courage to go for a drink in town, he had inadvertently knocked into someone at the bar. 'You're lucky to be out,' came the response. 'Everyone knows you did it.' Tony had rarely been on a night out since.

He, like Dullah, railed helplessly against the misconception they had 'got off on a technicality'. The full heft of their appeal evidence had never been heard, the hearing brought to a close before they got their day in court. The tapes were one thing, but both men remained convinced the lid had been firmly kept shut on their unpalatable dossiers of corruption.

Dullah, still claiming police harassment, had 'turned himself inside out' to get the case reopened. But the whirlwind of campaigning, speaking engagements, his work at one time supported by left-wing activist and actor Corin Redgrave, had taken its toll.

He had collapsed with nervous exhaustion and woken to find himself in a psychiatric hospital, where he stayed for months. Once home, he vowed to make a clean start, but before long he slipped back into heavy drug use. Like a moth flitting at the edge of a flame, the same stop-start cycle would repeat, each time tightening his death spiral towards combustion.

The men's cynicism was understandable. The reinvestigation appeared to be making all the right noises, for all the good it would ultimately do.

◆ ◆ ◆

In May 2000, in the time-honoured tradition of murder mysteries, a stately home-turned hotel set in the affluent folds of the Oxfordshire countryside hosted the inaugural cold case conference.

Retired Lancashire detectives Hacking and Thornley thumped copies of their breeze block 477-page report and recommendations in front of each of the assembled players.

The report pulled no punches, dismissing the original inquiry out of hand. Not only was it deeply flawed, but in their experienced minds there was sufficient concern in some areas to warrant a criminal investigation.

It came as little surprise to O'Neill and Parry. They had scant prior knowledge of the case but surely, they had initially, maybe naively, thought, there had to be some basis of truth in the original investigation. But the deeper they waded through the case files, the more that belief waned. O'Neill at one stage thought to himself, 'Wow. Is that it? There's got to be more.'

Seated close by and gimlet-eyed was a pioneering independent advisory panel drafted in to scrutinise the police's every move. It comprised four South Wales-based professionals, once again diverse in ethnicity and expertise, which ranged from medicine and leadership to the law and multiculturalism. The group's redoubtable leader was Beverley Thompson, chair of the first panel of its kind appointed by the Metropolitan Police following The Macpherson Report.

In all honesty, for O'Neill the thought of his professionalism being questioned by members of the public with zero investigative experience felt like a monkey on his back. But personal pride aside, even at that early stage he appreciated how crucial the panel was to the integrity of the outcome, whatever the hell that was going to be.

Every system and strategy of the reinvestigation turned on the watch words of transparency, openness and accountability. Every conversation, meeting, witness approach, door-to-door inquiry, phone call, spend, was to be recorded, taped, conducted meticulously and obsessively by the book. Every inch of this case had to be beyond reproach, and the lay panel promised to rain down hell on any transgression.

Next in line to speak at the cold case conference was forensic scientist Dr Angela Gallop.

A specialist in investigating violent crime, she had risen to prominence after joining the Home Office's Forensic Science Service from university, where she had been researching sea slugs on the Isle of Wight. A friend had pointed out a job advert for the Forensic Science Service, suggesting it might answer her dilemma over what to do next.

Her first baptism-of-fire introduction to a murder scene had been in 1978 on a wet and windy night in Huddersfield, when the body of Helen Rytka, an eighteen-year-old victim of the Yorkshire Ripper, was found at the back of a timber yard under railways arches.

More recently, Dr Gallop had made headline news for her breakthrough in the investigation into the murder of Stephen Lawrence. A lack of forensic evidence in the original investigation had dealt a blow to his family's hopes of justice. Gallop had reviewed it, her innovative thinking revealing minute but compelling evidence that later secured the conviction of two of the five original suspects in 2012.

Scientists, Gallop had noted, always seemed nervous about using the word 'imagination'. Visual and intuitive thinking emanated from the right side of the brain; it was more subjective. Surely any scientist worth their salt was a left-brain thinker, analytical, orderly and objective? Forgetting, of course, that the two sides are intrinsically connected.

For her, the power of imagination had nothing to do with the rigorous methodology of laboratory experiments but with the process of examining a crime scene and looking for material to test in the first place. Thinking beyond the usual, from a different angle or simply heeding the blindingly obvious, her investigative attributes of boundless curiosity and eagle-eyed observation had been put to astonishing use in cracking some of the UK's most puzzling cases.

Her career evenly split between working for defence and prosecution teams, she had set up Forensic Alliance in 1997, one of the UK's first independent alternative services for police cold cases.

Work conducted by the Forensic Science Service in the original Cardiff Five case had been heavily criticised, with more than an underlying suspicion it had been in cahoots with the police. With DNA advances unfolding at dizzying speed, forensic science likely held the key to unlocking the truth of Lynette White's murder. Given that and the review's credo of impeccability, open-mindedness and independence, Dr Gallop's credentials dovetailed perfectly.

During her initial review of crime scene evidence, she had visited 7 James Street accompanied by Parry, leading forensic and clinical psychologist Adrian West, and Dave Barclay of the National Crime and Operations Faculty.

While the flat had been repainted a couple of times, the room in which the murder took place had remained largely unaltered since Valentine's Day 1988.

Original reports showed exactly where Lynette's throat had been cut and where she had been dragged the small distance to the light of the window and where the rest of the countless knife wounds had been inflicted.

Unidentified blood had been found on her clothes and wallpaper close to her body. The pattern of it suggested it was cast-off blood flicked from the killer, likely injured, as was so often the case during a struggle or when a hand, wet with blood, had slipped from the knife handle on to the cutting edge during an attack.

Crime scene photographs showed other blood marks, some on the walls outside the room. Barclay, blindfolded, pretended to flee the scene in a rush, blundering along the right angle turns of the narrow passageway to the flat's exit, cracking his head on a corner turn before stumbling down the communal stairs to the street-level door.

The contact marks of his hand on the wall were noted to see if they corresponded with those on the wallpaper from 1988, all of which had been carefully removed and preserved.

Adrian West's assessment informed by the scene chimed with the original offender profile: the actions of a single person, likely a client; one person in, one person out.

There were doubts about that at the cold case conference. The leap from nine people at the scene – the five defendants and four witnesses – as the original prosecution had insisted and, more to the point, a jury had believed, to an unrelated stranger? Besides, among Hacking and Thornley's 107 recommendations was that the original witnesses – Leanne Vilday, Mark Grommek, Angela Psaila and Paul Atkins – be investigated as possible suspects.

But Dr Gallop reported to the hotel meeting that proving or disproving any theory about the events that had unfolded that night was going to be an uphill climb.

The two sources of foreign blood at the murder scene were useless. Spatter on the wallpaper had been corrupted by ninhydrin, a chemical used to dust for fingerprints. Marks on Lynette White's clothing had either been tested to near death or dye from the denim of her jeans interfered with the results.

Getting anywhere near the realms of a DNA profile of the killer was hopeless unless they found more sources of his blood.

In another of Dr Gallop's celebrated cases, she had exposed the truth behind the murder of Italian banker Roberto Calvi, dubbed 'God's banker' due to his association with Vatican City. He had been found hanged from scaffolding under London's Blackfriars Bridge, his pockets stuffed with brick and rocks. The verdict of his death switched from suicide to murder following a series of Dr Gallop's imaginative reconstructions.

And so, the manuscripts of woodchip wallpaper stripped from the walls of 7 James Street were unfurled into the light of day for the first time in over ten years to be rehung and re-read in a summoning of the past, as South Wales Police announced a full-scale reinvestigation to settle the score of Lynette White's murder once and for all.

It was given the codename Operation Mistral.

Mistral, derived from the Latin *magistralis*, meaning 'masterly', pertaining to a teacher or expert, is the name of a fierce north-westerly wind which roars as cold as hell down the Rhône Valley in southern France, turning stones on the ground of its excoriating path and scouring the sky above clear of clouds as it skids into storms out on the Mediterranean Sea.

Dr Gallop grappled and tugged as she manhandled an assistant, dragging her by the heels along the floor in the reconstructed murder scene at Forensic Alliance's base at Oxfordshire's Culham Science Centre.

All eyes may well have been on DNA, the poster boy of forensic science, but long before it entered the lexicon of everyday parlance, a tried-and-tested discipline of unlocking the secrets of crime scenes still held its own.

Bloodshed.

Akin to hieroglyphics carved on to an ancient wall, the outline and patterns of blood – whether pooled, sprayed, splashed, smudged, misted, or spattered – can be read like spectral ink, revealing a story of murder and mayhem.

With the exact proportions of the room built, along with the twists and turns of its hallway, the wallpaper and related crime scene photographs read like scrolls denoting clues as to where the killer's blood likely fell that night.

DNA testing did not come cheap, and O'Neill's budgets had their limits. Finding the blood of the killer or killers from Lynette White's heavily stained clothing was akin to searching for a needle in a haystack. Focus was imperative. Where might the sources of blood be that had been previously overlooked?

Dr Gallop had got hold of a jacket similar to the one found pulled from one arm of Lynette White and twisted back to front around her body. Grappling with an assistant to determine the actions necessary to tug and pull it into that position, she identified areas around the cuffs where the killer's blood might be. It turned out, they had not been tested.

Meanwhile, an interminable treasure hunt to track down a total of 954 pieces of evidence – debris from the murder scene, coins, condoms, carpet, clothing, the entire 1988 wardrobes of John and his co-accused – had trailed from one storeroom, cupboard and archive to another strewn across the expansive force area.

During one of the regular case conferences in Oxfordshire, Parry and a colleague, Detective Constable Paul Williams, compared each area of the reconstructed crime scene with photographs taken in 1988. They were checking for any missing material, small pieces of rubbish or cigarette butts, for example, which they would then cross-check with an inventory of retrieved crime scene exhibits to see if they still existed.

Williams homed in on a trampled, incidental piece of cellophane on the floor close to the body. It blended into the scene and looked like it could have been discarded from the top of a cigarette packet. He noted that it had never been tested, but who knew if it even still existed?

Their search for the cellophane finally ended on Thursday, 11 September 2001, amid the fervour of breaking news from the World Trade Center in New York. The wrapper, perfectly sealed and protected, was unearthed among a packed library of evidence bags.

Among the smears of blood on its surface, Dr Gallop noticed a tiny stain that bore a defined, circular outline typical of droplets cast off from the swinging blows of a knife. In the New Year of 2002, a partial DNA profile of an unidentified male heralded the first major breakthrough in the hunt for the identity of the killer. Fittingly, the reinvestigation named him 'Cellophane Man'.

Stains on cardboard boxes in the corner of the room not far from Lynette White's head yielded further matches. Progress undoubtedly, but still not enough. They needed more.

In 1988, scenes-of-crime officers had found blood splashes on wallpaper and the skirting board next to Lynette White's body. Traditional blood grouping tests done at the time had first revealed it as both foreign and male, the same rare blood grouping that had coincidentally and, as time would soon tell, unrelatedly matched that of Angela Psaila.

A large drop of blood had dripped down the wallpaper on to the skirting board, where, photographs showed, an additional two splashes had landed, their outline and shape showing they had clearly been airborne and, as such, had possibly come from the killer. It was a long shot. Even if the skirting board was still in place, a vigorous cleaning process before fresh coats of paint were applied could have eliminated any traces. But there was a chance.

In the two years of the reinvestigation, the scope of DNA testing had dramatically evolved, the required sample size shrinking from that of a ten pence piece to the tiniest traces of blood, from which more discriminating profiles could now be yielded.

To the excitement and fascination of the James Street flat's current tenant, Parry had supervised the removal of the section of skirting along with the original front door, where traces of blood had also been found at the time of the murder.

A skilled scientist at Forensic Alliance embarked on the painstaking process, requiring a microscopic focus and the manual dexterity of a surgeon's hand, to intricately scrape between two layers of paint – not deep enough and no traces would be revealed; go too deep and they would be missed and wrecked. But, it became clear, the blood had not been cleaned off before paint was slapped on top. Blood amid the paint was found, as well as a perfectly preserved sample that had seeped through a small gap between the skirting and the wall.

In headline news, fourteen years after the murder, South Wales Police announced they had a full DNA profile of a man at the scene, and appealed for thousands to volunteer for screening. A tough ask given the force's reputation. Who in their right mind, many in the city thought, would willingly walk into that lion's den?

The genetic fingerprints of all five original suspects were eliminated, along with any key players involved in the 1988 inquiry. If nothing else, the reinvestigation had at least exonerated the innocent and wrongly stigmatised men.

The profile was run through the UK database. No matches. Two ships had docked in Cardiff at the time of the murder which had never been followed up. There was a chance Interpol's database of 140 countries would throw up a match. Again, nothing.

Interestingly, the launch of the Lynette White reinvestigation had prompted the formation of South Wales Police's cold case unit, one of the first of its kind in the UK. It had recently piqued world interest with its success in solving another troubling murder case, forty-odd miles west of Cardiff.

On a Sunday morning in September 1973, a man out for a stroll had stumbled upon the body of a young girl in countryside surrounding the village of Llandarcy, near Neath in south-west Wales. Close by in the densely wooded copse, police later discovered the body of her friend. Pauline Floyd and Geraldine Hughes, both sixteen, had last been seen hitch-hiking the night before. Both had been sexually assaulted, beaten and strangled, length of ropes left around their necks.

Two months before, another sixteen-year-old, Sandra Newton, had been found murdered six miles away. Young girls were urged to be on their guard, as police feared they were dealing with a serial killer. He was dubbed the Saturday Night Strangler.

Despite a fervent murder hunt, police had drawn a blank. The case remained unsolved until DNA advances meant sperm samples found on the victims' clothes could be tested. With no matches to a profile on the database, the case looked in danger of foundering once again.

The cold case team noted two of the alleles or numbers within the tapestry of the DNA fingerprint were extremely rare. With a DNA profile comprising a number of pairs, half of the chromosomes inherited from a father, the other half from a mother, a child of the killer would share a significant amount of the killer's profile numbers.

A forensic scientist had the idea of using the unusual traits to identify possible relatives on the database. A profile of a car thief was found to be a close match. Using the profiles of the thief's sister and his mother, the scientist was able to determine the likely identity of the killer.

The remains of Joseph Kappen, a former lorry driver and nightclub bouncer who had died of lung cancer ten years before, showed a perfect DNA match following exhumation, making history in what was heralded as a world first in solving a murder with familial DNA.

It was not long after, as the mass screening in the hunt for Lynette White's killer took detectives around the country, that exhibits officer Detective Constable Paul Williams made a startling observation: the number twenty-seven present in the DNA profile from the murder scene hardly ever appeared in any of the DNA records of all the men who had been sampled.

An arduous search of all samples submitted by South Wales Police over the years containing the unusual twenty-seven component highlighted six hundred profiles. Long before the days when computer technology would have saved him the task, Williams began a complex mathematical game of bingo, sifting through the list and whittling it down to seventy profiles that shared at least ten matching elements. Of those, one profile of a fourteen-year-old boy arrested for joyriding, yet to be born at the time of the murder, matched twelve.

Detectives called at his address in the Ely area of Cardiff and tested his father and later an uncle. The matches were closer but not exact. There was one other brother, they said, but they had been out of touch for years.

That brother was a man called Jeffrey Gafoor, who would have been twenty-two in 1988. Detectives called at his semi-detached house in the village of Llanharan, eighteen miles west of Cardiff, the home of a man regarded as a hermit, a man who never spoke to anyone in the community. There was no one at home.

The following day, 27 February 2003, Gafoor responded to a calling card posted through his letterbox and arranged to meet Williams and a colleague at his place of work, an office block near the city centre where he was the night watchman.

Agreeing to a mouth swab, Gafoor told the detectives out of the blue, 'I knew Lynette. I had sex with her . . . a week before she was murdered, in the flat, the one in which she was murdered.'

A media and poster campaign in nine different languages had escaped few people's attentions over the preceding months. Gafoor, there is no doubt, knew police had a DNA profile but he did not know the type of fluid at the source of it.

'Anyway,' Gafoor asked the officers, 'I thought you had people for this?' Williams remained poker-faced.

Immediately, the swab was driven up to the laboratory in Oxfordshire, where scientists cautioned an excited Williams against being too hopeful, reminding him of how many dead ends they had encountered over the past two years.

Scientist Andrew McDonald set the sample running and waited nervously by the computer monitor, a copy of Cellophane Man's profile in his hand. His heart rate increased as his eyes flitted between the two, the rows of colourful, patterned columns slowly emerging on the screen unfolding and taking shape like an image developing in a photographer's darkroom.

It was a match.

A whirr of meetings and phone calls ensued to ensure the next vital stage left no margin for error or criticism. Arrangements were hurriedly made for specialist interviewers assigned to conduct the questioning in a room fitted with cameras where a member of the lay advisory group would supervise. And in the meantime, a surveillance team was to be assigned to keep tabs on Gafoor's every move.

The following day, as O'Neill settled in for a Friday night at home with his family, he took a call from Parry. Gafoor, followed home from work, had bought boxes of paracetamol from three different shops and garages. O'Neill gave the OK to break into his house.

Lying in bed, Gafoor initially denied he had taken any tablets before admitting he had actually swallowed sixty-four. During the journey by ambulance to hospital, he confessed.

'Just for the record, I did kill Lynette White,' he said. 'I've been waiting for this for fifteen years. Whatever happens to me I deserve . . . I sincerely hope that I die . . .'

He went on to say that at work he had prayed to God to show Himself moments before Williams had arrived to ask if he could take a mouth swab from him.

With officers guarding his bed, medical staff made it clear to Gafoor that if he continued to refuse treatment then he would surely die.

'Actually, it's quite a relief being found out, not having to hide anymore,' he said. 'At least I can die with a clear conscience for what it's worth . . . This might be my last two days on earth. I'm quite looking forward to seeing if God or the devil exists.'

Eventually he agreed to have his stomach pumped declaring that it was 'time to face the music'.

'The reason they are concerned,' Gafoor confided in a nurse, 'is because I killed someone fifteen years ago and they want me alive to go and stand trial.'

◆ ◆ ◆

Released four days later, thirty-six-year-old Gafoor refused legal help that had been arranged by his frantic father, who had not seen or spoken to his son for the past nine years. He also refused to divulge any details of the murder other than to confirm his date of birth, that he was guilty and had acted alone. He wanted to go to court and get it over and done with.

As news spread on radio bulletins that a man had been charged, a neighbour called out to John Actie as he walked near his home. They got him, it was on the news. Got who? A guy for Lynette White. After the news sunk in, John felt ecstatic. He could have cried. In an instant, he felt the burden lift from his shoulders and for the first time in fifteen years he felt freed. From that moment on, he vowed, he would never again smoke crack cocaine.

By the time Gafoor was charged, advances in DNA had identified thirteen separate sources of blood used to confirm a complete DNA profile. As well as the cellophane, cardboard box and skirting board, his blood was found on Lynette's jeans, her sock, on the walls of the murder scene, the hallway corridor and the communal doorway to the flat.

Dr Gallop had read the room to reveal Lynette had been dragged a short distance across the carpet to where the majority of the attack likely took place, in the process of which Gafoor had been injured, likely a cut to his hand. After that he made his way out of the flat, blundering along what would have probably been a pitch-black hall and passageway and then down the stairs and, after fumbling to find the catch on the front door, out into the street.

◆　◆　◆

On 4 July 2003, Gafoor, dressed in blue trousers and sweater, was led handcuffed from a prison van into a side entrance of Cardiff Crown Court. With chin-length greased-back hair, he bore an uncanny resemblance to the artist's impression released by police back in 1988 of the man seen crying and clutching his bleeding hand outside the murder scene. The same description that had matched a man suspiciously searching wasteland where Lynette White's keys had been found. His thin-rimmed glasses chimed with a barmaid's statement in response to the *Crimewatch* appeal of an 'odd character' who frequently stood at the back of the pub not far from the docks, staring at sex workers.

Gafoor had killed Lynette White in a row over £30, the court heard, money he wanted back after he changed his mind about wanting sex. She had refused and a fight broke out.

Ever since, he had retreated into the shadows, his only other conviction being in 1992, when he pleaded guilty to hitting a fellow security guard on the head with half a brick following a minor dispute for which he was given eighty hours' community service.

Gasps and cries from the packed public gallery, where Lynette White's sister, stepmother and aunties were seated, rang out around the court when he was read the charge to which he replied 'guilty'.

Terry White, Lynette's father, was not among the family present that day. He never lived to know the truth about his daughter's death. A short time before the announcement of a DNA profile, he had fallen down the stairs at his home and died. He was fifty-five.

Nine months later in late 2002, his son, Terrence, Lynette's twenty-nine-year-old half-brother, was also found dead. He had died from an overdose. An inquest into his death heard how his life had become blighted by his sister's murder. He had never got over it.

Their wife and mother, Carol White, had gone to court to look Gafoor in the eye; she needed to see him in the flesh. He was a monster, she had said, whose actions had made the family feel on countless occasions over the past fifteen years that they could not go on.

Gafoor's barrister, John Charles Rees QC, who had defended John Actie during the second trial, addressed the court before sentencing.

'My Lord, may I say straightaway that the defendant accepts full responsibility for the killing of Lynette White. He accepts that he will receive a life sentence and accepts that he will spend many years in prison and, as he said to the police, he knows he deserves it.

'He also asks me to state, and perhaps I can use his words, that he is very sorry for the killing of Lynette White, taking such a young life. He is very sorry for the hurt and suffering caused to her family, and he is also very sorry for the five men who were falsely accused of her murder, who stood trial and were incarcerated for a long period of time, some for up to four years in prison . . .

'. . . those men have been stigmatised ever since. I want to say on Mr Gafoor's instructions that they had absolutely nothing to do with the killing of Lynette White.

'Mr Gafoor had no connection with the docks area. He didn't know the five men at all and had no connection with them. The alleged motives at the time, which varied between a drugs deal gone wrong, for which Lynette White was being punished, or control of prostitution, were again wholly erroneous and untrue. If ever there was a case to stop calls for the reintroduction of capital punishment, this is it.

'. . . I repeat: none of those men had anything at all to do with the killing of Lynette White.'

Gafoor was sentenced to life in prison with a tariff of twelve years and eight months, the time he would need to serve before being eligible for parole, the aggravating factor that he allowed innocent men to take the hit for his actions having been taken into account. It was less than the tariffs imposed on Tony, Stephen and Dullah.

Next door, on the steps of Cardiff Central Police Station, Detective Chief Superintendent Wynne Phillips read a statement,

O'Neill and Parry either side of him like bodyguards. Parry, it was obvious to everyone assembled, felt awkward. He had wanted a press conference indoors, not some show in front of the cameras. They had undeniably led an outstanding police investigation, an exemplar of good practice from a force beset by allegations of corruption that could finally make peace with the wrongdoings of the past.

Phillips had wanted to say sorry publicly to the men wrongly stigmatised for the murder, but he had been advised against it. As John Actie and Dullah stood by, Tony vociferously heckled for an apology; Phillips resisted. 'I think today,' Phillips said, 'is about the conviction of the man who killed Lynette White.' His stance was ill-conceived. Everyone knew the outcome of the original inquiry into her murder had never been about that.

The Cardiff Five had made legal history as the first miscarriage-of-justice victims to be vindicated by advances in DNA testing. Surely now reparation could be made for the shameful injustice.

For O'Neill and Parry, the case had been the pinnacle of their career with South Wales Police, a watershed for the force they had served so passionately, the beginning of repairing its reputation left in tatters by the Lynette White murder inquiry.

But shortly after Gafoor's conviction, O'Neill received a phone call from a duty inspector congratulating him on the success of the reinvestigation.

'Great,' the inspector said, 'you've got him. But what about the others?'

'They didn't do it,' O'Neill replied.

'Oh no, come on. The Acties were involved somehow.'

'No,' O'Neill replied firmly. 'They weren't.'

Four years of his career had been devoted to proving that. And if the many doubters needed more than the indisputable facts of forensic science, then there was far more to come.

Chapter Twelve

'You keep accusing me of being there. I was acquitted. It seems like I am the one on trial!'

The nightmare had sprung back into life. It was happening all over again. Only this time it felt even worse.

John Actie, his jaw clenched, beckoned to the jury, jabbing his finger at the dock.

'It is them who fitted me up!' he said, before snapping his glare back to the barristers' bench in front of him. 'These accusations you're putting to me, they're all wrong. I wasn't there. I was acquitted. You know what? It seems like I am on trial and they are sitting there doing nothing!'

How could this be happening?

For the *third* time he was stood in the witness box of Swansea Crown Court defending his innocence of the murder of a woman he had never known in a flat he had never been into.

He wondered, certainly not for the first time, if the world had gone mad.

Way back in the mists of time at the start of the original trials, the prosecutor, David Elfer QC, had begun his address to the jury, setting the scene with the stigmatised depiction of the 'upside-down world' of Butetown.

The judgement of the ne'er-do-wells of Tiger Bay, sleeping by day and prowling by night, knives flashing in handkerchief pockets, hit far beyond the men in the dock.

Chastened, Elfer later apologised, but only with the surety of three convictions under his belt. His regret was as may be, but looking back, it seemed Elfer had unwittingly set in motion an enduring theme – many over the years would nervously hint at it being more of a curse – of a world turned on its head.

It was a Wednesday in late September 2011 when John stepped into the witness box. By then it was nearly three months since the detectives had first filed into the dock at the start of the UK's biggest ever police corruption trial.

Even the usually dependably miserable Welsh weather had flipped, the customary damp and grey of autumn sent packing by the surprise and welcome blaze of an Indian summer. John, in a light pink polo shirt and jeans, had dressed accordingly for this, his long-awaited day in the sun. Or so he had hoped.

He, along with a full cast of players thrust in and out of the limelight ever since the tragic opening scene at 7 James Street twenty-three years before, was now assembled for a final reckoning.

The dénouement.

It had been a thousand-mile journey to get to this point.

The first step was taken early on Monday, 7 July 2003, the next working day following Jeffrey Gafoor's conviction, when Detective Superintendent Chris Coutts, at the time head of South Wales Police's cold case unit, was summoned to force headquarters.

Coutts, who had transferred to the force in 1986, having spent the early years of his career with the Metropolitan Police, had been selected on the basis of his investigative experience and was deemed to be the officer most capable of handling the complexities of the inevitably fraught and controversial next steps picking up where Operation Mistral had left off.

A poisoned chalice, a colleague had commented. Coutts, ambitious and meticulous, regarded by some as the closest to a perfectionist they had ever worked with, preferred to see it as a challenge.

That same day, South Wales Police had publicly apologised to the wrongly accused men, announcing a further criminal investigation 'to identify and investigate any criminal or disciplinary offences arising from the original investigation'.

In other words, a lone man, a client of Lynette White's had confessed to murdering her in a row over money before slipping unseen into the night. So how on earth did a stranger-than-fiction story of ritualistic revenge meted out by a random group of unconnected men ever come about?

Even before it got off the ground, Coutts's investigation was mired in controversy. It was ludicrous, John and the other men protested, that South Wales Police be allowed to investigate its own, officers who had at one time been bosses and colleagues. How could integrity and objectivity be guaranteed?

With questionable logic, the Independent Police Complaints Commission, charged with allocating and supervising the case, deemed it in the interests of restoring the morale of a battered force that it should be seen to be clearing out its own backyard.

The first of several arrests of officers had been made in April 2005 during a series of early morning raids on their homes. Executed by officers from Gloucestershire, Dorset and Hampshire constabularies, it had been given the codename Operation Rubicon.

'Crossing the Rubicon' refers to a river, a forbidden boundary, over which a defiant Julius Caesar led his army and ignited a Roman civil war.

The phrase has come to mean 'passing a point of no return'. The wholesale arrest of comfortably retired officers, the high-ranking and highly commended among them, was momentous. This had the potential to expose alleged corruption on an unprecedented scale. There was no going back.

With every arrest, a courier would be dispatched to each of the Cardiff Five's homes to deliver a letter informing them of the latest officer to be taken in for questioning. To John, it felt great, at least in that moment. But cynicism burned in his mind; there was no way on God's earth those detectives were going to jail. The system simply would not allow it.

Operation Rubicon had been predicated on admissions by the witnesses in the original trials. They had come clean; their entire story had been a pack of lies.

Angela Psaila, Mark Grommek and Paul Atkins had already confessed during Operation Mistral, long before Jeffrey Gafoor had been caught. They said they had been forced to adopt a fictional story after being bullied and manipulated. Leanne Vilday at that stage had refused to be interviewed.

But in October 2008, she along with Psaila and Grommek appeared at Cardiff Crown Court charged with perjury. Paul Atkins, it had been decided, would not be charged after a psychological assessment deemed his mental disability so severe he was incapable of the intent necessary for the offence of lying on oath.

Psaila and Vilday duly entered pleas of guilty, while Grommek hobbled into court, now a man in his late fifties in poor health and unable to walk without the aid of a stick, to plead not guilty on the grounds of duress.

He had been threatened with violence and had only given evidence because he was petrified the police would do him harm. The judge rejected his defence, ruling that it did not meet the strict criteria for duress. With nowhere to turn, Grommek changed his plea to guilty.

Representing Vilday, prominent barrister Lord Carlile QC did not hold back in court with a blistering condemnation of her ordeal.

'The sheer wickedness and dishonesty of the police,' he said, 'and remorseless systemic corruption in this case is difficult to believe, but it's true beyond a doubt and it is accepted by the prosecution.'

It would be an utter scandal, Lord Carlile added, if none of the police officers involved in the case were brought to trial themselves.

The judge, Mr Justice Maddison, deemed it as bad a case of perjury likely to come before any court and passed sentence, taking into account 'police behaviour that was simply unacceptable in a civilised society'.

Addressing the three, he said each of them, vulnerable in different ways, had been 'seriously hounded, bullied, threatened, abused and manipulated' to the extent they felt compelled to agree to false accounts suggested to them.

All three were jailed for eighteen months. A greatly reduced sentence, but in Vilday's case it still meant leaving young children without their mother while she served it.

The news was of little comfort to John. To him, the witnesses were scapegoats, vulnerable people held over a barrel. Any anger he and the others felt towards them had faded over the years. He even disagreed with members of his family who believed they absolutely deserved to go to prison. For him, the only real justice would be to see the puppet masters, as he saw them, being held accountable in the same way.

John, Tony, Dullah and Stephen and their lawyers attended victim liaison meetings with Coutts and his team every few months to keep abreast of the timeline of the investigation.

John had been an eager participant, but at the end of each session would repeat the same mantra: 'This is never going to make it to the jury, you know.' Tony was horrified. It was as plain as the nose on his face what had happened. These people were going to jail, he protested. Mark my words, John told him.

Aside from those briefings, the men had barely been in contact since the appeal. John would chat briefly on the rare occasion he bumped into Tony on the street and nod a civil but perfunctory acknowledgement in the case of Dullah.

As for Ronnie, by the autumn of 2007, aged just forty-nine, he was dead. The cause was deep vein thrombosis, although anyone who had seen him of late would have pointed more to his spiralling mental health.

During his final years, his mind had seemed to implode. His relationship, which had borne him a daughter on whom he doted, had broken up and he had moved into a flat on his own. Seemingly unable to cope with the everyday chores of life, his mail piled up unopened and he was evicted from the flat for failing to fill in a required form. Turning down offers from family to live with them, he had hunkered down in the garden shed of a friend's house close to where he grew up. Ronnie vehemently refused any help. He remained close to his siblings, calling to see one of his sisters the day before he died, when he had talked to her about the case, which he always did. Ronnie, like a wounded animal, had retreated to die.

His family, as well as the other four men, would later receive a letter of apology from the chief constable of South Wales Police at the time, Barbara Wilding, in which she said she could not begin to imagine what his experience had been like. Not only had he lost his liberty and been separated from his family, but he had also been 'branded with involvement in a most brutal murder in the most public way possible'.

John had seen Ronnie maybe a handful of times over the years. One of the last occasions had been in the early hours of the morning at a garage forecourt cloaked in freezing fog. Ronnie was buying milk. It was all he ever drank. John offered to drive him the mile or so to his home to save him the cold, icy walk. Ronnie thanked him but would not have it. Same old stubborn Ronnie, John thought.

He had attended Ronnie's funeral just eight months before his own brother's. Stephen, his biggest cheerleader throughout this interminable ordeal, succumbed to cancer aged forty-nine. John was inconsolable at his loss and harrowed by the image of his older brother, the once upbeat irrepressible ladies' man, wasted to nothing, a replay of his father's end so many years before.

The two oldest grandchildren of Cardiff's infamous Actie clan had died. John felt gripped by a fear that he would be next, dead and buried before he had the chance to see his injustice avenged.

After overcoming his addiction to crack cocaine, he had leant on the crutch of alcohol, but that too had now been kicked into touch. For a man who had spent his life fighting, he faced a new battle to protect his health, fired by his belief that, for some, it would be all too convenient if he also slipped away before his time.

By that stage, he had reconnected with Taryn. After settling in London, she had thrived on a fresh start away from the docks and the spectre of John and the case. Having recently finished a logistics role during the building of the Westfield shopping centre in Shepherds Bush, she was now working with the marketing team at the under-construction Shard, set to elevate the city's skyline ever closer to the heavens.

Their relationship had been wrecked in the aftershocks of injustice. Now, maybe, there was a chance the two of them could rebuild it on the studier ground of vindication.

After the officers were charged in 2009, the wait for their trial to begin seemed never-ending, delayed in part by the heavy burden of disclosure, an operation overseen from the investigation's major incident room, removed and secure at a Ministry of Defence base in St Athan, some fifteen miles west of Cardiff.

The process of disclosure in judicial proceedings can be defined simply as the sharing of material capable of undermining the prosecution's case or assisting the defence. In many ways it is akin to the prosecution shooting itself in the foot, but nonetheless it is integral to ensuring a fair trial and is wholly embraced in the spirit of justice.

In reality, the process is anything but straightforward. Subject to complex policy and protocols, it has bedevilled criminal justice for years, its failings prompting the collapse of countless trials. At best, material can fall through a myriad administrative cracks; at worst it can be deliberately withheld.

The disclosure challenge for Coutts and his team was nothing short of colossal. A mountain of eight hundred thousand documents gathered since 1988 had to be sifted through into piles of what should and should not be divulged.

Coutts had no qualms about the rigour of his investigation; his faith in the Crown Prosecution Service (CPS), however, was another matter. CPS Wales had forgone handling the case in the interests of independence, the matter charged to counterparts in London.

Rightly or wrongly, Coutts saw his investigation sniffed at by 'London types', and was left with the distinct impression that they saw it as just a Welsh case, provincial and not of UK-wide importance. A trial of thirteen police officers conspiring to frame five innocent men for murder in one of the UK's longest-running legal scandals: how could that not be significant, regardless of where in the country it had happened?

Coutts's uphill struggle had led to angry outbursts during fraught meetings as he pushed for more senior handling further up the CPS chain and more money. When told by some CPS lawyers that the case was ill-advised and likely to fail, relations broke down, eventually smoothed over by the intervention of the then Director of Public Prosecutions Keir Starmer.

Even so, Coutts continued to feel he was swimming against the tide.

When the chief prosecutor, Nicholas Dean QC, strained by the immense workload of such a massive case, requested a second silk or experienced junior barrister to help, he was turned down flat due to 'budgetary concerns'.

Compared to the weight of Elfer's team during the original trials, the resource afforded the prosecution for the police trial, which faced way more challenges and pitfalls, was woeful.

In the run-up to the start of proceedings, Coutts had sounded a grave warning. 'The only way this case will fail,' he said, 'is through disclosure.'

To compound matters, the CPS had insisted on appointing a 'baby barrister', a relative junior, to oversee its labyrinthine disclosure responsibilities.

Coutts, I have little doubt, must have shuddered at the thought of the top-flight legal teams appointed by the indicted police officers circling like sharks around a chum bucket.

After an eight-year investigation, thirteen retired and serving officers faced charges. A *nolle prosequi* had been entered against one of them, Rachel O'Brien, on the grounds of ill health.

For logistical reasons, the challenge of physically fitting so many people into a single dock included, it was decided the case would be split into two with a second trial of four officers – John Murray, Wayne Pugh, Stephen Hicks and John Gillard – due to begin the following year.

With the first trial assigned to a highly respected and experienced judge, Mr Justice Sweeney, in early July 2011, eight retired officers filed into the glass-panelled dock of Swansea Crown Court. Graham Mouncher, Richard Powell, Thomas Page, Michael

Daniels, Paul Jennings, Paul Stephen, Peter Greenwood and John Seaford, charged with conspiracy to do acts tending and intended to pervert the course of public justice.

The health centre receptionist and yacht club bar worker, Violet Elizabeth Perriam, also known as Wendy, stood alongside charged with perjury, accused of deliberately telling lies about seeing John Actie outside the murder scene.

Next in line was convicted armed robber Ian Albert Massey, also charged with perjury over his false account that Tony Paris had confessed his guilt to him while awaiting trial in Cardiff Prison.

Graham Mouncher, the lead detective in the original murder hunt, who had liaised with Massey and had taken that statement from him, faced an additional charge of perjury relating to his sworn testimony that he had not offered the inducement of assistance with parole.

All ten vehemently denied the charges.

By its conclusion, Operation Rubicon had arrested nineteen retired and serving police officers, including the former head of CID, John Williams, and his deputy, Ken Davies, who were later released without charge.

Nicholas Dean QC led the jury on a meandering and prescriptive three-day opening statement. Laying bare the detail of alleged corruption in a flowing, captivating narrative was challenging to say the least. The devil was in the detail.

But at the heart of his case, he told the jury, was the framing of five men in a fantasy story manufactured after a murder hunt ran aground.

The stone-cold truth about what had happened to Lynette White was dramatically different to what had been alleged back in 1988.

How can it be that police gathered compelling evidence, evidence sufficiently persuasive that three men were convicted of murder, about events that simply didn't happen?

How is it possible, when the truth turned out to be really rather simple, that a hugely elaborate story was built up involving a very unlikely combination of five men killing a girl for no apparent reason in an attack witnessed by a dubious combination of witnesses?

'What happened in 1988 can now quite easily be explained,' Dean said, 'but is no less shocking for that.'

With the police having no idea who killed Lynette White, he told how a conspiracy grew after officers decided a small number of men were guilty, spinning a wildly unravelling fictional story built on rumour, gossip and the imaginations of the detectives themselves.

The jury heard that the police had moved away from investigating a murder, and with a gross disregard for truth, not due to any lack of competence or innocent error, were instead busy trying to implicate completely innocent people.

The packed courtroom heard how six months into a foundering inquiry, a newly promoted detective inspector, Graham Mouncher, a man known for getting results, had been parachuted in on a rescue mission. His landing proved abortive when he set his sights on Mr X, a sex offender and former client of Lynette White's, the original suspect, details of whom had first emerged publicly at the Court of Appeal.

In a report, Mouncher had outlined how Mr X aligned with several points on the offender profile commissioned at the beginning of the hunt. Up until weeks before the five men's arrests,

Mouncher had believed correctly the most likely offender was a lone client who had argued with Lynette White.

But on 9 November 1988, midway through intense surveillance, results of DNA analysis showed Mr X's blood did not match spatter from the murder scene.

Mouncher, a man who did not take defeat on the chin, found himself back at square one, the jury heard. Becoming emotionally embroiled and setting aside any semblance of a professional lens, his influence, Dean alleged, contaminated a 'team effort' that cut at the heart of truth and justice.

The next day, the court heard, two detectives, Seaford and Greenwood, the same duo who would later be part of Stephen Miller's interrogation, were dispatched to the home of Wendy Perriam, the yacht club bar worker and health centre receptionist described in the original trials as a gossip and a busybody.

A detective on the case, Jock Mitchell, had been having a late-night drink with her in late October, during which they had talked about the murder inquiry. He said he was investigating and had gone there looking for witnesses he felt might have been driving home at the time of the murder. Mitchell later told the original trials he had 'picked up on her by way of his sixth sense'. He passed a note on to the incident room saying it might be worth having another word with her.

Ten months after the murder, Perriam suddenly recalled seeing four 'coloured men' near 7 James Street having a heated discussion. No names, only vague descriptions. Hardly a breakthrough. James Street was a busy area, with the usual comings and goings from a nearby block of flats mixed in with weekend reverie.

Whether she was being honest at that stage, who knows, Dean said. But what was to come two days later? That, he said, was an outright lie.

In a new statement, she had placed someone who resembled John Actie and a more certain sighting of another innocent man, Rashid Omar, among the group.

Why lie? Dean asked. Maybe she was malicious, or maybe she had been primed and prompted by officers desperate for help, he said, a favour done without realising what would be involved and what it would lead to.

Regardless of her reason, her statement on 16 November 1988 signalled a turning point in the inquiry, providing a story template, a scene-setter on which the rest of the tale could build.

The lives of Vilday and Psaila had been made unbearable in the immediate aftermath of the murder by the police, who, not unreasonably, suspected they might know more than they were letting on. Vilday after all had been a close friend of Lynette's, she had led police to her body and had been staying at the time with Psaila in her flat across the road.

But in recent months, the women had fallen off the radar, left to get on with their lives, both having moved to new, separate addresses. Now, though, Psaila was pulled back in to the frame.

Some 2,884 witness statements had been taken by the inquiry. Detectives homed in on one taken a few weeks after the murder from a neighbour, living in the same block of flats as Psaila. She described arriving home late at night on Friday, the night before Lynette White was killed, to find Psaila crouching down and peering out of her doorway. 'Sorry,' Psaila had said. 'I was looking for a friend.'

Psaila acting weirdly. Nothing new there, thought the neighbour. She disliked her intensely on account of the commotion coming from her flat at all times of the day and night – knocking, shouting, babies crying.

A month later, the neighbour got in touch with the police to add more detail. She recalled Psaila disposing of property in a communal rubbish chute while looking 'scared and nervous'. Then at the beginning of November she spoke to the police yet again to say come to think of it, this did not occur on the Friday but on the actual night of the murder at around 2.15 a.m. She was convinced Psaila knew more.

After a further chat with the neighbour, officers promptly collected Psaila from her home and brought her in for questioning, where she remained for eight hours.

Insisting as she always had that she knew nothing, at some point she had rambled on about Stephen Miller calling round. He had done so, looking for Lynette, but that was three days before. Somehow, during Psaila's discussions with officers that day, that was conflated with the night of the murder.

Midway through her questioning, police diaries showed Psaila had been taken aside by Mouncher. He told the original trials it was to give her assurance of her safety. Following the chat, her story dramatically changed.

She subsequently signed a statement explaining how she had been home alone, babysitting Vilday's child, and had seen Stephen Miller with John Actie standing on the communal veranda of her block of flats. She then watched them meeting up on James Street with Ronnie and Dullah. Shortly after, she heard screaming from 7 James Street, outside of which a taxi had pulled up. Tony Paris, she said, had been coming back and forth as if he was trying to sell drugs to the men.

Psaila had also placed at the scene a man called Tony Brace, the doorman at the North Star. There later emerged a problem with this 'fact', given that Brace had recently died in a road accident on the outskirts of the city. Without explanation Brace disappeared from the narrative.

For the next twenty days, the court heard how a number of witnesses, Psaila, Vilday, Grommek and Atkins among them, filed into the station, 'voluntarily' according to records. During this time, Dean said, in which all accounts changed dramatically, each was held for long periods until police had either got from them what they wanted or until it became clear that no matter the pressure exerted, they would not play ball.

The jury heard that a pattern began to emerge of people being spoken to alone by Mouncher or another senior officer in between interviews. They were also shown shocking photographs of Lynette White's injuries to drive home the seriousness of this crime, one that, it was made clear, they were at risk of being accused of.

The police were no longer investigating the murder of Lynette White, but were involved in a criminal conspiracy 'fitting in evidence to suit their view of what had happened to her', Dean told the court.

In the witness box, Psaila, whose IQ of 55 put her squarely in the category of mild learning difficulties, described enduring 'evil' and unrelenting mental abuse.

'It was as if they were making a film,' she said. 'They were putting people where they wanted them to be . . . I told them I wasn't there. There was no way on God's earth they were going to believe me.'

Detectives berated her, she said, shouted and screamed, making her feel like 'a beaten dog'. Whenever she asked to go home, she said she was told she was going nowhere. Could she speak to a lawyer? 'Oh, we tried ringing him but he's busy,' came the reply.

As she sat there, she told the court, detectives suggested the names of a group of men they wanted off the streets, feeding her a story that they would write in a statement, telling her it was her legal obligation to sign it. It was the police's story, she insisted, not hers.

A week later, by 22 November 1988, Psaila's version of events had changed again to say Vilday was not out that night but with her in the flat. They had both heard screams and seen men hanging around.

At this point, the prosecution alleged, whether spoken about openly or not, there was a deliberate policy to break further witnesses.

Dean explained that a carefully coordinated and choreographed web of meetings and conferences were used to mould and manipulate witness evidence by means of threat, intimidation and outright fabrication.

While normal to confer and hold meetings in the midst of an inquiry, Dean explained, evidence showed they had become 'part of the criminal conspiracy' rather than integral to a proper investigation.

That same day, two officers called at the home of Mark Grommek, a man who was taking prescribed medication at the time for his nerves, and told him he had to come to the station.

Led through the back entrance, he was walked past rooms in which other witnesses were being questioned. He remained at the station for nine hours, the majority of the time alone in an empty room.

At one stage, Grommek told the jury, Mouncher had come in, yelling homophobic epithets and calling him a liar as he banged tables and threw a chair.

Just as with Psaila, Grommek recalled being told he could only go home when he told the police what they wanted to know. And why would he need a solicitor? He clearly had something to hide, they said. He never asked for one again after that.

Grommek was subjected to a good cop-bad cop routine. One officer, he maintained it was Powell, was tough and shouty, accusing him of being the only witnesses holding back. He told the court that he was threatened with a 'blanket job', which he later found out meant being taken down to the cells and beaten while covered in a blanket to hide the marks.

The good cop, Murray, who had played a similar role during Stephen Miller's interrogation, told him softly not to worry, that their bark was worse than their bite. If he just told the truth, and helped corroborate Atkins's and Psaila's stories, things would be a lot easier for him.

'I felt I was on the verge of a nervous breakdown,' Grommek said. 'My nerves got the better of me and I just broke down crying and said I would tell them what they wanted to know, anything they wanted to know.'

It was the worst thing he had ever done, he said, explaining how the police would write the statements, ask him if they were true, he would say yes and they would congratulate him for doing the right thing.

Giving evidence in court via video link, he said his life in late November 1988 had become a living nightmare, being picked up if not every day, then every other day by the police. He remained terrified for years to come.

Of whom, he was asked.

'Them,' he replied. 'I'm frightened of, as I said, police in the dock. Either they might find out where I live and come and do something to me, or if I bump into them, something might happen.'

The jury also heard from others who had been pulled into the station but were better equipped with 'courage and moral strength' to resist pressure.

Joanne Smith, a young mother-of-two who had been living in the top-floor flat of 7 James Street at the time of the murder, said she was surrounded by threatening and intimidating police officers.

During aggressive questioning, she told that the five men's names were given to her and that detectives had lied, saying they had a witness who had seen her letting them into the property.

Smith remained as steadfast as she had been from day one; she had heard nothing out of the ordinary the night Lynette White died.

Then there was taxi driver Jack Ellis, the man who had appeared on the *Crimewatch* TV reconstruction talking fondly of Lynette. He was picked up from his family home and escorted to the station, where he was shown into a small, cupboard-style room. After again being left alone for long periods, detectives accused him of pimping women and dealing drugs. Why else would he like working with the scum at the North Star?

'I thought it only happened in American films and not British officers operating as policemen,' he later recalled.

Four officers, one shouting in his face, one in each ear and another behind his back, must have asked him fifty questions, he said, only ever giving him the chance to answer a couple of them before he was cut off for the verbal assault to resume.

Fear rooted him to the spot as they told him his cab had been seen outside the James Street flat, that he wanted Lynette and because he could not have her, he had murdered her. Left alone, isolated, in between bouts of interrogation, he also recalled the cries and sobs of a man coming from a nearby room.

Resisting the coercion, Ellis was eventually allowed to leave twelve hours later. Shaking with fear as he waited to be driven home, he asked a woman who had been taking notes of his interview if officers were allowed to behave in that way. 'Well,' she retorted, 'it is a murder case.' No statement or records were to ever emerge of Ellis being questioned that day.

His wife would later tell Tom Mangold's *Panorama* programme that when officers dropped him home, he looked gravely ill and they had casually told her he might need a doctor as he looked on the verge of a heart attack.

But Ellis had not played ball. And so, he and his taxi were airbrushed out of the picture. In the latest flurry of statements, accounts that had previously been unequivocal about his car being outside the flat now changed it to a green Ford Cortina, the vehicle police mistakenly thought Ronnie Actie was driving at the time.

The consistent and abrupt editing of the story continued as Dean explained how each of the four witness accounts U-turned, backtracked and zigzagged, all damningly in sync with one another to maintain consistency as the story lurched to its final version.

More telling was a single fact contained in only one account. Take Atkins's statement, for example, Dean said.

DNA testing being in its infancy in 1988, the inquiry had focussed on fingerprints, identifying 1,747 marks at the scene, a few of which matched Atkins and Vilday. No surprise, given that Vilday had rented the flat and Atkins, it had already been established, had visited the previous occupants on many occasions.

In reality, Atkins had been nowhere near James Street, let alone in Grommek's flat, on the night of the murder, but an early statement under his name described how he and Vilday had entered the flat in complete darkness and 'felt our way along the wall'.

Remarkably, the only three locations of the flat Atkins mentioned touching, Dean told the jury – the passageway, chimney breast and light switch – matched exactly the points his fingerprints had been found.

Taking into account Atkins's cognitive challenges and that his account was made up, if, as the police insisted, it was freely given rather than forced on him, it begged the question of how he got the detail of where his fingerprints were found.

But the corrupt inquiry, Dean told the court, was about to plumb new depths.

On the afternoon of 6 December 1988, Leanne Vilday was picked up and, as had become routine, led along a corridor to a back room.

Detectives confronted her: they now had a witness who said, contrary to her previous statement, that she, on hearing screams and seeing men go into the flat, had in fact run over and had actually been in the room with Lynette when she died.

In disbelief she asked who this witness was. Angela Psaila, she was told.

Psaila, her head bowed, was then led into the room, she told the jury. 'You were there, Leanne,' she said without making eye contact before being ushered away.

'What have you done to Angela?' Vilday said.

The court then heard she was taken to another room, where she was held with a female officer for what seemed like hours, not being allowed to sleep. Over the months, Vilday, who had been used to dealing with the detectives, intuited that something about the atmosphere around the station was different; it felt off, she said.

She then saw Mouncher, who rounded on her. The two argued and shouted until such point he produced photographs of children who looked like they had been beaten. They, like her own son, were of mixed heritage.

Vilday, the jury heard, was told that this is what would happen to her son when she went to prison and he was put into care. Unable to bear the thought, she said, 'Alright you tell me and I will say I was there.'

'My head was gone. I didn't know what to do,' she told the court. 'I cracked and said that I was there.'

The threat was clear, the jury heard: play ball or be charged with murder.

The upshot of Vilday being held at the station on that occasion for seventeen hours was an eight-page statement. In it, she apologised for not being honest previously but she had neglected to tell how she had run over to the murder scene on hearing screams and witnessed a gang killing.

Once it was signed, Mouncher got up and left. Moments later, she told how she heard the sound of champagne being opened, as if they knew they were going to crack the case that night.

'I could hear voices, like a little party going on,' she told the jury. 'I just remembered hearing bottles, like a cork being popped and them all bloody hurray-ing.'

At the same time, Dean said, the details of Grommek's and Atkins's statements were also 'updated' to comply with this new version of the story.

After Vilday had submitted to pressure, six men were arrested: Stephen Miller, his brother Anthony, Rashid Omar, Ronnie Actie, Yusef Abdullahi (Dullah) and a man called Martin Tucker, mentioned by Vilday, a man she knew from the North Star whom she disliked.

It soon became clear that Anthony Miller, who had never been implicated in any of the statements gathered by the time of his arrest, had an alibi. He had been at a wedding in London with his wife at the time of the murder.

By that stage, of course, another story thread began to be weaved into the narrative, that of Stephen Miller's. He had begun to crack under interrogation, details from existing accounts being incorporated into his coerced revelations.

With Tony Paris placed front and centre of Stephen's 'confession' and John being placed near the scene, two days later, on 9 December, both men were pulled in, Tony in an alleged sham arrest.

Then there was another startling development, the jury was told.

Vilday had been told by detectives that it was no longer safe for her to remain in Cardiff, so she had gone to a friend's house in Newport, where she had been staying for five days. On returning from a night out in the early hours of 10 December, she was startled to see four officers, Thomas Page among them, flying towards her. She was ordered into an awaiting car.

The development concerned an unrelated incident over a week before, when, on 2 December, Psaila had been attacked by a man on the street, a client. She had reported the assault and a blood sample had been taken during forensic examination.

On 9 December, the murder incident room was alerted by a scientist, also working on the murder inquiry at Chepstow's Forensic Science Service laboratory, that Psaila's blood grouping matched the fairly rare samples found at the James Street flat.

Even though the blood belonged to a male, this development, Dean held, prompted the story to shift in a fundamental way. Previously Psaila had never been put at the murder scene. But if they were to strengthen accounts with her blood at the scene, Dean said, detectives needed to find a way of explaining how it came to be there.

With time running out on how much longer the arrested men could be held without charge, a frantic search had ensued, scouring the streets of Cardiff and Newport to locate Vilday and Psaila. Both were dragged back in, the court heard, to update their stories.

Now they told how *both* women ran over to the murder scene on hearing screams and Psaila had bled when punched in the mouth by one of the men before being forced to take part and be drawn into a pact of silence.

Psaila's statement also said she had got rid of the clothing she was wearing that night via the communal rubbish chute of her block of flats, the jury heard, neatly tying in with her neighbour's account.

This latest raft of statements, the police insisted during the original trials, were unprompted, with no mention made of blood test results at any time to either woman.

But the blood was never Psaila's, Dean said. It was Gafoor's. She 'freely' volunteered false information at a time it so happened to be convenient to the police investigation to have her blood in Flat One. She was never there. How on earth could she know she had to explain the blood? How on earth could it be that what Psaila said came to be replicated in what Vilday said later the same day?

The simple truth, Dean continued, was that these accounts were written by police officers to clarify something they thought needed explaining.

Operation Safehouse would soon be implemented to secure the witnesses in accommodation at South Wales Police headquarters.

Grommek, who had moved to Swansea, was at work in a bar one day when he was accosted by two officers. They told him his flat had been broken into and that he was in grave danger. He was shipped to accommodation at police headquarters.

It was close to the house where Vilday had by then been installed. There, she was visited by officers regularly, her movements recorded in a diary and escorted at all times if ever she went out. She remained in the house for two years until the end of the second trial. Psaila, on the other hand, had stayed only a matter of weeks before she had had enough and went home to Cardiff.

The jury also heard expert testimony showing how detectives had doctored documents and forged one statement. This had been discovered via electrostatic detection apparatus, also known as ESDA – a process that examines indentations or impressions left on pages underneath paper being written on.

On four significant occasions, it was alleged, statements or parts of them had been destroyed and rewritten concerning key pieces of testimony.

It also proved, Dean added, that a further statement under Perriam's name had been forged. Not only did ESDA evidence show it had been written early in the morning, possibly as early as 5 a.m. but certainly before 8 a.m., but also that the signature was markedly different.

In it, Perriam updates her account to say a man she had previously been so emphatic about identifying, Rashid Omar, she was now certain she had not seen. And the presence of John Actie, about which she had been tentative, became a dead cert.

Rashid Omar's name had not been corroborated by the four witnesses or Stephen Miller, possibly because he was commonly known by his nickname Wibidi. Perriam's statement, Dean said, took care of the inconvenience, enabling him to be released and John Actie to be charged.

When questioned about the statement following her arrest, Perriam said she was baffled. You look confused, the interviewer said. Perriam asked if she could have a minute with her lawyer in private.

With Martin Tucker also dropped from the scenario abruptly when corroboration of his presence also proved tricky, most of the rough edges on the case theory had been smoothed over and the five men were gathered together to be charged.

But, Dean intoned, the conspiracy did not stop there.

Detectives, he said, continued their methods to either maintain or strengthen the case against the five men by putting 'the fear of God' into back-up witnesses.

Helen, a former girlfriend of Tony's, later told the jury how she was harassed and held for hours before a statement was thrown in front of her and she was told to sign it. Speaking angrily from the witness box at the trial of the police officers, she said the contents, that Tony held a knife to her throat and forced her on to the streets, that he had told her he knew who the killer was, were all lies. The account, Dean said, helped discredit Tony, changing the perception of him from a man known for running from trouble to one with a capacity for violence.

Dean showed how attempts to undermine Dullah's alibi led to detectives speaking to men who had been working on the same ship at the time of the murder. One was led to believe wrongly that Dullah had confessed. Others reported feeling intimidated, one presented with an album of photographs. He had refused to look beyond the first leaf, which showed Lynette White's near severed head.

Such actions demonstrated a willingness to secure evidence, Dean told the court, by hook or by crook, by fair means or foul.

Then there was the thorny issue of Ian Massey's claim that Tony had confessed to him.

The convicted armed robber, Dean said, was an opportunist, a self-interested liar who exploited his fellow inmate's naivety, helped by Mouncher to cynically and deliberately lie in the belief it would earn him brownie points towards parole.

During the original trials, Massey swore blind he had not been promised any inducement. Mouncher backed him, insisting on oath that his only motivation had been public duty; beyond that he had nothing to gain.

But the jury was shown correspondence from Mouncher, written to his superior after his first meeting with Massey, which clearly showed the issue of parole had been discussed from the off.

Then, in 1990, shortly before the start of the second trial, a message was left for detectives: Massey's probation officer had called to say his parole hearing was coming up and he was hoping for a favourable report.

Mouncher had later handwritten a lengthy letter, later typed up and signed by an assistant chief constable. It was submitted to Massey's parole board hearing.

It said the convict had acted out of morality, only to be defamed by the media and suffer reprisals in prison for his evidence, which had almost certainly led to the conviction of a dangerous killer, Tony Paris. 'A debt of gratitude is owed by the public to Mr Massey,' the letter concluded.

In certain circumstances, a report of this nature might be acceptable for someone who had testified, Dean explained, but only ever if the pre-condition was open and transparent in court. Mouncher, he held, had known such an admission would ruin Massey's already flimsy credibility.

Before drawing to a close, Dean outlined the reaction of the former officers on being arrested. Some readily answered questions, others maintained their right to silence, Mouncher having done so over sixteen statements. Prepared statements were put forward by all defendants categorically denying any wrongdoing.

Page, who retired at the rank of chief inspector and acting deputy divisional commander, said he was not formally part of the inquiry and that he would have willingly attended any police station to assist with Coutts's investigation, but in view of the fact he had been arrested like a common criminal, he did not intend to cooperate.

Aggrieved by what he described as bullying and intimidation, Powell, who described Grommek's allegations as a complete fabrication, claiming he could prove he was not working on the inquiry at the time of his allegations, agreed that the original suspects had been the victims of a miscarriage of justice.

He pointed to the help he had given years before during the Hacking and Thornley review. 'You should have used me as a witness and I would have remembered a lot more,' he had commented. 'Now I can't remember. If another force investigates this enquiry, maybe we can do business.'

Regarding the ESDA evidence, Seaford had recalled spilling a cup of tea or coffee over a statement taken by Grommek and that he had to rewrite it.

'But I just hope,' he said, 'there's no suggestion that I added something into that page, because I certainly didn't.'

During his first interview, Greenwood said he still believed the men were guilty and blamed himself in part for their successful appeal. It was his interrogation of Stephen Miller, alongside Seaford, that had been so heavily criticised.

At the end of his epic 375-page opening, Dean left the jurors with the words of Greenwood giving evidence on Stephen's confession during one of the original trials.

They were chilling, Dean intoned, and brought into sharp relief what had gone so catastrophically wrong in the hunt for the killer of Lynette White.

'I was going to speak to Miller until he gave me the truth that he was involved,' Greenwood had said. 'He was going to be interviewed until he recognised that.'

These officers, Dean said, were not interested in the truth but in a version they had decided was the truth.

But above all else, if the jury was to take anything from what he had told them over the last three days it was this: Jeffrey Gafoor was the lone killer of Lynette White, and the five men charged in December 1988 had nothing to do with it.

Common sense, he said, offers no alternative.

Chapter Thirteen

Any doubts over the upside-down complexion of this entire case would have almost certainly been dispelled with the examination of the first witness to take the stand at the trial of the police officers in July 2011.

Prison guards standing by, the jury looked on as Jeffrey Gafoor relived the night of the murder, the unleashing of a deadly dimension of his character never before detected by anyone who had known him.

A self-confessed murderer caught by the incontrovertible trail of his own DNA, he had skulked for fifteen years in the misanthropic shadows of his reclusive life as five innocent men, their families and community were dragged through the mud for a crime committed by his hand. Surely only in an upturned world would anyone try to convince him that he was in fact innocent?

Gafoor gave short, dislocated answers lacking detail or the faintest flicker of emotion. His recall of events, he said, was fragmented.

It was not so much that he had tried to forget that night, he could never forget but it felt vague and hazy, he did not want to use the word dream-like but that was how it played out in his mind.

Dean persisted with his blood-from-a-stone questioning to determine that Gafoor had no recollection of walking to the flat that night, but in all likelihood he had picked Lynette up in one of the pubs, the Custom House by the bridge or the Ship and Pilot on the opposite side of James Street. It was dark, night-time, Gafoor said, but beyond that he could not be specific about the time, although he would have been surprised if it was any later than 11 p.m.

There was no doubt he would have been drinking beforehand. In those days, he had been a binge drinker, one of many secrets kept from his family. He had no friends to conceal them from.

At the time of the murder, Gafoor lived with his sister and her husband in a flat above a corner shop the couple ran, Malefant Stores in Cathays, a mixed residential and student district a little over three miles from the docks. He would help out in the store three or four evenings a week in return for bed and board, shutting shop at 10 p.m. and retiring quietly to his room to read or watch television.

His sister, a mother of two young boys at the time, said she treated him to all intents and purposes like a third child. But then Gafoor had always been the baby of the family. Born in May 1965, the last of five children welcomed into the world by father Royce, the son of a Bengali sailor raised in Tiger Bay, and mother Jeanette, he was timid and quiet but biddable, never causing any trouble and helping out around the house.

Gafoor's spare time would be spent digging through clogs of ash at old Victorian dumps, scanning for the glints of long-forgotten Codd bottles to add to his prized vintage collection. There had never been any friends to speak of. The extent of any social life, as far as his sister could recall, had ended with the youth club not far from the family's home in the Ely area of the city.

On leaving Glyn Derw High School at sixteen with no qualifications, Gafoor embarked on a youth training scheme at a warehouse at the top of Bute Street, loading lorries and occasionally going out on deliveries.

The warehouse was close to the Custom House and another couple of pubs where it was known women would ply their trade. His own aunt, a woman called Marjam, was a well-known sex worker, but the family, who had no connection with the docks, would see her rarely, perhaps at a funeral. He could not recall if Marjam was among the women he would pass regularly as he escorted a female cashier to make deposits at a bank in town.

Later, he said, he would venture inside the pubs during his breaktimes and likely it was then his interest in their services was piqued. He could not say for sure; his long-term memory had never been the best and now many years later it was even worse.

Gafoor recalled being inside the James Street flat, discerning the outline of a bed by the light from the windows. He presumed he had handed over the money then if not before. On top of the mattress, the torn wrapper of an unused condom was later found, a preparation likely interrupted by Gafoor's change of heart.

For what reason? Just changed his mind, he said, and demanded his money back. Lynette had rightly, in his retrospective view, flatly refused. The two had argued and were shouting by the time he pulled a knife from his pocket.

It was a hunting knife, the blade around six inches long and with a carved, decorative handle. He had taken it from a box where he kept a collection of knives, stowing the box away in a cupboard in his bedroom before going out.

He had carried one for self-protection ever since he had been robbed at knifepoint by three prostitutes a few months before. There had been another incident too. That time, they had not taken money but his jacket, flinging it on top of a wall. He had laughed off the humiliation as he climbed on a roof to retrieve it. Had Lynette White been involved? Not to his recollection. Had he ever used her services before? Not to his recollection. On both occasions, he had been 'very drunk', he said.

After threatening Lynette with the knife, Gafoor said she had tried to grab it from his hand. She may have screamed, he could not be sure; he recalled only that the scrabbling and jostling seemed to go on for a long time, it felt like forever but could have lasted only five minutes.

In front of the jury, he pointed to scars on his fingers, knuckle and wrist, indelible reminders of injuries sustained during the struggle and the ensuing attack, which he said was, as the police described, frenzied.

He remembered stabbing her but not where on her body, only 'feeling something', but could not recall inflicting particular injuries, although judging by the length of time his attack endured, he said there must have been many.

Lynette lay on the floor. He was certain she was dead. Slumped forward, he had sat on the edge of the bed for a few minutes before leaving in a panic. He had turned right out of the front door, wrapping his knee-length mac around him against the cold and rain, keeping his head down to avoid eye contact, detecting in his peripheral vision someone walking away on his left, and some passers-by on the other side of the road.

He had likely gone for a drink afterwards, he said, passing off the cuts to his hands as the spoils of a fight. As for being covered in blood, he said he probably was but again he had no clear memory.

Maybe he had discarded clothing on his way. There had been talk in the area in the weeks after the murder of a blood-stained jumper found on waste ground nearby, although it had never featured in the inquiry. It was close to where Lynette's key fob had been found, a small green plastic frog and two keys attached.

In his seminal text *Traité de Criminalistique*, twentieth-century French criminologist Dr Edmond Locard, the godfather of forensic science, set out his famous exchange principle, which held that the perpetrator of a crime will bring something to the scene and leave with something from it.

Ever since his apprehension, Gafoor insisted he had left taking nothing from the flat but his knife. Lynette's shoe, where she had kept her money, lay discarded close to her head but he insisted he had taken no cash.

In a revelation that blindsided the defence and proved Locard's theory correct, entirely unprompted, Gafoor announced to the court that while in his jail cell in between the days of being called to give testimony, he had had a flash of memory. He now remembered that, as he sat on the bed, he had looked down and picked up three £10 notes and some keys from the carpet. It was a shock revelation. The keys had featured in Stephen Miller's interrogation, detectives convinced he had discarded them.

Maybe the memory had seeped through a fracture in his dissociative state or maybe Gafoor remembered a lot more than he was prepared to divulge. Not for the first time had he given the distinct impression he was a man prone to mind games.

It was as a result of his psychological one-upmanship that the defence found something to hook their wagon to so they could continue to blame the five men.

Following his arrest, Gafoor had refused the legal help organised by his estranged father and was instead appointed a duty solicitor from the on-call rota.

This resulted in Gafoor being assisted by Cardiff solicitor Bernard De Maid, who had represented Dullah on his murder charge and appeal. De Maid in turn instructed arguably the city's leading QC, John Charles Rees, who had been counsel for John Actie during the original trials.

Rees told the court that he had found Gafoor to be extremely difficult, disconcertingly emotionless and secretive. Gafoor had told him he would rather not give details of his crime due to his deep shame that he had 'used a prostitute and took it out on her'. The nature of 'it' remained unclear.

He did not want to talk, and insisted at all times on pleading guilty to get it over and done with. Rees had urged him to explore possible grounds of diminished responsibility, but Gafoor stopped his attempts to organise a psychological assessment.

A short time after sentencing, Rees prepared a document for tax purposes, setting out his fees and attaching what was described as an 'assessment of case', an outline of the work he had carried out.

Surprisingly, and for no reason that could be nailed down, it had come into the possession of the reviewing lawyer from the CPS. Its contents were such that it had to be disclosed to the defence. A document of this nature would usually be afforded privilege or privacy, but Judge Sweeney ruled it had now lost that status and, as such, was admissible as evidence.

It contained details that revealed a little more of the inner workings of Gafoor's mind. At all times during meetings with his legal team post-arrest, he had admitted the murder and that he had acted alone. The only time, Rees had noted, that his blank demeanour broke into animation was on mention of the men who had been wrongly accused.

They deserved it, he had said, appearing blasé; one of them was her pimp after all. When asked about the two women who said they had witnessed the murder, Gafoor had smiled and called them liars.

Like a cat playing with a mouse, he would vary his accounts, at one stage saying he had been with Lynette the week before and on the night she died he had asked for his money back when told unprotected sex would cost more.

Chopping and changing, he then said that was untrue but introduced a new scenario that Lynette had come at him with a knife from the nearby kitchen. After discounting that, he then said that as he walked on to the street, he had passed a woman who looked like she was heading to the address and that there was a couple crossing the road, a man and a woman. Another time he said maybe someone had been on the narrow staircase as he passed.

As far as the number of wounds inflicted was concerned, he was surprised; he could only remember about twelve. Smirking, he added, 'I think maybe others got involved later to make themselves look bigger over the people they were with.'

Tired of his own game, Gafoor's final account was unequivocal: it had only ever been him and Lynette anywhere near the flat, he had stabbed her in the struggle, and once he realised the trouble he was in, he continued, cutting her throat and stabbing her until she was dead.

Nevertheless, his game-playing had inadvertently handed the police officers on trial their defence. They held that the Cardiff Five were still guilty, contending that Gafoor had only ever stabbed Lynette White twelve times and that she was still alive when found by the five men, who then killed her.

Added to that was the thinly veiled inference that Gafoor's mea culpa statement had been managed by two highly regarded legal professionals, De Maid and Rees, who might still have had allegiance to their erstwhile Cardiff Five clients, any hint of which was given short shrift by both from the witness box.

The anomalies in the defence's thesis were considerable.

What were the chances of five men with no connection to one another coming together for an indiscernible motive, happening upon a stricken Lynette White and, instead of helping her, deciding to injure her further?

With so many people alleged to have been at the scene, why was there a total lack of forensic evidence?

And Vilday, Psaila and Grommek had gone to jail on account of their lies: did they plead guilty for no reason?

The defence claimed that Stephen Miller had used Gafoor to get Lynette into a room in order to confront her. If he knew she was about the area, why not confront her himself? And why would he require the company of a gang of unlikely supporters to do so?

And why, if all that was the case, had Stephen's 'confession' – which some of the defendants believed to be true – failed to mention anything about it?

There was also the pathologist's evidence. Lynette died at an early stage of the attack, with the majority of the wounds inflicted after she had died. Scientifically, the theory did not fit.

As for Gafoor, he said he bitterly regretted saying such things, explaining his mindset at the time was unhinged.

He struggled to explain why he had behaved that way, but rationalised it as defensiveness; he had just been arrested for murder and his thinking was 'half-crazy'.

No one else had been in the flat, he insisted. He had left alone and eventually walked home, his mind numbed to his surroundings. At some stage, he had quietly let himself in the side door to the shop, rinsed blood from his hands and dressed his cuts in plasters, telling his sister he had fallen off his bike.

After taking his clothes to the launderette, he braced himself for a knock on the door by the police. As for the knife, he assumed he had cleaned it and sold it.

From that point on, he stopped going out. The headlines on the newspapers he sold in the shop, the television coverage of the arrests and trials he must have been aware of but had no clear remembrance of them, explaining he would have worked hard to block them from his mind.

A few months after the murder, Gafoor's parents took over running the shop and he continued living there until his mother died suddenly in 1993. Her death hit him like a ton of bricks, his sister had told the court, describing as strange his lack of emotion at the funeral. It was as if he had bottled it all up, she said.

From then on, he cut ties with his family as if they had never existed. In between living in a van and rented accommodation in the city, he had worked in Germany on a construction site, where he was remembered for voicing a vehement disapproval of pornography.

In 2000, his sister tracked him down on the electoral role and called at his address to let him know their grandmother had died. Gafoor closed the door in her face.

A year later, when she was diagnosed with cancer and needed a bone marrow transplant, she had written to him but never heard back. By that stage, two years before his arrest, he had moved, buying a home tucked out of the way in the village of Llanharan.

Lawyers for the accused police officers asked how he had raised the deposit for his mortgage on low wages. He had saved money; he never went out, Gafoor said. They asked conspiratorially if he was sure nobody else gave him some money to keep his mouth shut? The original defendants maybe? Gafoor looked confused. No, no one had.

Did he only plead guilty and cover for others to get a minimum term? Gafoor shrugged; that had been of no interest to him. He had found contentment in prison. His life had improved inside? Vastly, he replied. Busy with rehabilitation courses and listening to the World Service and Radio Three, he would, of course, apply for parole one day but he was in no rush.

'Those men had absolutely nothing to do with the murder if that's what you're implying,' Gafoor interrupted. He had never met them; they were completely innocent.

He was lying through his teeth, the defence retorted.

A dismayed Gafoor fixed his stare. 'What I've said here, because it's the highest authority, more than the police, more than my solicitor, more than my parents, more than anyone else, is absolutely the truth.'

The surviving members of the Cardiff Five had always known they would be called to give evidence. It was all they had waited for: a chance to finally air their version of events for the world to hear.

Once a date had been set for the trial, Dullah's children, Tiffany and Joseph, noted an overwhelming change in their father. Less depressed, he had curbed his drug use and become more relaxed and sociable, his spirits buttressed by the return of a long-lost sense of hope.

Finally, they felt like they had their father back. Their lives had been blighted as far as their memories served. Before the start of the original trials, they had moved out of the city to the anonymity of the Valleys. But it had not taken long for word to get around.

Both required the help of child psychologists to process the trauma of being spat at in school and, on one occasion Tiffany recalled, made to stand on the stage as a teacher explained to the morning assembly that their father was a convicted murderer. Home life offered no respite. Racially abused by neighbours, they had cowered as windows were smashed and their car petrol-bombed.

After Dullah's release, he and Jackie had attempted to reunite, but the resumption of incessant and violent rows led to them cutting ties not long after. In the long run, the children grew closer to their father, who, despite his struggle to get back on an even keel, never failed to remind them how much he loved them.

In the New Year of 2011, six months before the trial was to start, Dullah had been in bed for days suffering episodes of hematemesis. Terrified by hospitals since his treatment in a psychiatric ward, he had refused to get help. Eventually he was blue-lighted to Accident and Emergency after taking a serious turn for the worse. After falling into a coma, he died the next day. He, like Ronnie, was forty-nine. A burst ulcer was entered on his death certificate, an official cause his children knew belied the true story of his fate.

Any dream Dullah had of redressing the balance died with him but, as the remaining three men were about to discover, it was never destined to be anything but a nightmare.

In a societal and psychological ritual as old as time, scapegoats blamed and outcast for the shame and wrongdoing of others are burdened with a stigma never willingly lifted. To do so conjures the spectre of unconscionable dread that the wrongdoing, looking for its rightful home, might just come knocking.

Refusing to accept the men's innocence, the defence baited each of them with accusations and re-branded them guilty. At least during the original trials, they had the small mercy of a defence barrister, someone to watch their back, to blow the whistle on unfair play. This time, though, they were ruthlessly exposed.

The defence kept John Actie on view for the least amount of time out of the three men. During heated cross-examination, John talked directly to the jury, some of them leaning forward with interest as he fired back at pugnacious questioning with rough-edged honesty.

The old themes of the original prosecution reconverged, wild imaginings, conjecture and character assassination. Playing on the Actie family's reputation, several witnesses called to give evidence during the police corruption trial had been asked, apropos of nothing, if they had been cowed into their testimony, threatened to keep their mouths shut. No, they had each insisted.

Raking over John's lifestyle in the 1980s, the objectification of Butetown persisted, with incessant questions about drug dealing and prostitution. Yes, there had been a drugs trade, he had sold cannabis in the past, John fired back wearily. Yes, there was a red-light district which served the city outside. The sum total of any connection the vast majority of the community had with it was, like his, walking past the women and men loitering in nearby cars on their way home under the bridge.

'Anyone would think we are in bleeding Harlem,' John said. 'Everyone is walking around with fur coats and fur hats and everyone is pimps and drug dealers because we are in a black area.'

That was not the case, he argued, there was black and white, everyone mixed together. It was a good community where people looked out for one another and it got ripped apart in 1988. And anyway, he continued his fire, that was not the reason he had come to court. Over there, he appealed to members of the jury, the police officers, sitting in the dock, are the only reason we are all here.

Back in the day, John Actie was an intimidating man, the defence said reproachfully, a 'terrifying prospect'. To some maybe, John replied, to others not so much; regardless, the last time he checked he did not have horns growing out of his head, he said. For the very attributes they were projecting on to him, John added, gesturing once again to the dock, they need look no further than their clients.

A letter from Stephen Miller, an apology for including John in his 'confession', written as they awaited trial back in 1989, was held aloft as incriminating. John had pressured him into writing it, the defence held. John looked confused. Stephen had been held separately and neither he nor any of his co-accused had any means of contact with him.

Then there was the matter of compensation. Defence counsel had petitioned the judge to be permitted to discuss the matter of money the men had been awarded in a civil case against South Wales Police. As if to add insult to injury, John had winced when the police officers' defence teams were given access to his medical records. Included in John's records was an assessment for post-traumatic stress disorder. It had been conducted by experts at Cambridge University, who had scored him in the extreme category.

John had been awarded £250,000 in compensation, a similar amount to Tony, with Stephen Miller being awarded slightly more due to the ordeal of his interrogation. Each of the payments was accompanied by another written apology from the serving South Wales Police chief constable.

The cash must have given him a fair bit of power, the defence suggested. Had he used it to influence witnesses in this case? John was in disbelief.

In an arched tone, a defence barrister reminded him he had attended the court hearing when Gafoor pleaded guilty. Yes, John replied, there were a lot of people there. Did his influence bring any pressure on Gafoor to accept sole blame? No, John said, I did not know him, that is why I went there to see what he looked like.

Mr Actie, he was rebuked, you know a great deal more about that night than you are prepared to say. There was a pact of silence, wasn't there? Were you actually involved in the violence? Please tell the jury, Mr Actie, what happened in the Casablanca that Saturday night. He was asked if he had covered up then and whether he was still hiding something now.

Not for the first time, John pointed to his chest as he appealed to the jury. He was an innocent man, he said, not the one on trial. The only secrets in this courtroom, he countered, were kept by those 'crooked police' in the dock who had fitted him up.

Enduring the same treatment, Tony Paris felt like he was being tortured during three days of incessant and repetitive questioning. Before he was dismissed, the defence went in for the kill, taunting him with their belief he was still guilty.

Managing to hold back his tears but not his anger, Tony had finally had enough. 'I never done nothing. I never killed nobody,' he seethed. 'You understand what I'm saying? I'm not playing with you no more . . . I'm here to know why I was arrested, who gave my name to the witnesses, why officers were feeding Miller information. That's what I want to know.'

As a witness for the prosecution, Tony Paris would not have been eligible to attend the trial up until that point and had not been privy to Dean's opening statement when he had talked in some detail of Tony's sham arrest. Tony Paris, Dean told the jury, had initially been interrogated for four hours 'voluntarily', with no record or notes taken. Detectives insisted he was not arrested at that point. But why in that case, Dean asked, would officers have gone mob-handed to accost him in his home?

It was clear, Dean continued, that what detectives wanted was for Tony to implicate the other men, as Stephen Miller had done.

But Tony would not comply and so had paid a penalty for that. In effect, Dean said, that penalty was to elevate himself from mere presence, from someone on the periphery of events, to becoming an active participant, indeed to be the person who supplied the knife that killed Lynette White.

Refusing to be within physical proximity of the officers, Stephen Miller had travelled to Swansea to give evidence via video link. Early on in his testimony, he had cried as he was asked to recall the moment he learned of Lynette's death.

Delays and arguments had meant his testimony was dragged out over a period of a month, an ordeal made worse by having to listen as all nineteen tapes of his interrogation were played in court yet again.

'I have been dealing with this nightmare for twenty-two years and it is not easy,' he had sobbed. 'It is really, really difficult.'

Stephen had been inconsolable, removing his glasses to wipe his eyes and apologising to the court. The judge noted his bandaged hands; the stress had led to a flare-up of a skin condition. After word reached Judge Sweeney of the toll on his mental as well as physical health, he permitted Stephen to read the transcripts of the tapes while the sound being played to the rest of the courtroom was muted on the video link.

At several stages of cross-examination, a line-by-line scrutiny of his confession, picking holes in evidence in the original trials and questions about his sex life in the 1980s, Stephen broke down. How much more of this could he take?

'I need to get out of here,' he told the judge. 'It is like I can't breathe.'

Each time, proceedings were halted so he could sufficiently recover.

Asked about the dynamics of prostitution, he said he had never got involved. A barrister explained the scenario of punters approaching women in some detail. You know more about it than me, Stephen replied.

The defence held that his confession had been a true version of events. Struggling for composure, Stephen said the detectives had taken a sledgehammer to his head. It is pure fiction, he protested. The entire case was fiction. If it was not so serious, if it had not haunted him for the past twenty or so years, you could make a comic book out of it, he said.

'These officers know what they done,' he rounded, shouting towards the dock. 'Put your hands up and plead guilty, man!'

'I am surprised I have lasted this long,' he added. 'But you know what's kept me going, sir? My faith. I have a little bit of faith in the criminal justice system. I want justice for me and my co-accused, yes, sir, and particularly Lynette.'

By December 2011, the prosecution case was drawing to its close.

The preceding five months of the trial had been far from plain sailing. Beset with arguments over disclosure, the defence teams had complained to the judge of one failure after another.

More latterly, they homed in on incomplete records of meetings police had with John and the other men. The relationship had been too close, they claimed, and demonstrated a blinkered view by investigators that they had already decided the police were guilty. The lack of such clear information had hampered efforts at cross-examination.

Dean contended that it was all part of a tactical approach, a slow but determined war of attrition to ground the trial.

The prosecution had given assurances that, following innumerable mishaps, its house was now fully in order. In the interests of presiding over a fair trial, Judge Sweeney required reassurance of that.

So, he set a simple exercise – a litmus test, he called it. The prosecution was ordered to identify paperwork in a particular disclosure category: material that had been described as disclosable or potentially disclosable by the police but which had been overridden as undisclosable by the prosecution lawyers. This would enable the judge to evaluate performance and reasoning to decide if the regime was fit for purpose.

Confident that it could fulfil the straightforward challenge by the following day, the prosecution set to work.

But a problem emerged.

Two sets of documents germane to the exercise had been listed in a computerised catalogue but could not be located.

The files, copies of originals from the Independent Police Complaints Commission (IPCC), were in themselves innocuous enough. One related to accusations by John Actie of harassment made against officers unrelated to the case. Another concerned a complaint from an aggrieved officer who had been arrested under Operation Rubicon but not charged.

The IPCC was still in possession of the original copies of the documents, but that was of little help. The disclosure regime demands that the actual documents in the prosecution's possession are disclosed, as they might have contained additional information, handwritten notes, for example, which fresh copies would not.

As for their importance, it could have been argued by the defence, albeit weakly, that they should have been disclosed. They would have claimed, rightly or wrongly, that the complaints by John had not been upheld, and as such cast doubt on his credibility as a witness. But regardless of their worth, their disappearance further undermined the integrity of a disclosure regime already on a knife edge.

A flurry of dramatic phone calls ensued. During one of them, a comment was made, the consequence of which would prove fatal to the trial.

An officer on the disclosure team recalled he had been unable to find the same documents during an audit eighteen months before. There was then talk of a 'vague recollection' that at some point an instruction had been given by Coutts to shred some material.

Prosecutor Nicholas Dean QC telephoned Coutts. He asked him a single question. Had he ever asked for documents to be destroyed? Coutts's response was emphatic: never. Dean instructed him not to attend court the following day.

Without any more time being sought to conduct a proper search for the files, a decision – sanctioned by a furious Director of Public Prosecutions Keir Starmer, who had been told of a deliberate destruction of documents – was made to offer no further evidence.

Based on that understanding, there could be no guarantees that other material had not be treated in the same way.

Judge Sweeney explained to the jury that when a trial has become irretrievably unfair it must be stopped. They were directed to return 'not guilty' verdicts. The same verdicts were passed on the four officers due to stand trial the following year.

All ten defendants walked free from the dock.

The final chance of getting to any conclusive truth in the scandalous Lynette White murder investigation was gone.

John was told the news over the phone by his lawyer. Bitterly disappointed maybe, but shocked? Far from it. To him, it reeked of an establishment cover-up. It was what he had been expecting all along. The trial had been thrown, of that he was convinced.

In headline news around the UK, Ian Massey was seen emerging from court grinning and punching the air. At one point he threw his arms around Powell, a retired superintendent, who awkwardly patted the convicted armed robber on his back.

In TV interviews, the jubilant former officers reiterated their innocence and spoke of elation and relief that a 'harrowing' ordeal was over. Perriam was 'delighted'; she had lived with the proceedings for many years, her lawyer read from a statement, and the impact on her and her family was impossible to describe.

Coutts, meanwhile, was 'absolutely flabbergasted' by the trial's sudden collapse. Why had there been no meaningful discussion with him? And why was there no request for extra time to find the documents?

Lawyers acting on behalf of John, Tony and Stephen had wasted no time, immediately issuing proceedings for a judicial review and reiterating calls for a public inquiry.

A letter they wrote to the Home Secretary, Theresa May, made clear that police corruption and malpractice was suspected, that the circumstances that led to the abandonment of the trial had been falsely and dishonestly orchestrated.

It read: 'At the very least there must be a strong suspicion that one or more South Wales Police officers, aware that the judge had, in effect, given the prosecution a last chance to show that disclosure was now in order, took advantage of that situation to create a false picture of further disclosure shortcomings.'

But there was more to come.

After the police trial's collapse, the investigation's high-security incident room had been immediately locked down pending an investigation. Three weeks later, as he was preparing to retire, Coutts was escorted inside to collect belongings. Sorting through items inside his office, he noticed some Iron Mountain boxes, a distinctive cardboard storage used by the IPCC but not South Wales Police. Inside were the missing documents.

In time, it would become clear that no thorough search beyond a 'quick look' had been made of the incident room before the trial was ended.

A report in 2013 by Her Majesty's Chief Inspector of the Crown Prosecution Service was unremitting in its criticism of the prosecution's management of disclosure and its performance generally.

On the same day, the conclusions of an investigation by the IPCC also revealed that no instruction was ever given by a senior officer to destroy material. Mistakes had been made, it concluded, but ones that did not warrant formal misconduct action, and instead it recommended management performance reviews.

A year later, an investigation, Operation Dalecrest, conducted by Devon and Cornwall Police, found no evidence of gross misconduct or malice by any officer.

Despite persistent calls for a public inquiry, the Home Office rejected them, ordering instead an inquiry to be led by prominent barrister Richard Horwell QC.

The heat was on to establish exactly why Britain's biggest police corruption trial – estimated to have cost over £30m – had collapsed in such controversy. But before that could be set out, there was yet another court case.

The police officers who had walked free from court were not finished yet.

In a case funded by the Police Federation – the UK's largest staff association for rank-and-file officers – fifteen officers who had worked on the original Lynette White murder hunt sued South

Wales Police for false imprisonment and misfeasance in public office.

Coutts, they claimed, had seen himself as an 'avenging angel'. He had a closed mindset, determined to prove the officers' guilt and ignoring evidence that did not match his preconceived theories. John, who made a point of attending the two-month hearing, groaned audibly at the irony.

He had sat in the public gallery determined to make his presence felt. On one occasion while in the entrance lobby, Page had attempted to greet him. John had responded in a manner akin to hell fire.

In June 2016, Mr Justice Wyn Williams handed down his judgement, rejecting their claims for financial compensation for misfeasance in public office.

In his 213-page judgement, he set out how the former officers were arrested at their homes, which were searched for paperwork and police pocket books.

There were strong suspicions, the judge noted, that officers had been tipped off about their impending arrests. Mouncher, he wrote, was dressed in a suit and, apparently, was awaiting the arrival of officers when they called at 6.15 a.m.

In the case of Page, items were seized from his home, including a number of diaries from the 1990s, and numerous pieces of burnt paper found in his garden. He insisted they were the remains of diaries and notebooks from the 1960s and 70s which he had decided to get rid of a few weeks before because he was moving house. Pocket books relating to the murder inquiry, Page insisted, would have been kept at a designated police station for seven years before being destroyed in line with force policy.

Had he known about his impending arrest? Yes, Page said, 'it was the worst-kept secret and they were talking about it down the pub.'

Mr Justice Williams touched on the subject of the corruption trial's collapse, noting that 'to this day, a degree of mystery surrounds the "losing" and "finding" of those documents.'

I suppose, he said, it is conceivable an officer deliberately hid the documents knowing the effect this would likely have on proceedings.

'The probability is that the documents were misplaced through human error,' his report continued. 'Quite how they came to be found, apparently so easily, some weeks after the trial came to an end is a mystery which I cannot resolve and about which I decline to speculate.'

In his only public statement concerning the case, Coutts said he had been made a scapegoat for the trial's collapse. He had only ever sought to put right what South Wales Police had got wrong – actions for which five innocent men had spent a total of fifteen years in jail. During that time, he said he had come up against 'relentless pressure' to treat the officers he was investigating differently to how members of the public would be treated.

Six months shy of the thirtieth anniversary of the murder of Lynette White, Richard Horwell QC had completed his exhaustive forensic investigation into the collapse of the police corruption trial.

In a courtesy to three surviving members of the Cardiff Five, they had been invited to a private meeting with him in Cardiff city centre's Marriott Hotel. Before his findings were made public, they should be the first to be informed of them. John had been in two minds about going. When he eventually decided to go, he had shown up late. They could wait, he reasoned.

By the time John walked into the room, Tony and Stephen were already seated around a large mahogany desk, exchanging small talk over coffee and biscuits with the assembled lawyers. Here goes nothing, John thought to himself.

Within a short time, news headlines would resound with Horwell's fierce condemnation. The collapse of the trial was an 'embarrassment on a national scale', he told the three men, and had compounded one of the worst miscarriages of justice in UK history.

But, Horwell went on, it had failed due to human error and not corruption.

The documents had never been shredded and therefore, Horwell wrote, the main reason given for stopping the trial was erroneous. But he went on to explain that the trial would have still buckled under the weight of disclosure catastrophes.

The CPS, Horwell said, had inadequately managed the prosecution from the start, which had ongoing repercussions. Added to that, it had appointed disclosure counsel too inexperienced for the case's scale and complexity.

Any theory that 'wicked minds' had sabotaged the files did not pass muster, he revealed. The same documents could not be located on two other occasions in the years leading up to the trial. Even if someone had maliciously seized on that fact, then surely they would have destroyed the documents rather than merely mislaying them.

In the grip of deep confusion, there had been no meaningful search for the papers. What was the point? At the time, it was believed they had been destroyed. But a corrupt mind could not have predicted that, Horwell said. If there had been a search, the documents would likely have been found, for all the good that would have done.

Midway through the briefing, John stood up and without saying a word left the room, refusing to listen any further.

For his entire life, he had lived by his father's credo to never back down, to stand up and be counted. And he always would. But he had come to know that no glancing blow is more deadly to an enemy than the might of turning your back and walking away.

Quivers of heat rose from the baking pavements as he emerged into the city centre streets. Cutting through the commotion of shoppers and office workers, he carried on walking, emerging from under the bridge as he made his way home.

No vestige of the Custom House pub, the pavements on which Lynette White had waited or the dingy sprawl of warehouses where her murderer had once worked, remained to be seen. In their place, the curved façades of corporate headquarters in the city's new business district swept around a smart plaza.

John wound his way along the edge of the square, a public park with small gardens and benches overlooking pools from which fountains rose and fell in the July sun. In its centre stood a bronze statue, the cast of its ceremonial robes green with patina and streaked black with grime.

Once admired by the crowds at London's Great Exhibition, generations ago the statue had returned home, unveiled to great fanfare and given pride of place in the heart of the city.

Now, though, an inconvenience to town planners, the relic of the past had been shifted sideways across the city, the inscription on its granite plinth – 'John Marquis of Bute' – meaning nothing to the majority who passed by.

The legacy of a man whose vision had transformed insignificant marshland into one of the world's greatest seaports and its adjoining model village of terraced houses into one of its most famous communities, one that had dared to blur the lines between black and white to reveal a myriad of shades in between, had faded from modern memory.

John made his way along Bute Street, stopping off at his flat in the tower blocks of Loudoun Square. Tucked away and out of sight, Butetown now seemed to be even more confined and segregated from the aspirational real estate of the docklands that had sprung up like mushrooms around it.

In keeping with his routine, he and Seb, his ageing collie-cross who stuck close by his side requiring no lead, wandered down to the bay on their daily walk.

The Oval Basin, which had once been journey's end for untold voyages as the old entrance to the docks, had long since been filled in and landscaped, and now echoed with music from funfair rides and the shrieks of children, faces flushed with excitement and sticky with ice cream.

Crowds filed along Mermaid Quay, the site where the North Star had once stood now bustling with cafes and restaurants, their forecourts fringed with Tiki beach parasols. Below at the quayside, day-trippers queued for pleasure-boat rides, the barrage sluice gates fighting tirelessly to keep the tide from reclaiming its mudflats buried from view beneath the shimmering freshwater of a new-look Cardiff Bay.

Some things remained. Remnants of the forlorn architecture of the old docklands clung on in the hope of rescue. And 7 James Street, still a rental flat now above a vaping shop, held firm just a stone's throw from the Welsh government's Senedd building and the Millennium Centre, home to the Welsh National Opera and a venue for theatre and visiting West End shows.

John was not overly sentimental about the past. Time moves on and with it comes change. Although no longer cowed by the reaction of people on hearing his name, he was painfully aware of what some of them said.

There would always be those determined not be swayed by the facts, and others who would try to find an excuse for them.

'Those guys were no angels!' If it had been said once, it had been said a million times.

No, they were no angels. But far more than that, they were innocent men who had told the truth and shamed the devil.

The end.

Epilogue

On a sunny day in October 2022, hundreds of mourners gathered at the bottom of Bute Street, for Tony Paris's funeral.

'Many of us walked the length of Bute Road shouting for Tony's freedom and justice,' his sister Rosie said. 'But now this is the last time we walk the length of Bute Road for him.'

In line with Tiger Bay tradition, the funeral procession was on foot, a slow and solemn walk behind Tony's hearse as it made its way to St Mary the Virgin Church, not far from the bridge.

Just days before his death, I had visited Tony in his brand-new flat. He had only recently moved in, and the change of surroundings had buoyed his spirits. He enthusiastically told me of his plans to get fit and lose a few pounds, and I said goodbye to a Tony in optimistic form.

A few days later, his daughter had phoned him to arrange to bring over a Sunday roast dinner but could get no answer. Found in his reclining leather chair, her father looked for all the world like he had taken a nap, one from which he would never awake.

Consoling, perhaps, to think that a sense of peace, so absent for most of his adult life, had returned to grace the end of it. Tony Paris, aged just sixty-five, died of an aneurism on 11 September 2022.

Right up until the end, he tried and failed to understand why the police had picked on him in particular. Maybe, we discussed, it was down to his amenable nature; they saw him as easy prey. Maybe. 'Whatever the reason,' he would repeat so often I came to think of it as his catchphrase, 'they picked on the wrooooong family!'

His pride in his family and the dignity and strength with which his siblings had fought for him were his silver lining.

Tony had returned home from jail in 1992 but never felt a free man. On being sentenced to life imprisonment, he had told his wife, Denise, to divorce him. Happily, the couple reconciled and went on to have two more children, daughters this time. But they eventually separated and for the final few years of his life Tony lived alone.

In the time I knew him, he rarely went out, lacking the confidence or motivation to even attend family events. Try as he might, it was impossible to banish the spectre of the case, and he was profoundly saddened that something so awful had come to publicly define his life.

'It haunts me to this day,' he told me. 'It's never going away. I act like I'm OK. People see me in the street, you put your face on and you play the game. You don't want people feeling sorry for you. I smile and talk like I'm OK so when they leave you, they go home and say, "I saw Tony today, man. He's alright, he's cool." But I ain't. I'm not cool, never will be . . . no, they hurt me.'

In 2016, Malik Abdullahi, who helped lead the Cardiff Three freedom campaign, died, and a few years after that, the troubled life of Mark Grommek also came to an end. Leanne Vilday has since married and has striven to put her life on track. But my brief phone call with her in 2020 showed how painfully close to the surface her agony lay. Within a minute of our conversation, she had broken down, ruing the day she had lent her friend Lynette White the keys to Flat One, 7 James Street.

Angela Psaila still lives locally. Occasionally during visits to the post office, John Actie will find himself standing near to her in the queue. He is never sure if she recognises him, but even if she did and was to talk to him, he would be civil, recognising that she too remains scarred by all that happened. In 2012, she gave a television interview to BBC Wales in which she spoke candidly of her regret.

What happened, Psaila said, was not down to her – the police had given her no choice but to tell lies that had destroyed her life and for which she felt she would be forever judged.

As for John, he and Taryn, who still lives in London, are no longer together, but they remain connected through their daughter, Remi. It is obvious to anyone who knows him that Taryn remains the love of his life. His gratitude for her standing by him during the original trials is as heartfelt today as it was thirty-five years ago. Without her, his late brother, Stephen, his beloved mother, Maria, who died in 2017, and older sister, Natalie, who died six months later, he shudders to think how he would have coped.

Sharing his home with Louis, a Staffie, and Lola, a long-haired Chihuahua, John continues to live in a flat in one of the high-rises in Loudoun Square. The media exposure of the case in recent years has led to a much wider recognition of his vindication. It is rare that John will take a walk down the Bay and not have a member of the public approach to talk or shake his hand. There have been several police officers who have done the same, little knowing how much the gesture has moved him.

Long gone are the bad old days of crack cocaine, and it will be perhaps a surprise for many to learn that the only powder featuring in the life of John Actie these days is the superfood greens supplement heaped into his morning smoothie. Heeding medical advice to ease his arthritis, John adheres strictly to a gentle daily exercise and healthy eating regimen.

But, like Tony, Ronnie, Dullah and Stephen, he will never be free of the past. Regularly a black cloud descends on John and those closest to him, many of whom have been friends for life, are cognisant of the space and time required for it to lift.

For the first time in his life, he is exploring therapy for post-traumatic stress disorder. His expectations are realistic; it will never be resolved, but nonetheless, however small, it is a step in the right direction. For him and Stephen Miller, who still lives in south London, closely supported by his siblings, there can be no happy ever after.

The enduring debris of injustice, like the delayed fallout of a nuclear blast, is something too often overlooked.

A few months before Tony's death, in July of 2002, another procession had wound its way into St Mary's courtyard. This time led by a horse-drawn hearse and comprising mourners from a younger generation.

At the age of thirty-eight, Dullah's son, Joseph, had been found dead.

A fitness enthusiast and devoted father, he had made it his quest in life to transmute the trauma that had spilled like acid on to his life, into a force for good.

A thriving TikTok account called 'Goals and Growth' was to be the forerunner to a podcast series he was in the midst of planning, a platform to examine miscarriages of justice and the intergenerational trauma that can ensue.

In a cruel twist of fate, Joseph's lifeless body was found lying on a bed by his sister, Tiffany, when she returned home from a night away in the May of that year. The cause of his death proving so difficult to determine, it delayed his funeral for two months and heaped further agony on to his loved ones.

What would not have been discovered by any post-mortem but cannot be denied is the inextricable link between his early demise and the events that began in December of 1988; they not only upended his father's life but his too.

Those tempted to dismiss any continuing discussion of the case by saying, 'It's time to move on, that's all in the past', would have been met with short shrift from Joseph Ameed Abdullahi Harris. It is an inconvenient truth to many, but nothing about the case was in the past tense for him.

Aware of the insidious fallout of intergenerational trauma, how historical psychological and emotional wounds and fears can insidiously ripple from parent to child, from one generation to the next, he had grown determined to come to terms with his own trauma for the benefit of his young daughter.

It takes courage to recognise and understand some uncomfortable truths about our own behaviour, our habits and avoidance, to air them, talk about them and then work towards consigning them to the past, where they rightfully belong. Honest conflict is healthier than dishonest harmony, as the thinking goes.

The undoubted parallels with the Cardiff Five's ordeal were encapsulated by Operation Mistral's former Detective Chief Superintendent Kevin O'Neill when he said, 'What is incumbent on each new generation is to look at the past and not hate it but to understand where it was formed, what damage it did and change it.'

It would be comforting at this point to gather the loose ends of this extraordinary case and tie them into a neat bow of lessons learned. If only it were that simple.

There have been many experts, brilliant minds, who have helped lift the rug on this landmark case, the majority alerted of the need to do so by campaigning journalist Satish Sekar, whose unassailable fight for recognition for the Cardiff Five endured for decades.

Over the years, I have asked each of the experts their thoughts on the legacy of the Lynette White murder investigation. Its impact on policing is undoubted, as is its contribution to systemic change within the criminal justice system, but each spoke of the ever-present danger of history repeating itself, and a watchword common to all of them was the need for vigilance.

Human nature is infinitely fallible, its capacity for self-deception unbounded. Attitudes soften then harden again, lessons learned get forgotten, pressure leads to expediency, technological advances are open to abuse.

I leave the last words to Gareth Peirce, the publicity-shy lawyer whose human rights activism, so instrumental in this and countless other miscarriages of justice, has led her to be being credited with transforming the criminal justice system singlehandedly.

With particular resonance for the scapegoated district of Tiger Bay, this is an excerpt of her answer to my question about the legacy of the case and her warning for vigilance that can be applied across the board, far outside the remit of policing.

'If you have an environment where you take as your premise that society is entitled to look at particular groups of people in a certain way, as alien from society, then you have every building block for wrongful convictions. Police officers party to the mindset they pick up from the politics of the day, the media of the day, juries are susceptible and "here you go again".'

AUTHOR'S NOTE

Throughout the reporting of this case over the past thirty-seven years, the answer to one question in particular has remained a mystery.

Where was Lynette White in the five days leading up to her death?

All those closest to her, family and friends, insisted they did not know where she had stayed and detectives consistently said they had drawn a blank. At the time there was speculation in the press that Lynette may have had a new boyfriend, someone who had shielded her and who had later been afraid to come forward to the police.

But that was not the case.

As I trawled through the files, every so often I would come across a statement that shed some light on the mystery, and gradually I compiled a small pile that, when pieced together, revealed where she had been during the final days of her life.

During that period there were numerous sightings of Lynette White in and around her usual haunts, walking along streets and tucked into doorways in the vicinity around the bridge, mostly alone and, as usual, dressed casually and free of make-up.

As to where she slept during this time, a fellow sex worker by the name of Theresa, who had met Lynette for the first time only weeks before, came forward and gave a statement to the police early on in the investigation.

Theresa told how she initially met Lynette in December 1987, bumping into her again on the evening of Monday, 8 February 1988. The two had gone for a late drink at a pub in Riverside, an area not far from the docks, and, before going their separate ways home that night, they had arranged to meet the following day.

And so, on Tuesday evening, not long after her boyfriend had dropped her off near the Custom House, Lynette, wearing jeans and a sweatshirt, had taken a taxi to Theresa's flat above a fish and chip shop in the Canton district, not far from the city centre. She had arrived with a carrier bag containing some clothes that she changed into before the two went out to work.

On the street that night Lynette had been approached by two police constables who reminded her to appear in court to give evidence later that week. She had told them of her reluctance. Even if she turned up, she had said, no one could make her talk. They asked for the whereabouts of her boyfriend. She did not know, she replied; they had split up.

Sometime after, two sex workers recalled Lynette telling them she feared reprisals over the court case and that she was 'going into hiding' to dodge the witness summons.

Indeed, as Stephen Miller waited to meet her as usual in the North Star, Lynette had returned with Theresa to sleep at her flat, breaking down in tears as the women chatted over a coffee, overwhelmed by her predicament and the end of her relationship.

On Wednesday morning, Lynette and Theresa said goodbye, not arranging to meet again, but they had, by chance, run into one another again that night.

The two women decided to finish work early and returned to Canton, where they went for an Indian meal, sharing a bottle of Asti Spumante before heading back to Theresa's flat, where they talked and played records long into the night, Lynette eventually falling asleep on the sofa.

Then, on Thursday, 11 February, not far away in the Grangetown area, a neighbour reported passing Lynette close to her home in Dorset Street, and saying hello. Lynette had regularly chatted with neighbours as she walked her dog, stopping to give money to their children for sweets. On this occasion, the man noted that she was carrying a black bin liner in both arms, a tear in which revealed clothing inside.

Staff at the local launderette confirmed Lynette would turn up like clockwork towards the end of every week to drop her washing off in a black bag, returning to collect it a few hours later.

Her visit there that day would account for the fact that it was noted that Lynette was wearing freshly laundered clothes at the time of her death. It is likely she had phoned the landline of the Dorset Street house to check there was no one home before venturing inside to pack some of her belongings; this was something she had been known to do in the past to avoid Stephen when they had fallen out.

As for where she slept on Thursday evening, a mother of two living in the Roath area, again not far from the city centre, told police that Lynette had stayed that night at her house. This had come about, she explained, when a woman living close by, someone she knew to be a sex worker, had asked if she would mind putting up a friend who had split up with her boyfriend.

The woman reluctantly agreed and, shortly before 10 p.m., Lynette arrived by taxi carrying a tartan suitcase and a black shoulder bag. The woman recognised her as Terry White's daughter and after having some dinner, the two chatted as they watched television, no mention being made of Lynette's private life.

At 9.30 a.m. the next morning, the woman had gone into the spare room to ask Lynette if she wanted a cup of tea but found she had already left, the bed appearing to have been barely slept in.

That leaves just Friday night to account for. During that day it was known Lynette had been in the docks area, having been seen outside 7 James Street at lunchtime and in the vicinity of the Custom House pub that evening.

It is only my theory and purely speculative but it is feasible that Lynette returned to Theresa's flat that night. She knew it would be empty as Theresa had gone to stay in London. She would not have needed a key as the entrance to the flat was actually inside the late-night chip shop, towards the back where a set of stairs led directly to the living room. This also fits with an account given by Leanne Vilday, who said a taxi driver had told her he had picked up Lynette in the early hours the day before she died, dropping her off in Canton.

It is also possible Lynette's suitcase and bag remained in the flat until it was re-let, at which point her belongings could have been mistakenly viewed as unwanted and left behind by the previous tenant. There would have been no reason to connect Lynette with the property and maybe they were thrown away by someone unaware of their connection to one of the city's most enduring murder cases.

Lynette's movements on the Saturday are, of course, well documented. She made her usual weekly trip to the chemist shop near Dorset Street to buy provisions and was seen that night in the city centre before, for the final time, she ventured under the bridge where she would cross paths with her murderer, Jeffrey Gafoor.

The minimum sentence Gafoor had been ordered to serve was thirteen years but it was in fact twelve years and eight months taking into account the time he had already spent in custody since his arrest. This made him eligible for parole in March 2016. Since then, Gafoor made five applications for parole, all of which were rejected, and he has spent eight additional years in prison for the protection of the public. In 2023 the parole board, an independent body which decides if prisoners can be released, confirmed that Gafoor, now in an open prison, was eligible for day release.

With his sixth parole hearing due the following year, an application was made by Lynette White's family and others for the hearing to be held in public, a call supported by the Secretary of State for Justice.

Up until 2022 there was a blanket ban on public hearings, but following controversy surrounding parole board decisions the law was changed to further consider the welfare of victims and to agree to requests for open hearings that were deemed to be in the 'interests of justice'.

Gafoor's legal representatives were not happy. Given the media attention the case had attracted, they said, a public hearing would impact negatively on the process. They also highlighted Gafoor's diagnosis with autism spectrum disorder, which meant he would be put under 'a significant amount of stress'.

A decision by the parole board went in his favour. The case did not warrant a public hearing. 'There are no special features to the case apart from the fact that a number of men were wrongly convicted of this offence before Mr Gafoor was convicted,' the parole board said.

And so, just as they had done before each of the previous parole hearings, the White family prepared and submitted a victim's personal statement for the board to consider, each one petitioning against Gafoor's release, the prospect of his freedom dealing yet another bitter blow to those relatives and friends still living and to the memory of those who had since died.

In October 2024, Gafoor, now fifty-nine, appeared before the parole board via video link. Shortly after, nearly four decades on from the first news reports of Lynette White's murder, news headlines and social media buzzed with the news that her killer would now be freed on licence.

An appeal was immediately launched. In its decision summary, the parole board itself had listed risk factors that Gafoor had once presented – willingness to use extreme violence, a lack of emotional control, rumination about events, holding grudges, being emotionally unresponsive and demonstrating poor victim empathy. Where was the evidence for his victims that any of this had changed? The appeal was refused.

A close relative of Lynette White's, who wanted to remain anonymous, described once again feeling 'utterly betrayed'.

The pain of the family's continuing ordeal is unimaginable, their grief already aggravated by instances of insensitive reporting and the interminable stream of headlines that reduced the memory of 'Little Lyn', as they called her, to two words – Cardiff prostitute.

To them, Lynette was a funny, upbeat, loving and beautiful young woman whose only dream in life was to find a man to love and to raise a family of her own, the chance to provide her children with the security and consistency that had been denied her.

One of her aunts who had helped raise her had tried so many times to steer her away from the path she had strayed onto, pleading with her to realise her true value, but Lynette, riven by a lack of self-worth, was always beyond her reach.

But Lynette's sense of self had not always been so fragile.

An old school friend of hers called Christine with whom I recently spoke recalled her shock at first learning of Lynette's murder back in 1988. By then, it had been six years since they had last seen one another, and Christine struggled to connect the circumstances of her death with the quiet, yet self-assured, horse-mad fourteen-year-old she had once known, who, despite her loathing of school work, was convinced her proven affinity with animals would be enough to ensure a career as a vet.

Christine recalled how they would go to a local farm several times a week to escape troubles at school and home, and pay a small fee to ride horses, excitedly setting out for another adventure in the nearby countryside.

One horse in particular, Christine said, a hefty chestnut called Fella, was a real handful. His capriciousness terrified everyone except for Lynette. Fella, sensing within her an innate self-possession and confidence, never once played her up. One of Christine's abiding memories is of Fella and Lynette galloping across the fields, effortlessly clearing jumps as she tottered behind on a reluctant pony with no hope of catching them up.

It was soon after this time that Lynette began regularly truanting from school and dropped off Christine's radar. There has been mention in the media that around this time in her life Lynette was sex-trafficked and forced into prostitution. In all the many thousands of pages of material in the case files, I have found not a single mention of this, but in fact evidence to the contrary – many accounts that she had drifted into sex work of her own volition. The documents do mention an incident in Bristol where Lynette, aged eighteen at the time, had willingly gone with two men to a blues party. Various people recalled to the police that she had complained that, once there, the men had held her against her will and forced her to work for them for a couple of days before she made her way back to Cardiff.

One of the most poignant discoveries I made in the boxes of case files were photocopies of a few pages of a notebook that had been found among Lynette White's possessions. On the front was her name alongside that of a friend with whom she once briefly shared a flat.

Among the lists of phone numbers and love hearts containing the girls' names alongside boys they fancied were the handwritten lyrics of a song entitled 'On My Own', a 1986 hit for Patti LaBelle featuring Michael McDonald. It was a song that clearly meant enough to Lynette that she went to the trouble of writing out the words in order to commit them to memory, a common practice for 80s teenagers.

The timeless break-up ballad tells of two people struggling to come to terms with the heartbreak of a failed relationship. In neat cursive, Lynette's writing continues as the song builds to its climactic close, the singer, a newly single woman, resolute that it is time to find herself once more, that she has faith she will thrive in a new life on her own.

It certainly seemed that Lynette White had begun to turn a corner, seemingly intent on ending her relationship with Stephen, perhaps feeling the re-emergence of the strong sense of self that Fella had intuited and that her aunt had so wished for.

Of all the many injustices that emanated from Flat One, 7 James Street that rainy Valentine's night in 1988, none can be greater than that opportunity being ripped away from Lynette White by the hand of a man who claimed not to fully remember his dreadful act; one that everyone who had known and loved her – and so many more besides – would never be allowed to forget.

ABOUT THE AUTHOR

Photo © 2024 Amy Williams

Ceri Jackson is a journalist, born and raised in Cardiff, Wales.

Follow the Author on Amazon

If you enjoyed this book, follow Ceri Jackson on Amazon to be notified when the author releases a new book!
To do this, please follow these instructions:

Desktop:

1) Search for the author's name on Amazon or in the Amazon App.
2) Click on the author's name to arrive on their Amazon page.
3) Click the 'Follow' button.

Mobile and Tablet:

1) Search for the author's name on Amazon or in the Amazon App.
2) Click on one of the author's books.
3) Click on the author's name to arrive on their Amazon page.
4) Click the 'Follow' button.

Kindle eReader and Kindle App:

If you enjoyed this book on a Kindle eReader or in the Kindle App, you will find the author 'Follow' button after the last page.